Modern Masters Volume 26:

F.

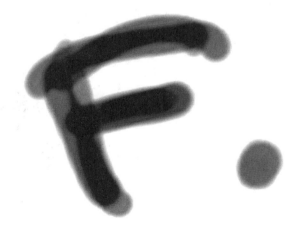

MODERN MASTERS VOLUME TWENTY-SIX:
FRAZER IRVING

edited by Nathan Wilson and Eric Nolen-Weathington
front cover by Frazer Irving
all interviews in this book were conducted and transcribed by Nathan Wilson

TwoMorrows Publishing
10407 Bedfordtown Dr.
Raleigh, North Carolina 27614
www.twomorrows.com • e-mail: twomorrow@aol.com

First Printing • September 2011 • Printed in Canada

Softcover ISBN: 978-1-60549-039-7

Dedication

I want to thank my wife Jan and children, Zoey and Connor, to whom this book is dedicated. — *Nathan*

Acknowledgements

Frazer Irving, *for giving so much of his time to discuss his life and career, and for his involvement in this book.*
Grant Morrison, *for agreeing to write an insightful foreword.*

Special Thanks
Joe Casey, Com.X Publishing, Andy Diggle, Nat Gertler of 24-Hour Comics Day,
Heritage Auctions (www.ha.com), Phil Hester, David Hine, Image Comics, Fabian Nicieza,
Rebellion/2000 AD, Si Spurrier, Christopher Teague of Pendragon Publishing,
Rick McGee and the crew of Foundation's Edge,
and John and Pam Morrow

Modern Masters Volume Twenty-Six:

FRAZER IRVING

Table of Contents

Introduction

When I discovered Frazer Irving's work in "Necronauts," his first of several collaborations with writer Gordon Rennie, I remember thinking he'd be good on a Batman story. Frazer's swirling, Gothic, woodcut lines and high-contrast compositions carried the frequency of the black-and-white horror anthologies — like Warren Comics' *Eerie* and *Creepy* and Dez Skinn's *Hammer House of Horror* — into the 21st century and seemed ideally suited for the Dark Knight's world of fetish noir. I tacked a conceptual Post-it note to my forebrain and made a point of keeping an eye on his progress.

And there were more surprises to come, with the acid super-hero strip "Storming Heaven," where the lysergic palette, the searing phosphorescent colour blocking, fish-eye distortions of perspective, innovative layouts, and carefully timed and edited storytelling were pure comics-as-music and demonstrated a mastery of light, atmosphere and tone that felt like hearing "Purple Haze" for the first time. When I finally met Frazer, it was music we talked about first, and how it could be represented visually in ways that were more visceral and psychedelic than anyone had dared attempted on paper before. Our first collaboration, on the Harry-Potter-for-Puritans series, *Klarion the Witch-Boy* at DC Comics, had nothing to do with music, of course, and neither did our later work on *Batman* so we still have to make good on that one.

(The work we did together on "Batman and Robin Must Die" is for me one of the high points of my run — but who knew the world would find in Frazer Irving the undisputed master, the dean, the king, of the small but perfectly formed and morally robust commonwealth of Puritan Fantasy comics?)

Often (not too often but often enough to sting) in the past, as a comic book writer, I've seen stories stripped of emotional nuance, effective staging, and storytelling clarity as a result of miscommunication with artists. One result of that is a tendency to over-direct the action at the script stage, but with Frazer no embroidery is necessary, and the creation of a comic book adventure becomes an exhilarating high-wire act with a trained and competent partner who inspires complete trust. As you'll learn, Frazer doesn't have to be told to put the first speaker in any comic panel on the left of the picture and the last speaker on the right. Frazer doesn't need to have the precise angle of a grief-stricken spine or the arch of a quizzical eyebrow described to him — he is already living the story, already inhabiting the characters, and with no instruction necessary he understands exactly what POV to choose for maximum impact, or how to skew a panel shape, heighten a mood, or flood a scene with fuming, unknown colour combinations and fogs of thickening shadow this mundane waking world is too drab and sensible to know. He is, quite simply, the kind of artist every comic book writer dreams of working with.

Nathan Wilson's interview/conversation with Frazer is one of the best of its kind that I've read on the subject of comics and their creators; Wilson's done his research and knows when to vary the tone or deepen the inquiry, but what makes this so much fun to read is his willingness to keep pace with Frazer's restless playful imagination. Wilson is unfazed by Irving's surreal digressions, and the best of the knockabout exchanges read as though they were scripted for a double act. As a portrait of the artist, it more than accomplishes its job. Frazer's honesty, humour, intelligence, and insight come across as vividly as the ultra-pinks and infra-violets with which he drenches in light his remarkable pages. If you're reading this, you probably already know and love Frazer Irving's work. Here's your chance to get to know and love the lad, himself.

— Grant Morrison
Scotland
June 2011

← CUT RIGHT HAND PAGE AT THIS LINE   DOUBLE PAGE SPREAD: CUT AS SHOWN, ABUT PAGE EDGES, TAPE ON BACK, DO NOT OVERLAP   CUT LEFT HAND PAGE AT THIS LINE →

5

Part 1: The Prophecy and Other Arty Things

MODERN MASTERS: Tell me about your early life.

FRAZER IRVING: I was hatched from a golden egg.

MM: Nice. You don't see that very often, at least not Stateside.

FRAZER: Neither did the goat herders that found me.

MM: See, I knew this early period of your life would be interesting. I know you live outside London, but tell us a little bit about your past. When and where were you born?

FRAZER: In Ilford, the birthplace of Ilford photographic film and the location of the only mammoth skeleton found in the UK.

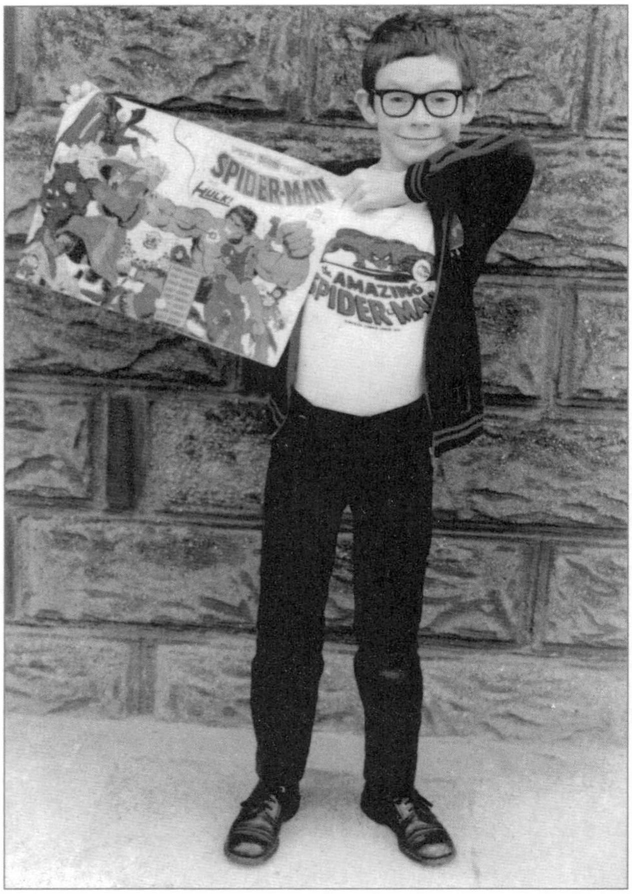
SPIDER-MAN
HULK
AMAZING
SPIDER-MAN

MM: I'm assuming here that the skeleton discovery didn't correspond with your birth though right?

FRAZER: Naw, it was about 70 years prior to that, but I consider it an omen nonetheless.

MM: A sign of the coming of Frazer then?

FRAZER: In a previous incarnation I slew that mammoth, or maybe it was my friend and it delivered my message of arrival to the primitive peoples that lived here. If it was my friend, it would have spoken to them in English. Would have confused them all and probably spawned many, many myths.

MM: Mammoth bones and prophecies aside though, it was 1972 correct?

FRAZER: Yup. Two years too late to enjoy the Beatles.

MM: Tell me about Ilford. What type of city was it in 1972?

FRAZER: A boring one? Suburbia, mixed, though probably less so than it is now. I was small, it was big. There were more trees then than now as well.

MM: So not an industrial city or agricultural area then, but mostly commuters to work in London?

FRAZER: Well, there were local shops, and there was the photographic place and so on, but, yeah, a commuter town, in essence. The kind of place *Halloween* would have been filmed if it was made in the UK. Long, boring streets, and lots of dog poo.

MM: [*laughs*] Probably not something they put out in the travel brochures, I suppose.

FRAZER: They should, to warn people about it. "When walking through Ilford, keep thine eyes downward in case of excremental deposits, and wear galoshes."

MM: The horrors of Ilford aside, where do you currently live?

FRAZER: Ilford. [*laughter*] I tried to escape a few times, but kept getting dragged back. I suspect that I have unfinished business here. I reckon the magnetic forces here are quite clingy and that some ancient force demands I wrap up my business here before I leave.

MM: It's the prophecy. You are the youngest of three children. Do you have older brothers, sisters, or both?

FRAZER: I have a brother and a sister, yes. Both split this town ages ago, one to Australia and the other into deepest, darkest Essex. I got left holding the prophecy down. Though to be fair, it was my prophecy anyway.

MM: How far apart in age are you?

FRAZER: Four years and seven years. They were both aliens to me.

MM: How about your parents? What did they do at the time you were born?

FRAZER: We were raised by just my mum, after I was two, due to divorce, and she worked in a nursery part-time; the rest of our income came from state benefits. The state owns me.

MM: Oh, I'm sorry to hear that about your parents. Were your parents from your hometown of Ilford?

FRAZER: No, but from Essex. The apples didn't fall so far in those days. It seems that Ilford was a good choice, though, as we could have gone in the other direction further out of London, which I wouldn't have liked.

MM: Too distant from the metropolis and its advantages?

FRAZER: Too distant from civilization in general. I liked growing up in a mixed environment, and in hindsight it was the right sort of melting pot for a kid of my generation.

MM: How so?

FRAZER: Well, with the increase in ethnic and cultural diversity, since I grew up I have noticed the more remote places have had a harder time adjusting to what could be perceived as an invasion. I was allowed to grow up in a place that already had everything in it, so none of the changes were scary. After I was a kid, the integration was more widespread, especially due to TV, etc., so modern kids are less affected by it, but people my age from villages have shown some real resentment to the idea of the global village, in my experience.

MM: Were you at all aware as a child of the state's role in your family or what could be a working class life, as well as this melting pot diversity of Ilford, or did this awareness come later on?

FRAZER: Much later. I knew we were poor, because the clothes I wore had already had my sister's and brother's names stitched on them previously, plus I got free school meals—at the end of the dinner line, though—but an awareness of it all eluded me, as there was nothing to compare it to. The melting pot was also just something I assumed happened all over. I had no idea about the world outside beyond what comics and TV showed me, and that was almost always New York, which itself was very mixed. I think I based my worldview on the X-Men, in fact. The way the new X-Men were a mixed bunch of international freaks. I kind of grew up seeing everyone in those terms, judging by content of character, not color, age, language, etc.

X-Men was amazing. In terms of communicating fundamental notions about diversity, responsibility, tragedy, cause and effect. It was genius that I got it all without them ever being blatant and patronizing about it. The humanity of Thunderbird's sacrifice in those first few issues. I knew nothing of the history of the Native Americans back then, so I was confused as to why he was so angry, but I still understood the error of pride from that one story. His death haunted me for years. For ages I couldn't read that story, because he was so frickin' stupid. "Get off the plane! Prof X can handle it! *Get off the plane*!" Such a waste.

Another comic that deeply affected me

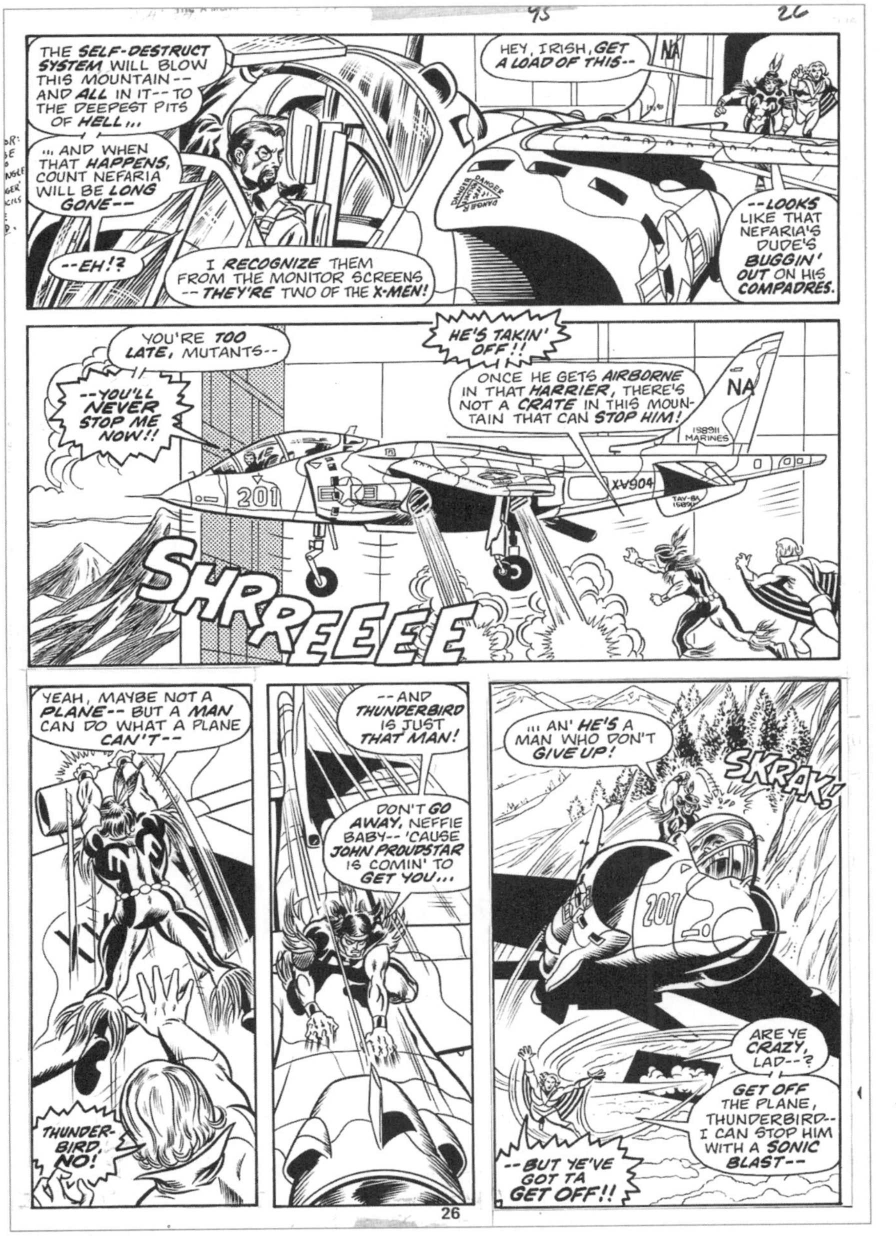
95
26
THE SELF-DESTRUCT SYSTEM WILL BLOW THIS MOUNTAIN-- AND ALL IN IT-- TO THE DEEPEST PITS OF HELL...
... AND WHEN THAT HAPPENS, COUNT NEFARIA WILL BE LONG GONE--
--EH!?
HEY, IRISH, GET A LOAD OF THIS--
I RECOGNIZE THEM FROM THE MONITOR SCREENS --THEY'RE TWO OF THE X-MEN!
--LOOKS LIKE THAT NEFARIA'S DUDE'S BUGGIN' OUT ON HIS COMPADRES.
YOU'RE TOO LATE, MUTANTS--
--YOU'LL NEVER STOP ME NOW!!
HE'S TAKIN' OFF!!
ONCE HE GETS AIRBORNE IN THAT HARRIER, THERE'S NOT A CRATE IN THIS MOUNTAIN THAT CAN STOP HIM!
201
XV904
SHRREEEE
YEAH, MAYBE NOT A PLANE-- BUT A MAN CAN DO WHAT A PLANE CAN'T--
THUNDER-BIRD, NO!
--AND THUNDERBIRD IS JUST THAT MAN!
DON'T GO AWAY, NEFFIE BABY-- 'CAUSE JOHN PROUDSTAR IS COMIN' TO GET YOU...
... AN' HE'S A MAN WHO DON'T GIVE UP!
SKRAK!
201
ARE YE CRAZY, LAD--?
GET OFF THE PLANE, THUNDERBIRD-- I CAN STOP HIM WITH A SONIC BLAST--
--BUT YE'VE GOT TA GET OFF!!
26

Previous Page: A 1982 photo of young Frazer proudly displaying his copy of Marvel UK's *Spider-Man* #500, a weekly black-&-white reprint magazine. **Above:** Page 26 of *X-Men* #95 [Oct., 1995], with art by Dave Cockrum and Sam Grainger. This scene had a tremendous effect on Frazer.

around that time was the one after Phoenix died—the first time. It was a eulogy piece, giving snapshots of their lives together, and was the first time I'd ever considered tragedy and loss on such a scale. It really did me good as I reference those emotions at other stages in my life, almost as if it was an inoculation of sorts. Obviously I couldn't read that comic for years, either.

MM: Do you ever go back to those books today?

FRAZER: I have done, but in a different frame of mind at the time, so I was distant from the emotional content. Part of me is wary in case the artistry I once revered is in fact no longer there. After all, most of my old comics now look so shoddy by today's standards.

I look back at some old comics and I'm horrified to see the same level of competence applied to comics I used to think were genius! It makes me reconsider each time that the quality of art is all in the eye of the beholder. I would never have liked Dave McKean's art as a kid, but I think he's pretty swish now.

MM: Different times equal a different set of standards, though, as well as how you perceive or understand the art.

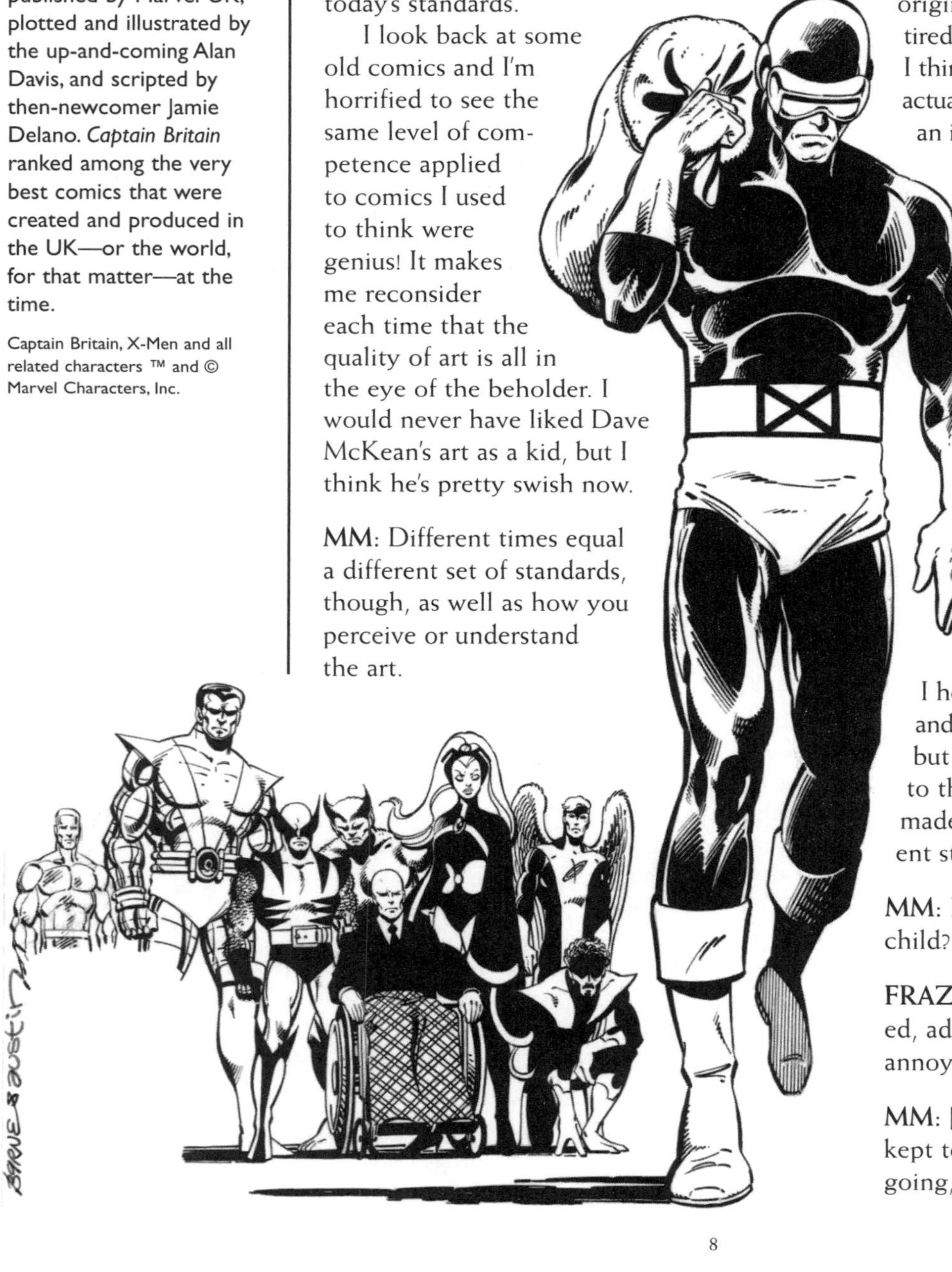

Below: Cover art for *Uncanny X-Men* #138, an issue devoted to the aftermath of the death of Phoenix which introduced Frazer to the concept of tragedy. Pencils by John Byrne and inks by Terry Austin. **Next Page:** Page 3 of *Captain Britain* #3, published by Marvel UK, plotted and illustrated by the up-and-coming Alan Davis, and scripted by then-newcomer Jamie Delano. *Captain Britain* ranked among the very best comics that were created and produced in the UK—or the world, for that matter—at the time.

FRAZER: *Star Wars*. As a kid it was awesome. Watch it three months ago? Meh.

MM: The story is still solid, since it's such a classic tale, but the film itself hasn't held up when we're inundated constantly with big budget effects and films where story often takes a back seat to action.

FRAZER: It's not the effects, it's the storytelling. It's one big cliché. But as a kid I'd never seen *Seven Samurai* or the other films it was referencing, like *Flash Gordon*. I watched it with my girlfriend and she was all bewildered, and she likes science fiction, *Battle Star Galactica*, etc.

I do remember that, as a kid, *Star Wars* was all about the surface—the sound effects, the spaceships, the light sabers—but I never really dug the characters or the plot. Sure, it was original to my innocent, virginal mind, but I tired of it real quick, unlike the *X-Men*, which I think was far more progressive in terms of actual story. Even as a tiny Fraze, I think I had an instinctive attraction to the weird and different. It was somehow inherent in the art itself. The magical X ingredient.

MM: *Star Wars* is a retelling of classic tales and stories anew versus *X-Men*, which can be more relevant to the age. The hidden secret of the "X."

FRAZER: I have no problems with recycling old tales, but I do have a problem using old frameworks and hanging the same rags on them just painted different colors. It's like those movie pitches I hear all the time: "It's *Jaws*, but with a wasp!" One of the worst ones I heard recently was a pitched aimed at me, and it was described, "It's the tale of Oedipus, but set in a cyberpunk world." Instant "no" to that. There could be a good wasp movie made, though it would have to have a different structure and subtext than *Jaws*.

MM: How would you describe yourself as a child?

FRAZER: Extremely intelligent, cute, talented, adorable. Everyone else would say, "small, annoying." I am right, though.

MM: [*laughs*] Did you find that as a child you kept to yourself primarily, or were you outgoing, social, active?

FRAZER: I was social and active, but I had that inner world, as well, where I could amuse myself by playing with stones. I had glasses. It's amazing how much damage glasses had on my ego.

MM: How so?

FRAZER: Everyone I know who had specs as a kid was brutally trashed by them. Well, we were instantly perceived as inferior. "Speccy kid: thou art defective. Ahahahaha!" etc., and judged by all others as, "He has glasses, he must be brainy."

MM: Jeez, that seems a lot more harsh than the occasional jibing I received as "four eyes" as a kid.

FRAZER: Maybe I was more perceptive of it. But also the disability of glasses. No swimming, can't fall over, if I lose them I'm screwed, etc. Another aspect is that because I was in the minority in terms of eyewear, my glasses seemed to define me socially. Frazer is the kid with *glasses*. It devalued everything else. And as a kid with such enormous ambition, that was quite a blow. Though I believe, like a "Boy Named Sue," that it made me tougher. Most of my other four-eyed mates felt the same way, so it's just we had a crappy childhood, but an awesome adulthood in exchange.

MM: It's interesting how times have changed with kids now purposely wearing Harry Potter specs.

FRAZER: I know. My girlfriend's sister wears those awful specs with no lenses because it's hip. They don't know our pain!

MM: Revenge against the sighted!

FRAZER: All normals will be impaired, and the strong will wear braces of lead! [*laughter*]

MM: Were you into drawing and art as a child, or did this develop later in your life?

FRAZER: I doodled as a kid like all others did, but it was my obsession with comics that took it the extra mile.

MM: Was anyone in your household also artistic?

FRAZER: Not really. My mum did amateur dramatics, pantomime, etc., but, no, the rest of 'em were pretty much normal. It is odd that I ended up doing all the arty things.

MM: Was your family supportive of your artistic talents and the arts in general?

FRAZER: I think so. I mean, I was never prevented in any way, though it was rarely treated in any other way than any normal hobby was until I actually started making stuff properly, like at college. My mum did try to fob me off as a child actor, but sadly for her, when I was at the audition I decided I didn't want to be an actor after all.

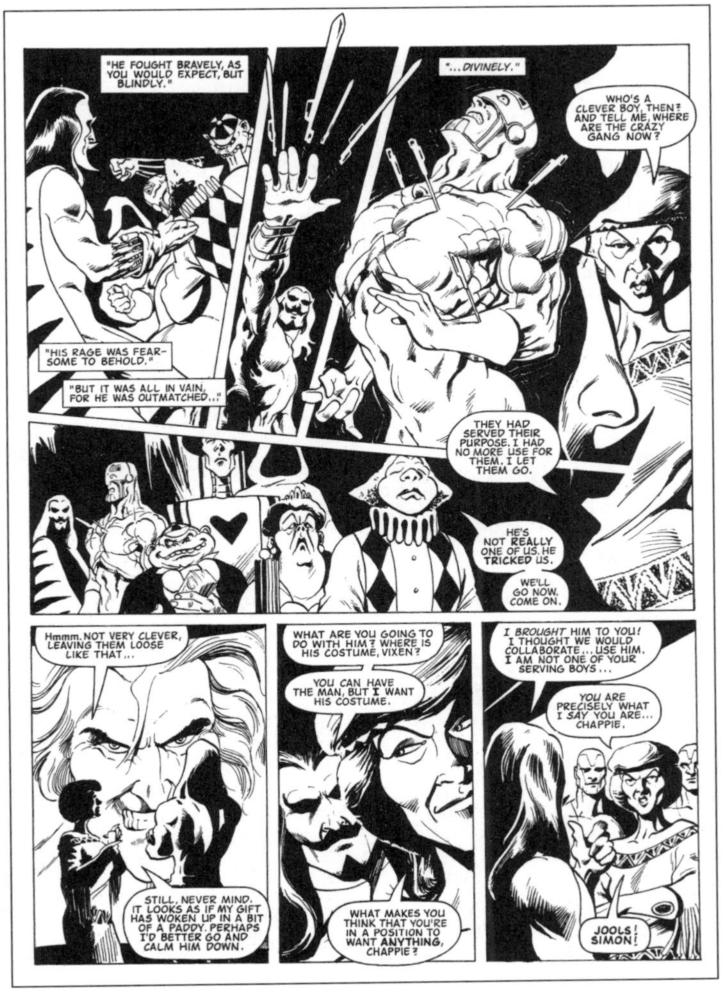

"HE FOUGHT BRAVELY, AS YOU WOULD EXPECT, BUT BLINDLY."
"...DIVINELY."
WHO'S A CLEVER BOY, THEN? AND TELL ME, WHERE ARE THE CRAZY GANG NOW?
"HIS RAGE WAS FEARSOME TO BEHOLD."
"BUT IT WAS ALL IN VAIN, FOR HE WAS OUTMATCHED..."
THEY HAD SERVED THEIR PURPOSE. I HAD NO MORE USE FOR THEM. I LET THEM GO.
HE'S NOT REALLY ONE OF US. HE TRICKED US.
WE'LL GO NOW. COME ON.
Hmmm. NOT VERY CLEVER, LEAVING THEM LOOSE LIKE THAT...
STILL, NEVER MIND. IT LOOKS AS IF MY GIFT HAS WOKEN UP IN A BIT OF A PADDY. PERHAPS I'D BETTER GO AND CALM HIM DOWN.
WHAT ARE YOU GOING TO DO WITH HIM? WHERE IS HIS COSTUME, VIXEN?
YOU CAN HAVE THE MAN, BUT I WANT HIS COSTUME.
WHAT MAKES YOU THINK THAT YOU'RE IN A POSITION TO WANT ANYTHING, CHAPPIE?
I BROUGHT HIM TO YOU! I THOUGHT WE WOULD COLLABORATE... USE HIM. I AM NOT ONE OF YOUR SERVING BOYS...
YOU ARE PRECISELY WHAT I SAY YOU ARE... CHAPPIE.
JOOLS! SIMON!

MM: Do you remember what the audition was for? How old were you?

FRAZER: Ten, I think, and it was a chat with Sylvia Young of the Sylvia Young Theatre School, which produced probably 90% of annoying Brit performers, including the Spice Girls. I think my mum used her amateur drama contacts to get me in. Those folks were all part of a big network, but Madam Young could tell I wasn't serious about it the moment she laid eyes on me. The other kids were loud and scary.

MM: [*laughs*] Do you remember how old you were when you first began reading comics?

FRAZER: I recall already being obsessed with comics at around five, so it must have been earlier than that. By seven I was already a proper hardcore comic nerd.

MM: The comics you read were largely black-&-white reprints, correct?

FRAZER: Yup, though I did start buying imported color comics, as well, quite early. Though, it was a lottery regarding if you could find actual runs of a series. I had so many gaps. I remember reading *X-Men* #120 as an American comic before I read any of the black-&-white reprints.

MM: What about British comics or Marvel UK books by British authors? Did you read those as well?

FRAZER: I never read *2000 AD*, because they had naked bums in them, and it scared me. Plus, I liked super-heroes, and *2000 AD* was devoid of that. I didn't want to read normal stuff. I wanted an escape from banality and suburbia and to dream that I could tap into that endless possibility that the Fantastic Four showed me.

Other Brit comics by the same folks were *Scream*, which was an awesome EC-style horror comic. But beyond that it was all American stuff. Marvel UK started later properly, and the first of that that I read was Alan Davis' *Captain Britain*, which was utterly spellbinding.

I think the art also had an effect. UK art back then was terribly dull, and the American art so varied and diverse: Byrne, Alcala, Trimpe, Pérez, Colan, etc. I used to use American words and I dreamt of visiting New York. What were Twinkies, eh? I had no idea. America was so amazing back then to my tiny British mind.

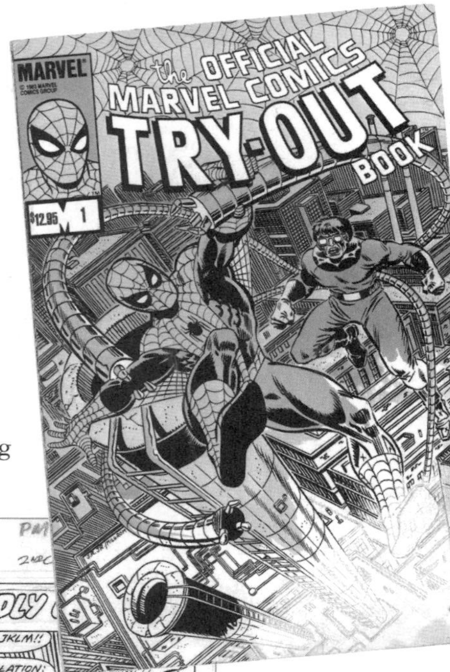

MARVEL
$12.95
1
the OFFICIAL MARVEL COMICS TRY-OUT BOOK

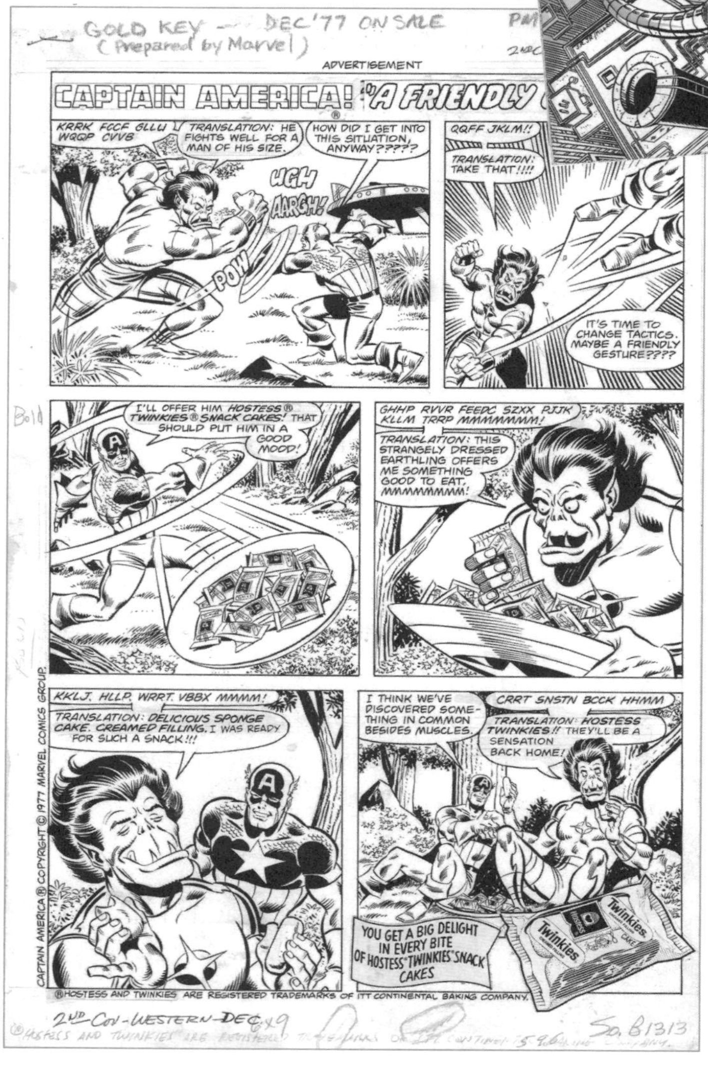

GOLD KEY — DEC '77 ON SALE
(Prepared by Marvel)
ADVERTISEMENT
CAPTAIN AMERICA!
"A FRIENDLY
KRRK FCCF GLLU WQQP CVVB
TRANSLATION: HE FIGHTS WELL FOR A MAN OF HIS SIZE.
HOW DID I GET INTO THIS SITUATION, ANYWAY?????
UGH
AARGH!
POW
QQFF JKLM!!
TRANSLATION: TAKE THAT!!!!
IT'S TIME TO CHANGE TACTICS. MAYBE A FRIENDLY GESTURE????
Bold
I'LL OFFER HIM HOSTESS® TWINKIES® SNACK CAKES! THAT SHOULD PUT HIM IN A GOOD MOOD!
GHHP RVVR FEEDC SZXX PJJK KLLM TRRP MMMMMMM!
TRANSLATION: THIS STRANGELY DRESSED EARTHLING OFFERS ME SOMETHING GOOD TO EAT. MMMMMMMM!
KKLJ. HLLP. WRRT. VBBX MMMM!
TRANSLATION: DELICIOUS SPONGE CAKE. CREAMED FILLING. I WAS READY FOR SUCH A SNACK!!!
I THINK WE'VE DISCOVERED SOMETHING IN COMMON BESIDES MUSCLES.
CRRT SNSTN BCCK HHMM
TRANSLATION: HOSTESS TWINKIES!! THEY'LL BE A SENSATION BACK HOME!
YOU GET A BIG DELIGHT IN EVERY BITE OF HOSTESS® TWINKIES® SNACK CAKES
Twinkies
CAPTAIN AMERICA® COPYRIGHT © 1977 MARVEL COMICS GROUP.
®HOSTESS AND TWINKIES ARE REGISTERED TRADEMARKS OF ITT CONTINENTAL BAKING COMPANY.
2ND COV-WESTERN-DEC 6x9
So. B1313

MM: Twinkies really? I never would have thought of that.

FRAZER: Hostess fruit pies. Man, those ads still enthrall me. Back in those days, Britain was still relatively impoverished, so a lot of the dazzle of America was strange and alien to us.

MM: The American dream in a pastry shell. How did you get your early comics?

FRAZER: Newsstands. I would strip those racks with all the pennies I could find/steal. Proper comic shops existed, but they were so far away, I couldn't visit them at that age. When I did, though, oh boy. I bought the *Marvel Comics Try-Out Book*. Well, I bugged my mum and step-dad to buy it, and I sold it to them on the promise that one day it would help me get a job, which he was less convinced by.

MM: Do you remember how old you were?

FRAZER: I must have been eleven or twelve. I got it pretty early, because I knew of it due to the house ads. I trashed it, though. I had no idea what I was doing, I just liked having that actual comic paper.

MM: Do you recall when you began to recognize the artists' names as a key ingredient in the storytelling?

FRAZER: I noticed that from day one. After I'd read the comic a million times, I started devouring the other stuff, like the indicia, the separation marks, the staples, the credits. I read those comics to death. And it was all good, as I learned a lot from those stories, about everything.

MM: What artists attracted your interest?

FRAZER: Probably Gil Kane and Romita Sr. due to *Spider-Man*, then Pérez on *Fantastic Four*, Byrne on *X-Men*, Colan on *Dr. Strange*, and the awesome and underrated Alfredo Alcala for his *Hulk* stuff. Out of those I still love Kane, Alcala, and Byrne. Byrne had a solidity that was amazing, and Pérez drew the best rubble ever. I also liked Dick Dillin's *Justice League of America* because it was so spooky. Barry Windsor-Smith's "Zukala's Daughter" [*Conan* #5] had some sort of magic that made me want to do comics myself.

MM: Outside of comics, what else entertained you?

FRAZER: We had TV, like *Dr. Who*, but I had to make do with comics and board games, like *Talisman*, which is still the best board game ever.

MM: I'm not familiar with that one.

FRAZER: Hand in you nerd card now. [*laughter*]

MM: What about books?

FRAZER: I hardly read anything. I got into fighting fantasy books massively for a few years before the quality dropped off, but I never read fiction. Books allowed my imagination to run off, so I could never finish one. I read like maybe ten books as a kid, and I can't remember them now. Everyone I knew read books. I had my comics, and they were better for me. I could read words and pictures. And I still maintain that comics are inherently a better form of reading matter for kids, because of this dual action in the brain. If only there were some better ones out there for them to read.

Comics really taught me emotion and context. They could say one thing, yet show another and let my brain figure out the connection, not just in terms of events, but in terms of meaning, too. And the panel shapes also controlled the pacing, yet allowed time to linger, which is why they were better than movies. Odd that I don't read comics anymore.

MM: You don't read any at all?

FRAZER: I read *Asterios Polyp* recently, which was good. But right now I'm writing the comic I want to read. Stuff out there just doesn't excite me. It's either poorly made or riddled with cliché. Even the good stuff makes me think, "Yeah, that's okay. Hmm, what's for dinner?" Old comics are good, and I like reading Judge Dredd stories from way back, especially some older classics from the '80s that I missed. But they have that freshness in them. I have the *Absolute Sandman* books here, and I am keen to read them.

I think one reason I don't read comics anymore is because I make them. As I read, I dissect. You can't have pets if you keep cutting them up. It is a shame, but I have other things to consume now. I did my comics reading during my spring years. Actually, this web piece by Emily Carroll is the most inspiring comic I've read in years. The storytelling, pacing, mood, it's all so excellent. As I read it, I was forced to engage to figure out what was being left out or implied. It made me work, and other comics treat me like I'm an idiot.

MM: Beyond comics, were you into sports at all?

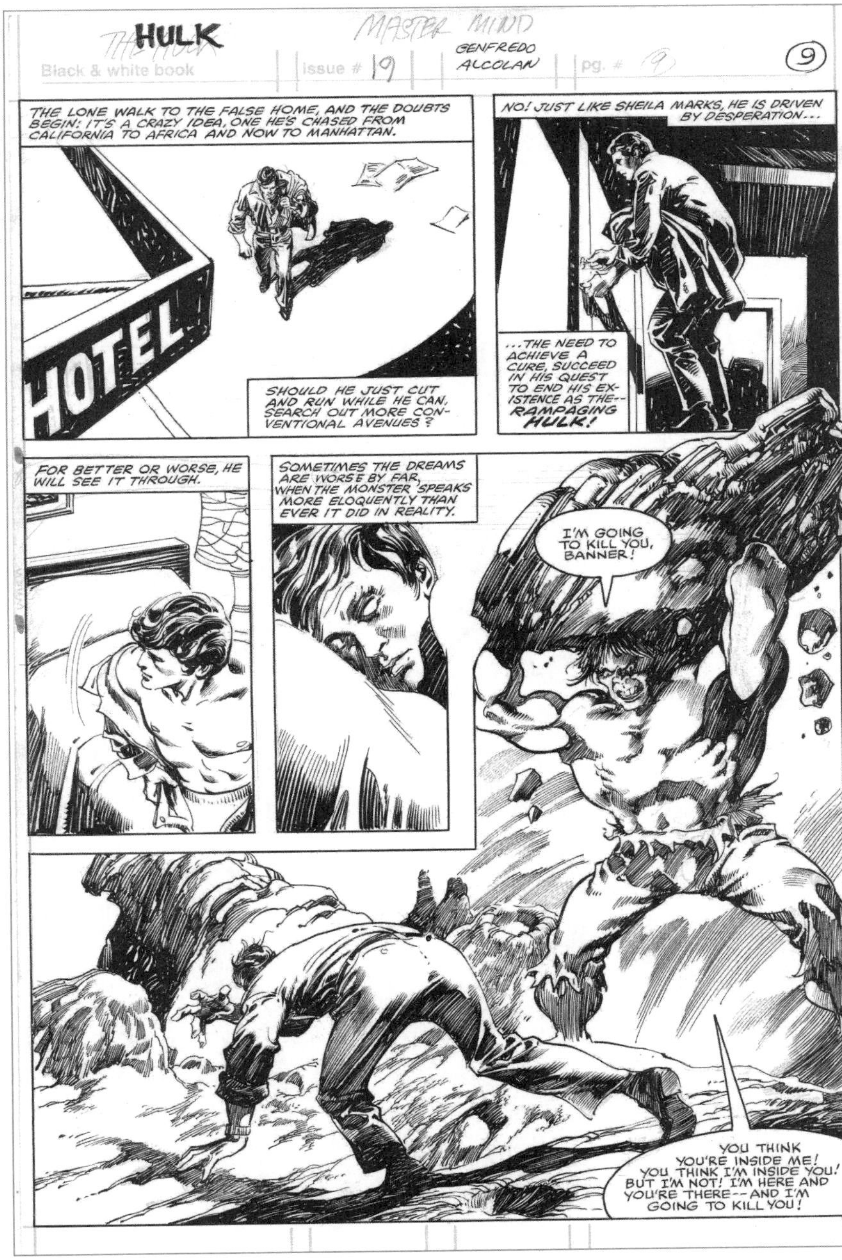

HULK
MASTER MIND
Black & white book
issue # 19
GENFREDO ALCOLAN
pg. # 9
9
THE LONE WALK TO THE FALSE HOME, AND THE DOUBTS BEGIN: IT'S A CRAZY IDEA, ONE HE'S CHASED FROM CALIFORNIA TO AFRICA AND NOW TO MANHATTAN.
HOTEL
SHOULD HE JUST CUT AND RUN WHILE HE CAN, SEARCH OUT MORE CONVENTIONAL AVENUES?
NO! JUST LIKE SHEILA MARKS, HE IS DRIVEN BY DESPERATION...
...THE NEED TO ACHIEVE A CURE, SUCCEED IN HIS QUEST TO END HIS EXISTENCE AS THE-- RAMPAGING HULK!
FOR BETTER OR WORSE, HE WILL SEE IT THROUGH.
SOMETIMES THE DREAMS ARE WORSE BY FAR, WHEN THE MONSTER SPEAKS MORE ELOQUENTLY THAN EVER IT DID IN REALITY.
I'M GOING TO KILL YOU, BANNER!
YOU THINK YOU'RE INSIDE ME! YOU THINK I'M INSIDE YOU! BUT I'M NOT! I'M HERE AND YOU'RE THERE-- AND I'M GOING TO KILL YOU!

FRAZER: I liked climbing and jumping, but hated team sports. I'm either a loner or a monkey.

MM: Well, I recently saw that some gorillas and apes have been trained to draw, so...

FRAZER: Ook! Ook! [*laughter*]

MM: What was school like for you as a child? Was it something you enjoyed?

FRAZER: Hated school. Hated. Like a zoo, it was, full of beasts and bars. Odd then that I studied for five more years.

MM: Was it the kids, the lessons, a combination of it all? So you had no enthusiastic art teacher during those formative years?

Previous Page: Ads like this convinced kids the world over that Twinkies were actually good—art by Sal Buscema. And *The Official Marvel Comics Try-Out* convinced kids the world over—Frazer included—to submit their artwork to Marvel. **Above:** Two of Frazer's favorites—Gene Colan and Alfredo Alcala—team up on this page from the black-&-white *Hulk* magazine.

FRAZER: The art teachers were supportive, but I hated being imprisoned like that. The kids were morons, the lessons primitive, the buildings cold and unforgiving. The whole experience was one of endurance for me. If we had had computers, well now, maybe I would have liked it more? Less kids, though. I would have liked it with less kids—less noisy, annoying, rude, bigoted, smelly, little, wretched brats. It wasn't a school where being smart or funny would get you anywhere. And they were my main skills until they all discovered I could draw, and then I became the kid with glasses who could draw. Plus, I was constantly pining for some girl or other, but never getting anywhere. The ultimate nerd. Wow, how things have changed!

MM: At 14, you submitted samples to Marvel from *Excalibur*. That's a bold move for someone so young. How did you come to the decision to send art to Marvel?

FRAZER: The *Try-Out Book*! They had all the info in it, plus *Marvel Age* often ran articles on submissions, so they were the ones I knew about. I had given up on DC at around 13 due to finances, and I didn't think there were any other publishers in existence.

MM: Do you remember what samples you sent? Did Marvel respond?

FRAZER: Marvel stuff from around that period started getting pretty lame, so I guess I was choosing based on the Alan Davis stuff in *Excalibur* at that point. It was four pages of rather bad storytelling. Boring stuff and a fight. A big panel with Captain Britain in the rain. They did reply a good few months later with a form letter saying, "Not good

enough yet, but keep trying!" It was only pencils back then. I lacked the confidence or the tools and skills to ink properly, and color terrified me. I had no schooling in color theory.

MM: You also produced work for an advertising company at the age of 16. How did you come to that, and what type of advertising work did you do?

FRAZER: That came about due to a friend of a friend. There was this dude who did caricatures down the road from my part of Ilford, and somehow he had made connection with a mutual school friend called Chaz, and Chaz had told him about me. I went over to check his stuff out with the aim of networking, and he took an instant shine to my doodles. He kept saying, "He could be the next Burne Hogarth," to his wife, though I was never that keen on Hogarth. Still, it was nice to have another artist have faith in me.

Anyway, he took me to a pub in London called The Cartoonist, where he introduced me to lots of old men who smelt of tobacco and booze. I spoke to quite a few of these chaps. This was the period when comics had become "cool," and there were younger dudes all excited by Sienkiewicz and McKean, and I was, like, totally not into that, and there were the older dudes who lettered *Prince Valiant* and stuff. Phil Collins' brother was there, too. Anyway, by the end of the night I met this cleaner, more respectable dude who was persuaded to give me a shot at some freelancing based on my buddy's recommendation, and the next week I took my folio up to his studio in Islington. They were a bit nonplused by my folio of fantasy crap and watercolor drawings of robot arms playing guitars.

Eventually they sat me down at a drawing table and gave me this brief to design a super-hero character for a company called Drupa in Germany. The gag was to call him Supadrupa. I was annoyed. I hadn't planned to be stuck there all day. So I drew and drew, eventually doing my best Kirby impression with the thing. They sort of liked it and then sent me off home to do a color comic page based on this character. I left it 'til the last moment and made what was the worst comic page ever. I took it back and they described it as a "rough," and then sat me back at the table to redraw it. I was annoyed a great deal. This wasn't comics. Besides, this was right in the middle of my rock star phase, so I was even less interested in this rubbish.

After a few hours the boss called me into his office and had a little chat. He thought the work was rough but that I had a lot of potential, so he offered me a job. I wasn't expecting this. I wanted freelance gigs drawing Spider-Man at home and playing gigs in the evening, not a job. Plus, there was a girl at school I was besotted with, and I was chasing my fantasies by opting to stay on at school for the extra two sixth-form years in order to do more drama.

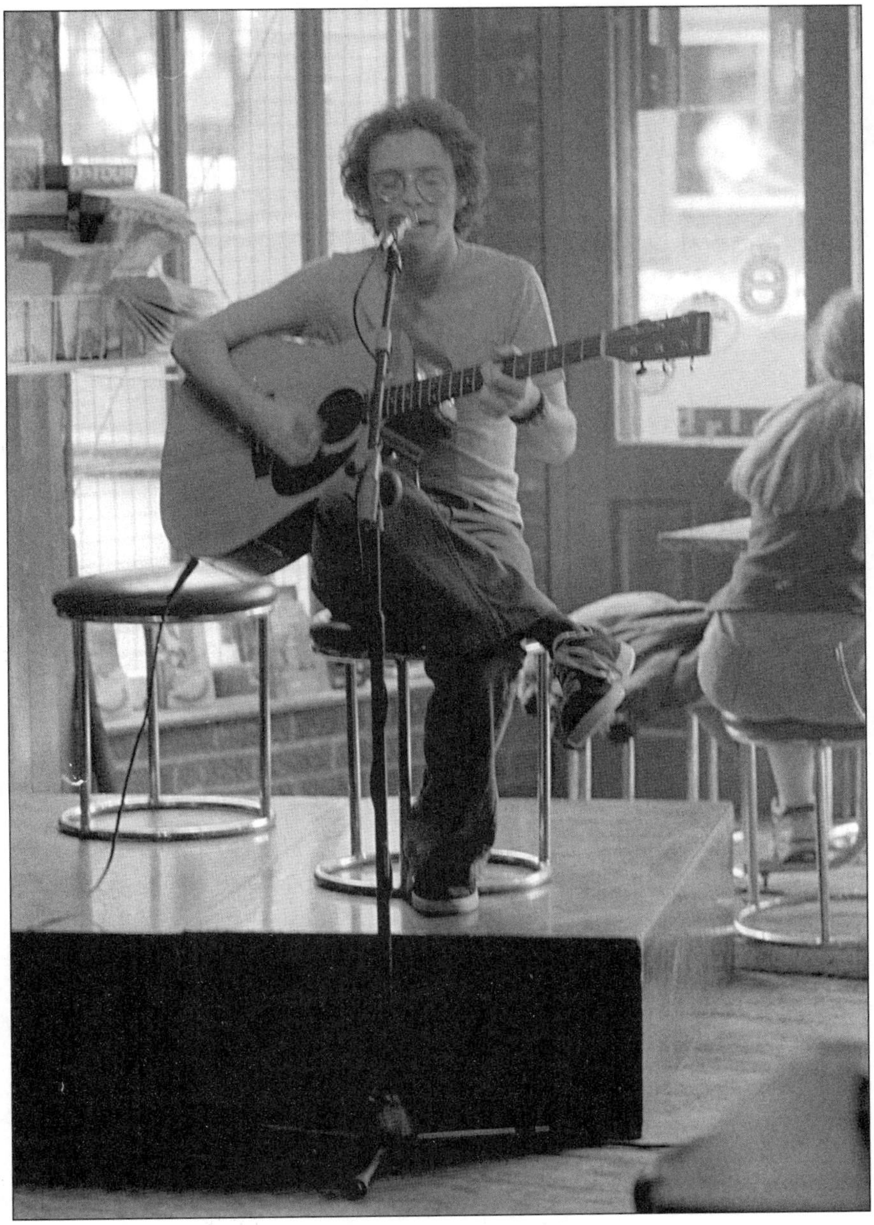

MM: How did this job affect your growth as an artist? What did you take away from it for your next art gig?

FRAZER: I knew what a rough looked like. That, and that in order to make any career as an artist, one must be able to turn crap into gold, even if the crap really, really stinks.

So I turned the job down, took the 30 pounds for the work I'd done, and bolted. His teenage daughter seemed to have liked me. I wonder what my life would have been if I had taken that offer. Mind you, she would have eaten me alive. [*laughs*] I spent the 30 pounds on my first bass guitar.

MM: When did you learn to play bass? Was this the musical awakening you mentioned at the age of 16?

FRAZER: Yar. I didn't actually learn to play bass. I bought a bass, figured out what the notes were, and improvised. I stole licks and figured out how basses worked, how music worked, by watching videos of musicians and digging around the fret board by myself. And that first bass? Fretless. Talk about in at the deep end.

MM: Pretty ambitious for a first bass.

FRAZER: I was into The Police, but I had no idea at all. Copied what Sting did on TV, and then I discovered Jack Bruce. Sadly, at school, sixth form, there were no other musicians to jam with until the second year there, when I met a tiny dude called Ashraful, who did the whole Paul Simon acoustic thing. We would jam, but there were no drums, and I wanted drums. I was a frustrated drummer, to be honest. I wrote my first song with him, and he was the one who got me into smoking, drinking, drugs, and bragging about how many women we had laid, which back then was nil. [*laughs*]

Previous Page: A late '90s illustration by Frazer entitled "Tongues Too Far."
Above: Frazer performing an acoustic solo set. By this time, he had a much better idea about what he was doing.

Part 2: On Being Dave McKean and Learning to Fly

MM: You graduated from Seven Kings High School in 1990 and gave yourself a four-year time frame to become a successful artist.

FRAZER: Four years seemed like a long time back then, and to be honest if I had stuck at it I would have been a lot better and likely to succeed. However, I got sidetracked by music and lust, so by 18 I wasn't into the whole idea anymore. I remember one night deciding to draw comics again. Yes, it was Captain Britain again, and I was inking with a dip pen onto proper board, doing far better work, but still very much lacking in proper storytelling skills. This, however, didn't last that long, as I was destined to go to art school.

Near the end of sixth form, I was going to apply to the nearest art school for a one-year prep course. Then about three weeks before my interview, my teacher told me they had a spot free the next day and did I want to go? I said no, I wasn't ready. Then, as with many times in my life, I felt that creeping shiver of cowardice, and I knew that I had to actually take this opportunity and not chicken out. So the next day I went along with my half-baked folio, and they offered me a place on the spot, unconditional of exam results.

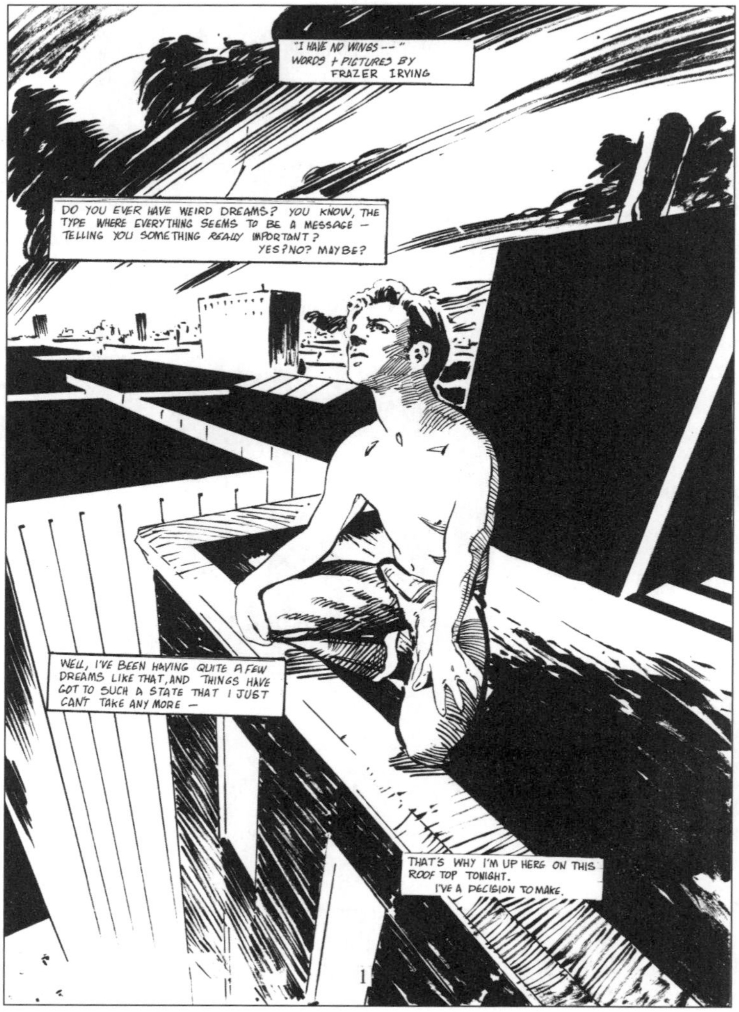
"I HAVE NO WINGS --"
WORDS + PICTURES BY
FRAZER IRVING
DO YOU EVER HAVE WEIRD DREAMS? YOU KNOW, THE TYPE WHERE EVERYTHING SEEMS TO BE A MESSAGE — TELLING YOU SOMETHING REALLY IMPORTANT? YES?NO? MAYBE?
WELL, I'VE BEEN HAVING QUITE A FEW DREAMS LIKE THAT, AND THINGS HAVE GOT TO SUCH A STATE THAT I JUST CAN'T TAKE ANY MORE —
THAT'S WHY I'M UP HERE ON THIS ROOF TOP TONIGHT.
I'VE A DECISION TO MAKE.
1

Straight after the holidays I enrolled at East Ham community college. My school mates all went to university, and so I was on my own for the first time. That first year at college, well aside from chasing tail, I got really into weed and hashish, thanks to my college mates and my new circle of local friends who all worked in banks and wanted to play metal guitar. This lifestyle totally trashed my first year.

MM: Barry Windsor-Smith attended the school and eventually taught there, and Ralph Steadman was an instructor there at some point. Did these factors affect your decision, and did you have the opportunity to learn under any similar caliber artists during your time?

FRAZER: No, I had no idea until after I left. If I had known, I would have used it to get in with the "in" crowd. The teachers were pretty lame, as well. The only one of the lot who taught me anything worth a damn was a part-time dude called Colin. He did paintings of the Moors. Boring stuff, but he knew the basics of painting, tone, drawing, etc., and knew the tricks to teach it. He showed us how a black can be lighter than a white. He also taught us how to shut one eye and flatten the scene and draw just the shapes. Invaluable stuff, I tell you.

MM: What types of art did you produce while at East Ham? Did you stick to drawing and illustration, or did you also study sculpture and other mediums?

FRAZER: The first year was a bit of everything: sculpture, illustration, graphics, textiles, etc. When I had to specialize, I chose fine art, because there was no other option that allowed for drawing. That was when I tried my hand at painting, and I got quite into it.

MM: Was it here where you learned about proper art tools and methods, or was that something you taught yourself?

FRAZER: No, I had taught myself that via books and reading interviews. East Ham wasn't all that hot, really. I got some basics, but it wasn't all it should have been. Kind of like the degree course at Portsmouth. What I learned at college was about socializing, people, weirdness, how to roll a joint, what variety there is in the world, etc. Art was almost like the extracurricular bit.

MM: From there, did you try applying to other art schools?

FRAZER: At the end of year two I applied for fine art courses. I went to two interviews, lugging around paintings and stuff—got rejected from both. After that I took a year out because I had to. I toyed with getting a job, but I didn't know how to, so I signed on the dole instead and started drawing comics again. This was also the year I joined my first proper band. We never got paid for gigs, so I survived on the dole.

MM: What types of music did your band play?

FRAZER: Pop-punk-funk-rock-jazz.

MM: So pretty experimental, improvisational stuff then?

FRAZER: Two guitars, one bass, drums, bad vocals. No, no, no. The jazz bit is just the chords we sometimes used. The rest of it was a bit like the Chili Peppers' *Blood Sugar Sex Magik*. We did jam on stage once, during my first and only gig with this band, when they all stopped in the middle of the song because they were stoned. I carried on by myself, lay-ing down a groovy twelve-bar bass line, and then they came back in, as did the audience. I saved that night, I tell you. My mate—who had defected to the bar after the second song—told me that the bass break got people interested again and they came back to see what would happen. He told me if I had stopped as well they would have lynched us.

MM: Do you find a lot of carry-over · between your music and art today in terms of drives and impulses? Do you ever see the rhythmic nature of music, beats, and time signatures affecting how you compose a page and tell a story?

FRAZER: Well, yeah, the whole comic thing is directly relatable to music. Panels are beats, volume; colors are chords, harmony; lines, melody; etc. I feel it instinctively when I make art. I hear music in my head, a direct translation of the mood I feel inside, and that works also with the art, though I have to

conform the art to the brief, so the experi-mentation is far less than with music. I like to jam with music. I can't jam with art.

MM: What finally convinced you to return to school and pursue art?

FRAZER: I had no other options. I went to university to form a band and to draw my own comics and sell them independently.

MM: And when did this decision occur?

FRAZER: Halfway through my year out. I decided I was good enough for art school, so I applied again. Again, I got in on the first interview, unconditional entry. They even showed my sketchbooks to the other inter-viewees to show them what they should be doing.

Previous Page: Page 3 of *The Man Who Learnt to Fly*, a comic strip Frazer wrote and drew during his time at college. It started out as a simple three-page experiment, but developed into something much bigger. **Above:** "Tempest" is an illustration done during Frazer's college days.

The Man Who Learnt to Fly ™ and © Frazer Irving. Tempest © Frazer Irving.

Below: Page 107 of *The Man Who Learnt to Fly*. **Next Page:** The first two pages of *Childeater*, done during Frazer's year-long break between community college and university. Page 2 gives a sample of the type of experimentation with lay-outs Frazer was working through.

MM: Was this your time at the University of Portsmouth?

FRAZER: Portsmouth was from '93 to '96. I got a second class degree, thanks mainly due to my thesis, which was a pile of crap, but I doubt they actually read it. They just saw the bibliography and said, "Yeah, he did the work."

MM: How did your course of study differ from East Ham? What was the thesis?

FRAZER: My thesis was on "adult comics," but not porn, more the "fantasy comics for adults." Portsmouth was a major disappointment. I went in the golden child and came out the McKean clone with the whole of the establishment hating him. University was far too academic for me. They didn't care about vocational art, only about grades and academia.

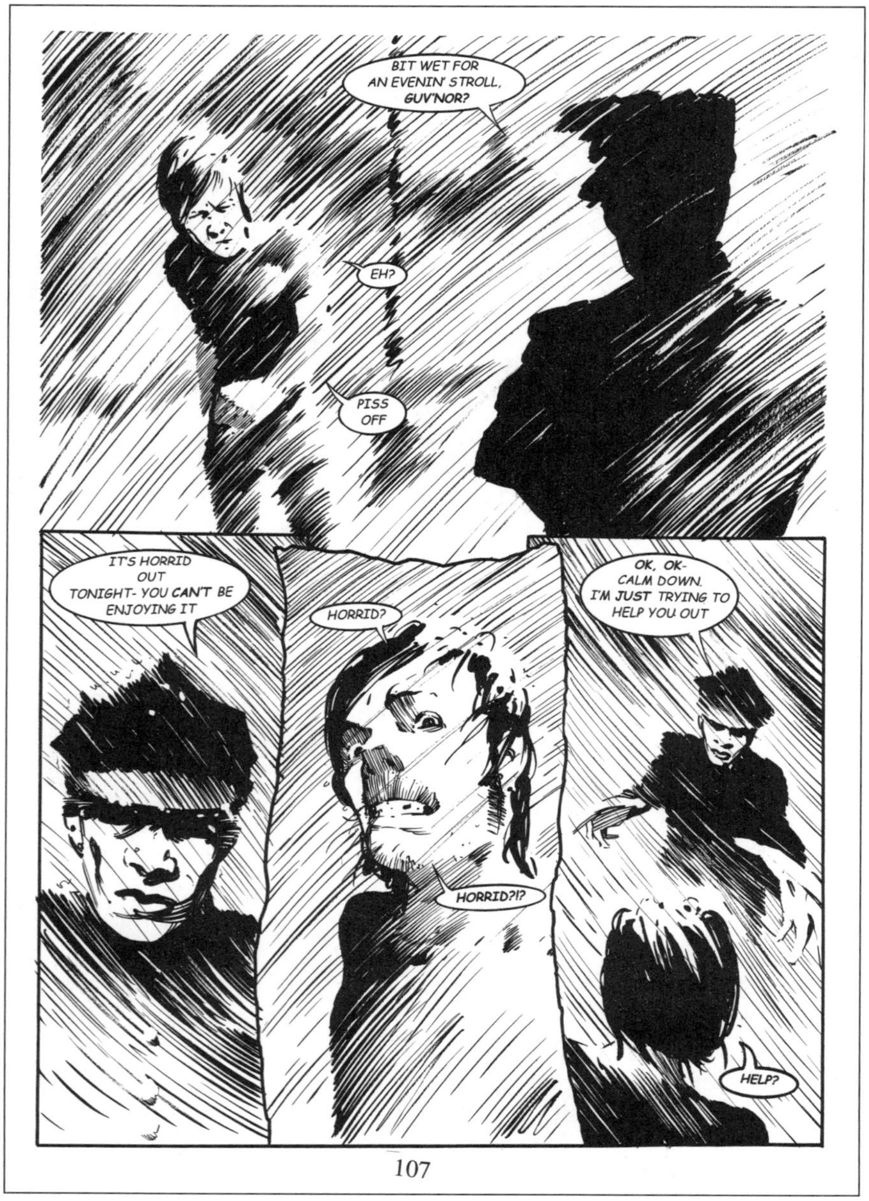
BIT WET FOR AN EVENIN' STROLL, GUV'NOR?
EH?
PISS OFF
IT'S HORRID OUT TONIGHT- YOU CAN'T BE ENJOYING IT
HORRID?
HORRID?!?
OK, OK- CALM DOWN. I'M JUST TRYING TO HELP YOU OUT
HELP?
107

I learned some good stuff about line in my first year, and the life drawing lessons were good practice, but on the whole it was all about method and exploring other avenues, which would have been okay if they cared about the aesthetics of the final product. The sort of project that would garner praise would have been a room full of tea bags. The sort of project that would have been reviled would have been a comic. So I just copied Dave McKean and slunk in between them.

MM: How do you see your time in this situation affecting your artistic output in terms of inspiration and drive?

FRAZER: Well, during this time my ambition to make comics was reborn, in part due to John Byrne's *Next Men*, and in part to *Hellboy*. Seeing those two dudes break the mold and do their own thing made me think I could do that as well. So I started my own comic strip called *The Man Who Learnt to Fly*, and that really was the saving grace of my time at college. I decided to create stuff, not because of college, but in spite of it. It made me the rebel once again.

MM: Was this during the same time period as the drawing sessions at Magic Torch? How did your peers influence and affect your art?

FRAZER: Magic Torch was the company my two mates formed and then told me about. It was to be an umbrella company for us all to work under, but they moved to Brighton and I moved to London, so I got shifted out. They were and still are very much into the image manipulation thing. My drawing never really fit in with it, and I did better with comics on my own. What I learnt from them, though, was how to use Photoshop. Playing around on that first Mac, man, it was like being reborn.

MM: I think you've said that your time in Portsmouth broke your Anglophile tendency towards American comics through exposure to other things. Can you tell me about some of these and how they changed your approach to art as you developed your own style?

FRAZER: Well, mainly it was the Legend imprint at Dark Horse that did it. The breaking free thing really struck me. I also got into Alphonse Mucha then, and then I discovered Abstract Expressionism and other forms of art that made me think. But *Understanding Comics* really showed the possibilities to me and made me more curious to try different things

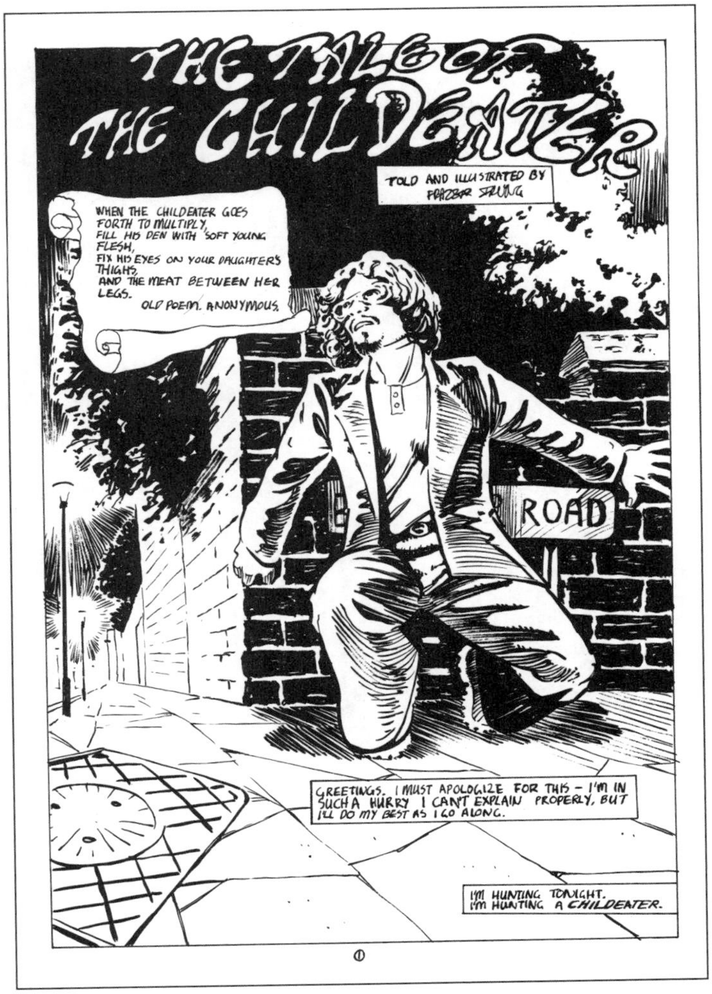
THE TALE OF THE CHILDEATER
TOLD AND ILLUSTRATED BY FRAZER IRVING
WHEN THE CHILDEATER GOES FORTH TO MULTIPLY, FILL HIS DEN WITH SOFT YOUNG FLESH, FIX HIS EYES ON YOUR DAUGHTER'S THIGHS, AND THE MEAT BETWEEN HER LEGS.
OLD POEM. ANONYMOUS.
ROAD
GREETINGS. I MUST APOLOGIZE FOR THIS – I'M IN SUCH A HURRY I CAN'T EXPLAIN PROPERLY, BUT I'LL DO MY BEST AS I GO ALONG.
I'M HUNTING TONIGHT. I'M HUNTING A CHILDEATER.
①

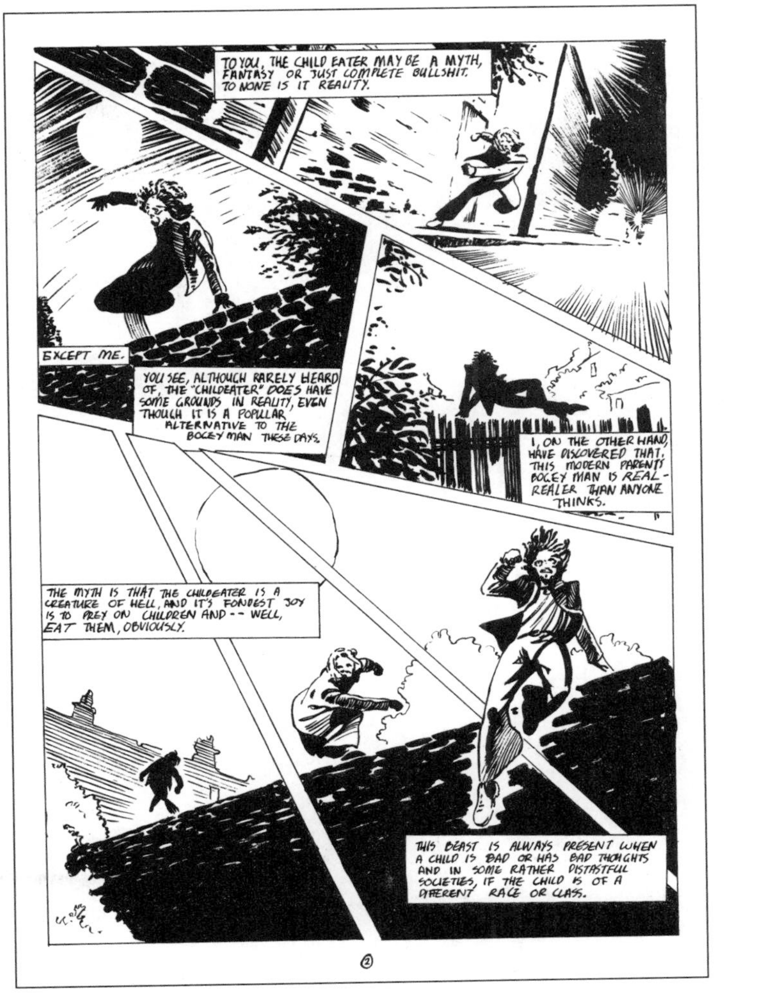
TO YOU, THE CHILD EATER MAY BE A MYTH, FANTASY OR JUST COMPLETE BULLSHIT. TO NONE IS IT REALITY.
EXCEPT ME.
YOU SEE, ALTHOUGH RARELY HEARD OF, THE "CHILDEATER" DOES HAVE SOME GROUNDS IN REALITY, EVEN THOUGH IT IS A POPULAR ALTERNATIVE TO THE BOGEY MAN THESE DAYS.
I, ON THE OTHER HAND, HAVE DISCOVERED THAT, THIS MODERN PARENTS BOGEY MAN IS REAL - REALER THAN ANYONE THINKS.
THE MYTH IS THAT THE CHILDEATER IS A CREATURE OF HELL, AND IT'S FONDEST JOY IS TO PREY ON CHILDREN AND -- WELL, EAT THEM, OBVIOUSLY.
THIS BEAST IS ALWAYS PRESENT WHEN A CHILD IS BAD OR HAS BAD THOUGHTS AND IN SOME RATHER DISTASTFUL SOCIETIES, IF THE CHILD IS OF A DIFFERENT RACE OR CLASS.
②

rather than just copy super-hero comics. I decided at university that I would try to develop stories that were anything but super-heroes, which is odd, since I ended up drawing Batman. It is good to do that, though, as it means I can bring some of those sensibilities to the super-hero world and thus add to the diversity for the readers.

I never figured I'd end up drawing men in tights. Once I turned my back on them, I figured that was it. I'm still shocked that anyone ever hired me to do that stuff, but I'm glad they did. I would never have pictured me doing work like this when I was 15. Of course, I would never have imagined balding back then, either. Or having a girlfriend.

MM: Is this the period that you refer to as your "Dave McKean phase"?

FRAZER: I emulated the photomontage art of McKean when I found Photoshop. I loved it so much, I figured that was my calling. Pffff. If you look at *The Man Who Learnt to Fly* you will see me go through several different styles as I tried to emulate different artists, but that was part of the process and not the end goal. I never really wanted to draw like someone else, I just didn't know how to find my own voice. I know now, of course.

MM: When did you begin *Childeater*?

FRAZER: Ooh, that was done in my year out. My first foray into my own comics. That was brought to an end, though, by university and the evils that came with it.

MM: From the few pages I've seen of *Childeater*, you wrote this story, as well?

FRAZER: Yeah. I wasn't a very good writer back then. It was all set pieces and fights, but some interesting themes did emerge. I noticed that gender issues and preconceptions based on appearance feature heavily in my work. It took me until, like, two years ago to figure out what a story really is, and what it is, is a vast growing thing that feeds and wails like a child, yet lives inside my head, tentacles popping out my ears.

MM: What stands out to me is that it's the first recorded attempt I have seen of what I consider to be trademark Frazer Irving in style: the layout on page two. You employ the off-angled, fractured panel style to the page. Where did you come up with this technique, and what inspired you to take such an approach?

FRAZER: That was stolen from Alan Davis and David Lloyd. I liked their layouts and they were readable, so I aped it. Since then, however, I've reined it back a lot to

LOU BEGAN CAUTIOUSLY, MOVING SLOWLY, OFTEN LOOKING BEHIND AS IF EXPECTING SOMEONE OR SOMETHING TO APPEAR... SILENTLY, SUDDENLY!
HE REMEMBERED HOW THE HOUSE HAD TERRIFIED HIM AS A BOY! THE WEEK HIS MOTHER WAS SICK, HE HAD COME TO STAY WITH HIS UNCLE!
HE HAD LAIN AWAKE NIGHTS, HEARING STRANGE SOUNDS, SPENT DAYS WANDERING ABOUT THE DREARY HALLWAYS FLANKED BY LOCKED ROOMS!
NOW, HE WAS NOT ANXIOUS TO DISCOVER THE SECRETS OF SHADOW HOUSE!
HE HADN'T LIKED THE PLAN, BUT HE HAD AGREED WITH MARIE! DIDN'T HE ALWAYS! THE MONEY WOULD BUY HER THINGS, MAKE HER HAPPY, MAKE HER LOVE HIM MORE! YES, HE HAD TO FIND IT!
HE MANAGED AN APPROVING SMILE TO BOLSTER HIS CONFIDENCE... AND MOUNTED THE WAITING STAIRWAY...
A DOZEN HEARTBEATS LATER, HE BEGAN TO SHRIEK...
LOU, WHAT IS IT?
IT...IT'S HIM! I SAW HIM! UNCLE!
IT'S ONLY HIS PORTAIT, YOU SPINELESS WORM! LOOK AT HIM ...SENILE, OLD UGLY!
IT MOVED! I SAW IT MOVE! IS IT MY NERVES?
HA!! CONSCIENCE... GUILTY CONSCIENCE!
4

avoid becoming confusing, such as with the Batman stuff, which was all pretty much regular panel shapes. Oh, also Steranko. He inspired a lot of that.

MM: What would you call then, if not "fractured," the layout device you use in *Batman and Robin* or *Batman: The Return of Bruce Wayne* in a few panels where it's a single image divided into two equal side-by-side panels. The image of Bruce reaching up to that necklace of Wonder Woman and Superman's symbols stands out in my mind.

FRAZER: Hmm. I'm not sure actually. I stole it from somewhere, I know. I love that gimmick so much, it features heavily in my own story, but until just now I never really thought about where it came from. Probably from Steranko...

Wait, it was that *Tower of Shadows* story he did ["At the Stroke of Midnight," *Tower of Shadows* #1]. The whole story used that gimmick, and I totally stole it. Though, I must say I used it in different ways. It is good for showing movement as well as isolating different elements. It's like beats or key changes in music. The overall scene is the same, because sometimes changing the whole scene to show a new element is too great a break, like that panel with the medallions in *Batman: Return of Bruce Wayne*. "Aspect-to-aspect" is how Scott McLoud termed it.

MM: I like how it forces me to engage the story differently, not abruptly or breaking the flow, but an unconscious guide within the rhythms of the page itself.

FRAZER: Yeah, that is something that irks me about a lot of scripts. They read like storyboards, not like comics. Steranko really did invent so many awesome toys; I'm glad he doesn't mind us using them.

MM: I can see the Steranko style carry over into *The Man Who Learnt to Fly*. How did you come up with the idea? Which came first, the story or the designs?

FRAZER: *The Man Who Learnt to Fly* started out as a three-page experiment to show some dude flying, to see how I would handle it. After I did that, the character loitered in my head, and eventually I got to wondering what his story was. I wrote it as a voyage of discovery piece, built around the flashback dream gimmick. Once I finished part one, I had no idea where it was going, a bit like how the writers of *Lost* must have felt each episode. The whole book was based around ideas of storytelling as opposed to the actual content of the story or the characters, a flaw I have isolated and corrected now. The gimmicks are there to serve the story and communicate the ideas, not the other way around.

MM: Is there a reason the main character has no name?

FRAZER: I felt back then that leaving him nameless made the connection between the reader and him closer, almost as if the two were so intimate that there was no need for names. I was less into creating brands as telling a story back then, so I didn't care if no one knew what to call him—that was never important. There's no info on his background, either, which I felt would also have distanced the reader.

MM: The placement of the panels and lettering denotes the story pacing. How difficult was it for you to understand and learn these story rhythms?

FRAZER: It was easy! I'd been toying with panel layouts for years, anyway, doing my own amateur comics at school and home, copying what I read in the proper printed things, but shortly before I began *The Man Who Learnt to Fly*, I'd spent a few weeks during summer break at college doing some test sheets of comic panels as examples of the variety of storytelling one could achieve. I did a bunch, ranging from frenetic action sequences to conversational sequences to sex sequences, and also a flying dude sequence. I was exploring how the shape of the panel and the arrangement would enhance the imagery within and create a very instant mood/feeling when one just regards the page as a collection of boxes. This really opened the imagination and clarified some of the gimmicks I'd been brewing for ages, such as the panels that are split up by gutters.

As for the lettering, that was all instinct. I hadn't heard the "first speaker on the left" rule—it seems so obvious now, but many folks still miss it—and I don't know if I broke that rule at any point in the story, I was just going with how it looked on the page. If the page was a slow change from one scene to another, then the lettering as graphics would have to enhance that. But it was all guess work.

MM: Did your script have extensive notes about panels and layouts? Did you do thumbnails beforehand to see how the story would transfer visually?

FRAZER: Oh, the whole thing was thumbnails with single sentence descriptions of the events. I didn't write full script at all. In fact, I'd be loathe to do so even now. It was all about the pictures telling the story. The notes would be a page of several pages thumbed out, with little arrows pointing to panels and a note that read, "lots of angels here, but looking creepy." There may well have been snippets of dialogue written out, too, but most of that was invented after the art was complete. I was basically working Marvel style. The whole story had been broken down into 22 sentences on a page, and that was my "plot."

MM: The entire work seems to get more polished as it proceeds, both in terms of more innovative and sophisticated use of panels, but also in the attention paid to the characters and the scenes. In some ways, the faces take on a style that is far more recognizable as your contemporary work. Was this a conscious move on your part?

FRAZER: This was a natural evolution, a product of actually just doing the work. When I started it, I was very unsure which illustrative path to follow. It was either Adam Hughes' smooth lines or Romita, Jr.'s horizontal hatching. I needed a focal point for the rendering and I went with Romita, Jr., because it just looked more solid. By actually doing the pages, though, I was forced into devising methods

Previous Page: Jim Steranko's bravura, "At the Stroke of Midnight," had a profound impact on Frazer during the period of time when he was finding his voice as an artist, as these panels from *Batman: The Return of Bruce Wayne* #2 would indicate.
Below: *The Man Who Learnt to Fly*, page 129.

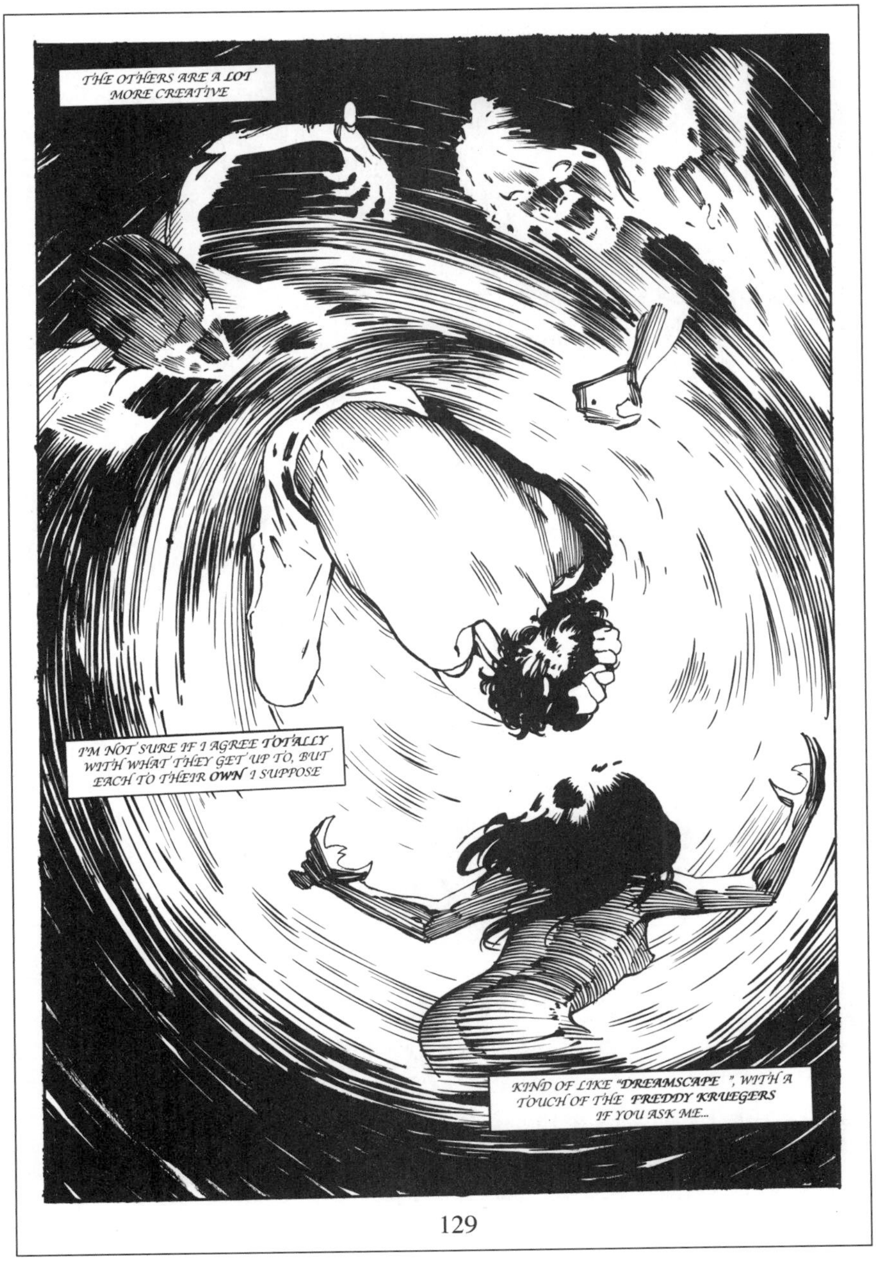
THE OTHERS ARE A LOT MORE CREATIVE
I'M NOT SURE IF I AGREE TOTALLY WITH WHAT THEY GET UP TO, BUT EACH TO THEIR OWN I SUPPOSE
KIND OF LIKE "DREAMSCAPE", WITH A TOUCH OF THE FREDDY KRUEGERS IF YOU ASK ME...
129

Below: Page 134 of The Man Who Learnt to Fly, along with the opening page of "Speak No Evil," which first appeared in the *Dreamy Comics Presents* anthology.
Next Page: Frazer based the eight-page strip, "I Hate This Job," on his eight-month long stint as a security guard at The Royal Academy of Art in 1996. Frazer says of his time there surrounded by works of art, "It probably did affect me, but not in any obvious way that I can recall."

to create textures and forms and to render complicated shapes without the benefit of ripping off another artist's style, which is where the art training of drawing from life came in handy, as I would actually study and experiment and stuff. But this is where style is born, in the struggle to solve problems. Each time I overcame a significant hurdle in terms of drawing or inking, my confidence increased, and I subscribed more to my set of lines than any derivative styles I may have been interested in before. There were key panels and key illustrative moments where I know I crossed certain levels, and I still carry some of those ideas with me today.

MM: When "Devils," the third issue, comes out, the typography is credited to Macintosh. What convinced you to employ a computer in your art?

FRAZER: I couldn't rely on Russ Hossain to do all the lettering at this point. I don't know if he had lost interest or if it was too much hard work, but contact had disintegrated somewhat. I was living with a mate who had a Mac Performa, so I was using that because it was there. The Mac was indeed the first Mac that the Magic Torch used. I think we called him Randall, after a character in a Tarantino movie, but that little feller started us all off on our digital paths.

MM: Can you tell me a little about what tools made up your art arsenal at the time you were working on *The Man Who Learnt to Fly*?

FRAZER: I had pencils, both regular and blue, pens of various sorts—mainly thin-tipped markers, though—and by the middle I was using nylon brushes and Indian ink for almost all of it, before reverting to pens with brushes near the end. I liked the clarity of the pens, but the brushes gave it more emotion. The best example of that is the opening to "Devils" with the rain. The brush just brings it to life, where a pen would have killed it.

MM: When you move into the "Voice" chapter, the entire project appears to get a lot wilder and bizarre. You have multiple, full-page splashes; lettering boxes that deviate between

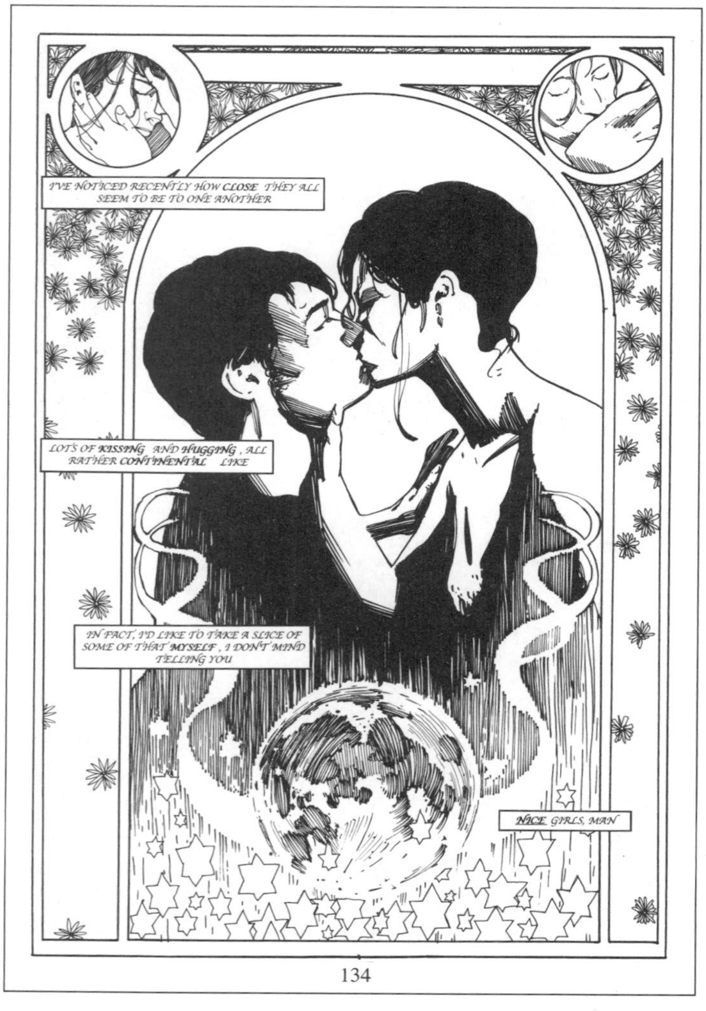
I'VE NOTICED RECENTLY HOW CLOSE THEY ALL SEEM TO BE TO ONE ANOTHER
LOTS OF KISSING AND HUGGING, ALL RATHER CONTINENTAL LIKE
IN FACT, I'D LIKE TO TAKE A SLICE OF SOME OF THAT MYSELF, I DON'T MIND TELLING YOU
NICE GIRLS, MAN
134

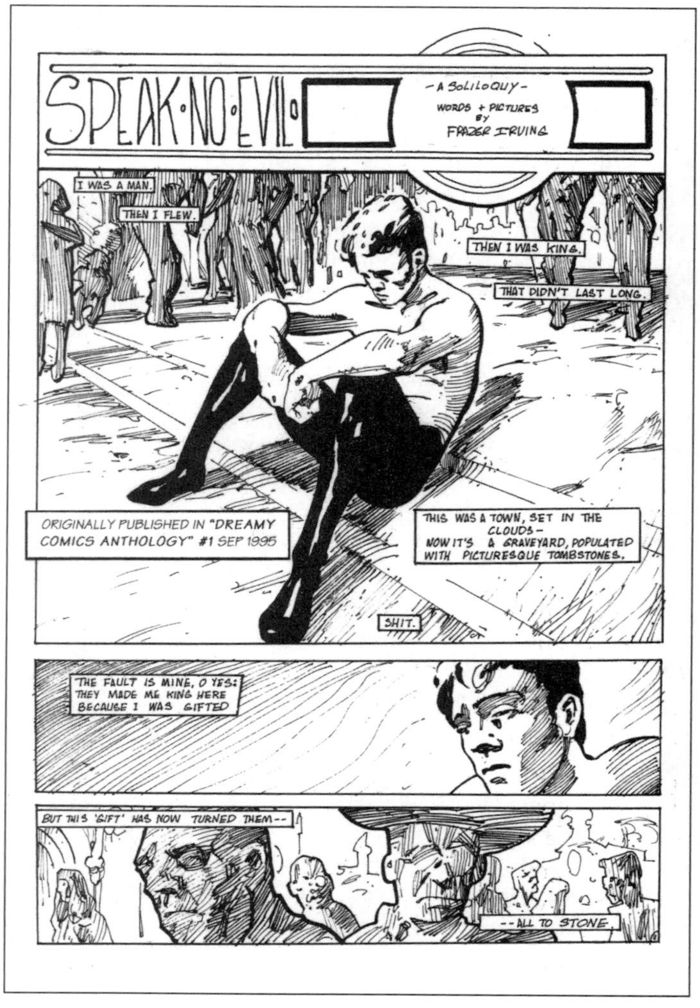
SPEAK·NO·EVIL
- A SOLILOQUY -
WORDS + PICTURES BY FRAZER IRVING
I WAS A MAN.
THEN I FLEW.
THEN I WAS KING.
THAT DIDN'T LAST LONG.
ORIGINALLY PUBLISHED IN "DREAMY COMICS ANTHOLOGY" #1 SEP 1995
THIS WAS A TOWN, SET IN THE CLOUDS— NOW IT'S A GRAVEYARD, POPULATED WITH PICTURESQUE TOMBSTONES.
SHIT.
THE FAULT IS MINE, O YES: THEY MADE ME KING HERE BECAUSE I WAS GIFTED
BUT THIS 'GIFT' HAS NOW TURNED THEM--
--ALL TO STONE.

rectangular and circular shapes; and these fantastic page frames. In fact, the frames break by page 137 and begin interacting with the images themselves. What explains this transformation and burst of new styles and designs?

FRAZER: The idea for that issue was to tell it all as single pages, all from the narrative/diary point of view of the dude as he shortens his entire experience with these strange people into 22 beats. Thus, there would be no dialogue per se, so I had the option of using the text as a design device, as well. The frames work in sets. The first set of pages was frameless to show there was very little different in his attitude—essentially he was still the same person. The second set of pages had very uniform frames where specific elements of the experience could be showcased as little design aspects or side images, which was to suggest that his attitude was shifting into a more glamorous phase. The third set of pages had the frames intersecting to represent the effects of the "voice," before the fourth set of pages ditched all frames and extended to full-bleed, which was my way of suggesting that after the transitions, he has now become totally immersed in this new life to the point where he doesn't even see it as anything unusual. The ideas behind this were just a frustration with having to produce the same sort of storytelling all the time. I wanted to do something that would drastically change the rhythm and reading of the story, give it some spice. I was well into Alphonse Mucha, and it seemed natural to follow all other comic artists and steal from him.

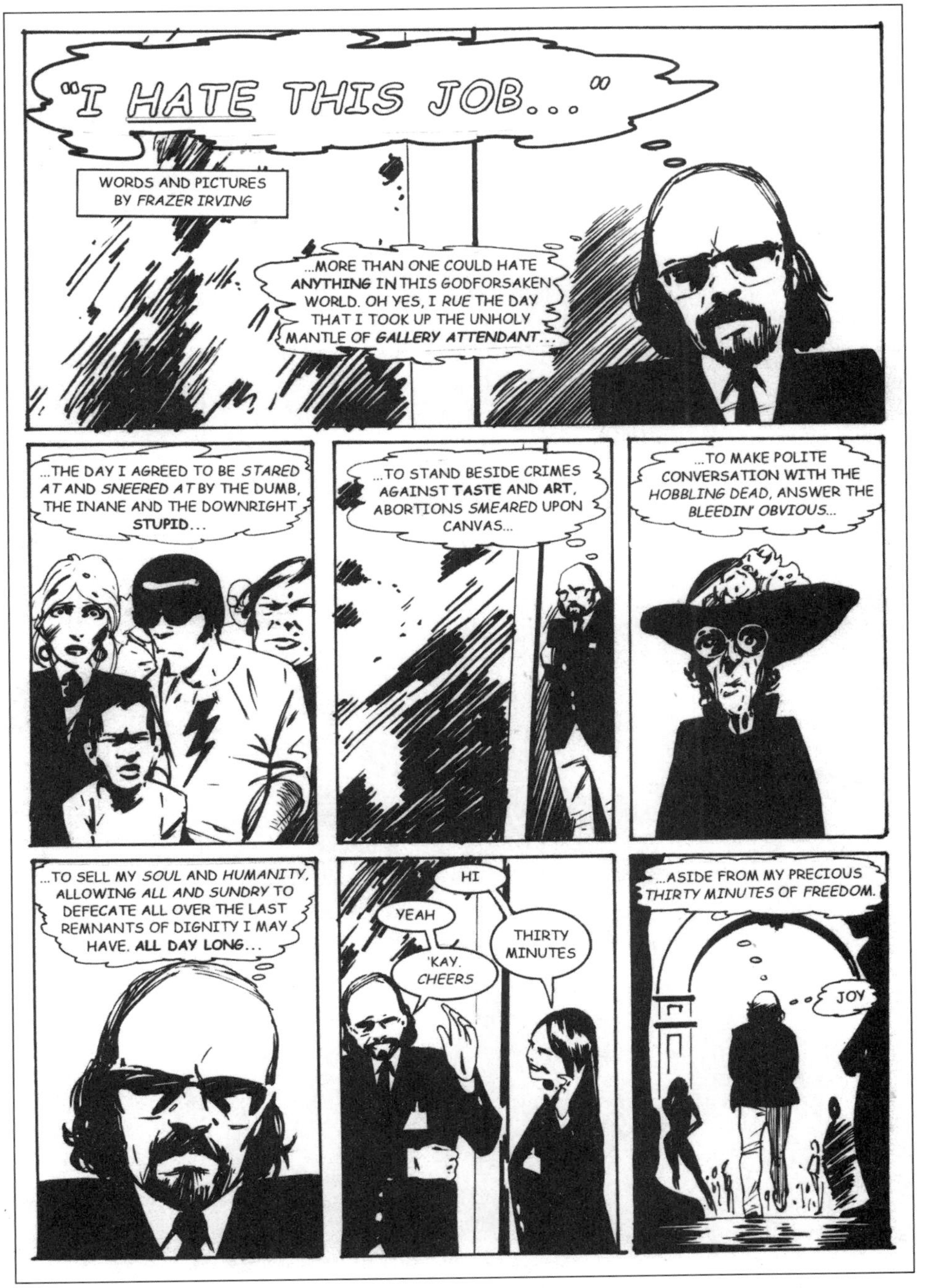

"I HATE THIS JOB..."
WORDS AND PICTURES BY FRAZER IRVING
...MORE THAN ONE COULD HATE ANYTHING IN THIS GODFORSAKEN WORLD. OH YES, I RUE THE DAY THAT I TOOK UP THE UNHOLY MANTLE OF GALLERY ATTENDANT...
...THE DAY I AGREED TO BE STARED AT AND SNEERED AT BY THE DUMB, THE INANE AND THE DOWNRIGHT STUPID...
...TO STAND BESIDE CRIMES AGAINST TASTE AND ART, ABORTIONS SMEARED UPON CANVAS...
...TO MAKE POLITE CONVERSATION WITH THE HOBBLING DEAD, ANSWER THE BLEEDIN' OBVIOUS...
...TO SELL MY SOUL AND HUMANITY, ALLOWING ALL AND SUNDRY TO DEFECATE ALL OVER THE LAST REMNANTS OF DIGNITY I MAY HAVE. ALL DAY LONG...
HI
YEAH
THIRTY MINUTES
'KAY. CHEERS
...ASIDE FROM MY PRECIOUS THIRTY MINUTES OF FREEDOM.
JOY

MM: *The Man Who Learnt to Fly* was eventually published by a small British press. How did this come about and when?

FRAZER: The whole thing started when I replied to an ad in *Comics International* seeking small press artists to contribute to an anthology called *Dreamy Comics Presents*. It was my first ever foray into such things, so I sent in samples of the first five pages of issue one and was delighted when the dudes replied saying that they'd love to have me contribute to their anthology as well as publish *The Man Who Learnt to Fly* properly as a series in its own right. Not knowing how it worked, I agreed and ended up funding half the printing bill—which was something like £37—and we launched the first issue at UKCAC 1994 or 1995. In the small press area there were quite a few folks who were very much the heart and soul of the small press scene of the '90s, including distributor and reviewer Pete Ashton. He seemed to like my stuff, despite him being into far more avant garde comics, and over the next year or so we ended up becoming quite good mates via letters and conventions.

The *Dreamy Comics* thing fizzled out at issue three. By this point the sales were very low, being dependant on conventions to sell them, and getting them into comic shops was difficult due to the low quality of the printing and overtly amateurish nature of it all, so the publisher was losing faith and eventually just stopped doing it. Thus, I was left with four issues to go and nowhere to publish it, until Pete suggested he publish the collected edition via his BugPowder distribution network. I think he was keen on starting a publishing empire and figured *The Man Who Learnt to Fly* was a good place to start. So I finished it and sent it off to him, and he photocopied, like, 25 copies and handbound them, and then sold them somehow. I think he sold half of them and sent the rest, unbound, to me to flog, and I gave them away.

MM: Did you primarily focus on developing a portfolio of work between 1996 and 1999? Is this where items such as "Porno Junkie" and "The Real Thing" come from?

FRAZER: "Porno Junkie" was a black-&-white illustration copied from one of my college pieces from my final year show. I figured it would look good in ink and so I did it. That was made around 1999, and it has all the hallmarks of the sable brush and the refined inking style I was developing back then. It was a pivotal piece for me. "The Real Thing" was a simple attempt to fill the folio with "social commentary" type illustrations. I always felt like a fraud doing that. But, yeah, during that period it was all about getting work, building a folio, etc. The comics dreams were to remain dreams until later.

MM: You admitted to being a technophobe in 1996, which seems shocking considering your workflow today. Why the fear and what caused the changeover to utilizing a computer in your art?

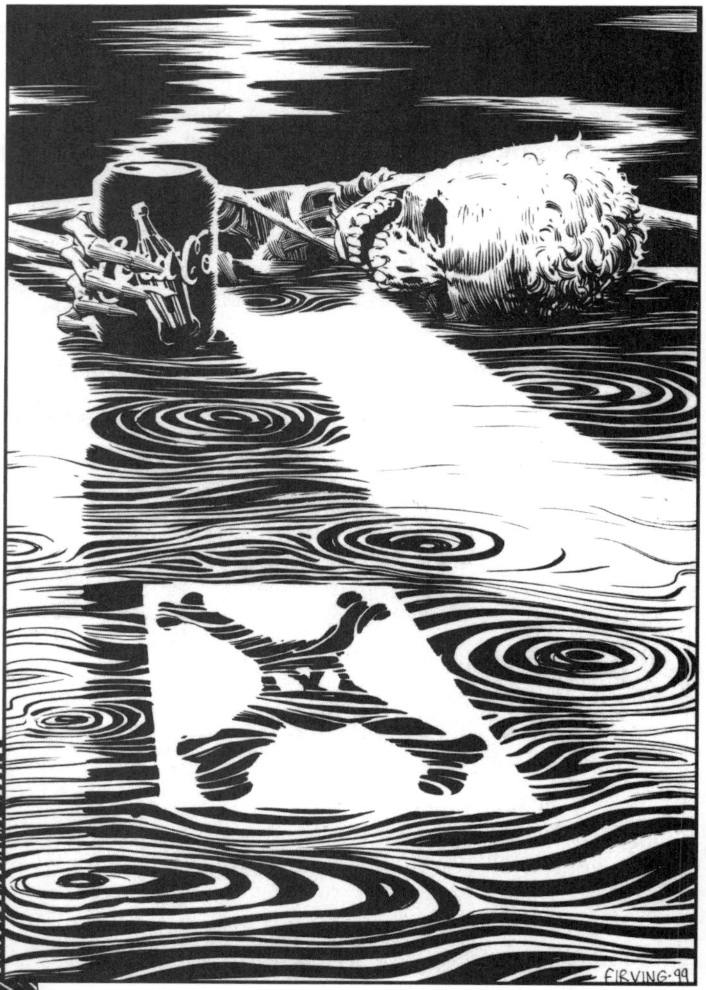

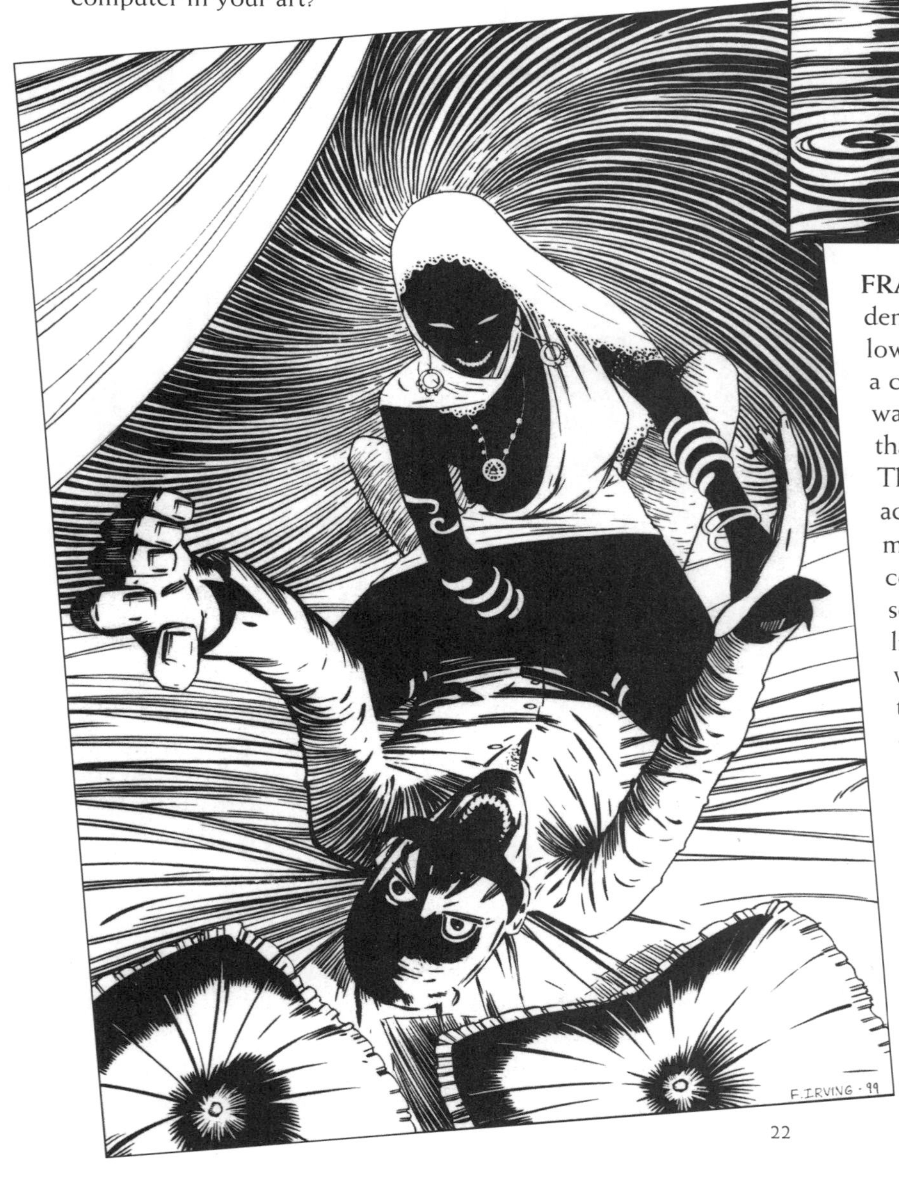

FRAZER: I was wary of it, because no one had ever demonstrated computer art to be anything more than low resolution, pixilated clip art to me. I'd never had a computer, never used one, so it was alien to me. It was only because my mate, Mike, was really into it that I decided to go along to one of the intro sessions. That was where they showed me Photoshop. A simple act of making a blob with the brush tool—using a mouse—and then erasing it set my brain on fire. I could draw on the computer? Oh, my God! As soon as I realized this had great potential, it was like a new box of toys. I started experimenting with it loads, so much in fact that it completely took over my art for the rest of the year, but I experimented loads with those primitive machines.

MM: What was your first computer?

FRAZER: My first computer that I worked on was Mike's Mac Performa 5200. The first computer I owned myself properly was a Mac G4. I bought that at the end of 1999 after I had finally got my mitts on the remains of an inheritance from my grandfather. He'd died in a motorcycling accident the year before, but the will was being contested by his new wife, and it wasted loads of the money

UH...

away in legal fees. At the time I hoped I'd get the money instantly to clear my debts and allow me to move out of my tiny box room, but the fates insisted that I wait a year until I was ready to spend it on something that would give me the means to get free and stay free, i.e., the Mac. The money wasn't much, a couple of grand, but it paid for the entire set-up.

MM: Were the Zodiac drawings your first attempts to merge traditional art with digital tools, beyond what you did with a Macintosh for *The Man Who Learnt to Fly*?

FRAZER: Yep. I was inspired by Jamie Hewlett's "Rola Girl" stickers that Virgin Cola were using to advertise their new product, and I figured I could do a bunch of cute chicks around a theme and color them in Photoshop. It was very simple, but I learned a bunch of new tricks doing it.

MM: Was it also around 1999 that you began submitting work to *2000 AD*?

FRAZER: Yeah, I started out sending off samples of my own stuff, and then I started using sample scripts. It all got ignored, until David Bircham [a *2000 AD* artist at the time] told me at a convention in 1999 that I should send in writing samples, as they needed writers. That was the catalyst, as it meant I struck a relationship with Assistant Editor Andy Diggle. He rejected my stuff in the end, but later recanted and said he would have bought it if he had known the level of samples that came in after that.

MM: Writing samples? Did you submit original scripts, and did they include art, as well?

FRAZER: I sent in four synopses, and developed one into full script. That was "The Gift of Laughter," which I wrote in 1998 and drew in 1999. No art attached, as they didn't do combo submissions back then.

MM: How did the submissions work exactly? Did they have a set policy that you followed or did you submit original artwork of your own creation unsolicited?

FRAZER: What I did was I sent in art of my own, hoping for them to send me a sample script back. I did this at college, and they sent me a "Future Shock" sample, but I just didn't draw it. The second time around I had just missed the folio review at the 1999 comic festival, and in my email I told them this and mailed in more new art. I got a "Dredd" sample back and did what I consider to be the worst pages ever on it.

MM: Why didn't you draw the "Future Shock" sample?

FRAZER: I left it too long to do the sample script. I figured it would be best to get something fresh to submit instead of drawing a script they sent out over a year previous.

MM: Did any of your submissions yield results?

FRAZER: My sample script work always sucked. I even got a rejection letter from Andy saying, "Your chances of working at *2000 AD* are virtually nil."

MM: Was this while you were working at Red Slap, or did that come about later? What exactly was Red Slap?

FRAZER: Red Slap was an agency formed by the wife of comic artist Colin MacNeil. I met them in 1999 at the comic festival. Not sure how, but I was at a table with Jock, Dom

Previous Page Top: Done for his portfolio, "The Real Thing" is Frazer's stab at social commentary through illustration, not to mention an attempt to get any kind of work. **Previous Page Bottom:** The final page of "The Amazing Adventures of Captain Cadwallader." Frazer: "It was just a pulpy story about some British Indiana Jones type. I was developing my brushwork back then. I ditched pens when I discovered the sable brush and made art that could stand on its own without color. It allowed me to explore the sensuality of the line." **Above:** Panels from "The Gift of Laughter," which were drawn after Frazer submitted the script for the story to *2000 AD* looking for work in any capacity.

Below: Andy Diggle told Frazer that it was this sample strip (only one page of which is shown here) that got him imagining how Frazer's art would look on the "Necronauts" strip. **Next Page:** A panel from Frazer's fifth installment of "Necronauts" for *2000 AD*.

Reardon, and some others as Karen MacNeil was telling us how comics are dead and RPGs are the way to go. I sent her my stuff, and during this time she did get me a few gigs, but they were small and low paying. The best thing about that was that at the next festival in 2000 I was at the 2000 *AD* panel when editor David Bishop announced he was leaving and that Andy—the fave of all newbies—was taking over. I knew instantly that this was my chance to move in as part of the new guard, but I needed an in. Colin MacNeil was on the panel, so when it ended I bounded over to him and introduced myself as "one of Karen's boys." He was very nice and instantly welcoming, so I'd sort of made contact with the elite in that respect, but Andy had vanished and I was left wondering if I'd ever actually get my shot at the big time.

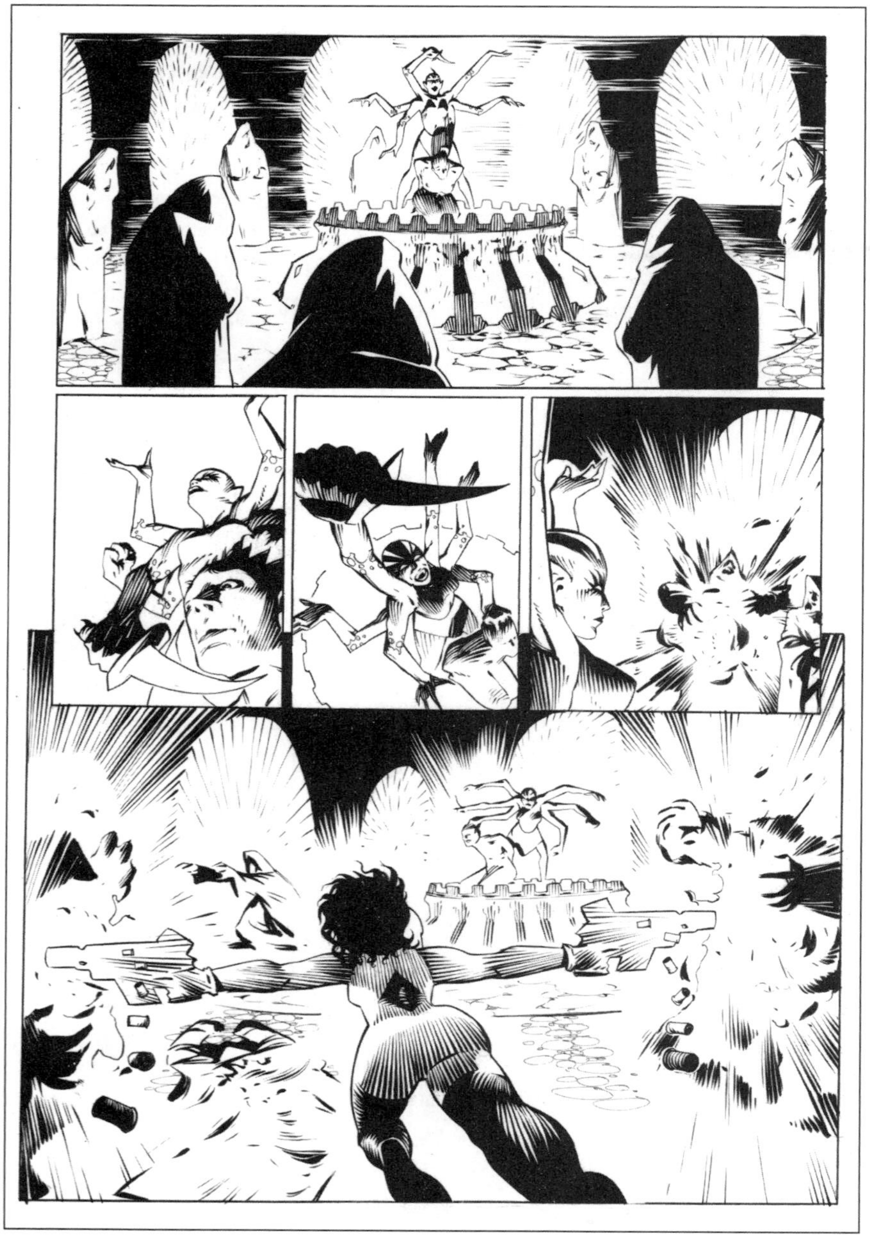

MM: What was your next move then?

FRAZER: I went to the bar. That's where everything happens, so I went there and vacantly loitered with the other wannabes. I was with a few small pressers who were whining about what to do and I just stood there, sending telepathic messages to Diggle. Then, when I wasn't looking, he came over and asked if I was Frazer Irving, as he'd seen my website and recognized my hairdo from the portrait I had on the front page. He asked if I'd had my script for "Sinister Dexter" from the editor, and I said no, at which point he suggested that I loiter around after the next panel and we'd chat.

After the panel, I joined the long, long line of people who were going to have their folios reviewed, and as he was leaving to get a pint of Guinness, he pulled me out of the line and said to wait 'til he came back and we'd have a chat. Naturally, I was excited, and the dudes in the line were giving me evil stares. Andy returned with a pint and another artist and sat at the back of the hall. I was being all polite and stood where I was, not wanting to intrude, yet a fellow newbie saw this and decided to just go ahead and walk over there, interrupt, and steal my spot! Once he'd butted in, Andy waved me over so I could intrude on legitimate grounds, and as he brushed this other dude's stuff aside, we sat down and I showed my new work. At that point Andy said I was too good for "Sin Dex" and that he had other plans for me, which was tantamount to being blessed by the godfather, in comics terms anyway. I'm glad I went to those two festivals.

MM: Were Andy's other plans "Necronauts"?

FRAZER: Yes. I think he saw the potential, not just for the "Necronauts," but for me spearheading their newly revamped black-&-white section of the magazine.

MM: Did you know about those plans or were they, no pun intended, cloaked in mystery here?

FRAZER: It was all mystery. They had decided to do one black-&-white strip every week, because it saved money, but most artists were only good at color art. When he saw my stuff, he saw that I could do full black-&-white art that worked on its own.

Part 3: Running on the 2000 AD Fast Track

"He was fast and professional, and the art looked great! I was wowed by Frazer's moody line work and hatching on 'Necronauts' and figured that was just his signature style. So I was doubly wowed by the psychedelic color effects on 'Storming Heaven.' It showed he wasn't a one-trick pony, and the readers loved it. I still think those two stories are the best work he's done. He draws real pretty."
— Andy Diggle

FRAZER: "Fast and professional," those were the days. He called me "the new Charlie Adlard." "Need a five-pager done in three days? Call Fraze!"

MM: And this was before you were the digital aficionado you are now, correct?

FRAZER: Yup. Little has changed, actually. I just take on too much work these days, hence the closeness of the deadlines. And thanks to *Gutsville* my reputation is now soiled.

MM: At the time you began 2000 *AD*, can you tell me about your process and the hybrid method by which you utilized digital tools in your art?

FRAZER: At first, I had the stupidest method ever. I'd draw the page in rough at print size, then blow it up to art board size, trace it with pencil to tighten it all up, then lightbox that tracing onto paper, and then ink it and scan it, and put it all together with any effects. It took way too long and wasted lots of paper.

Later on, I cut out a stage and just went from layouts to lightboxing and then to inks. All the panels were drawn separately, and I would arrange them and tidy them in Photoshop. My previous method had been to draw directly on the art

board, but now I had Photoshop I wanted to make sure I could expand the possibilities, and that meant I could re-ink panels if I ruined them.

MM: So was Photoshop pretty much just used for post-production arrangement of pages? What types of effects did you use early on?

FRAZER: It was, yes. Even though I had a Wacom tablet, the size of it plus the size and resolution of my monitor meant that drawing directly into Photoshop wasn't as good as me doing traditional inking. In those early days it was mainly scanned ink effects like spatters and patterns that I used, fills and stuff.

MM: Was the Wacom one of those full-screen tablets like you use nowadays or one of those smaller pen interfaces that sits alongside your keyboard?

FRAZER: The latter. It was an A5 tablet, Intuous 1. It was amazing, but I didn't really know how amazing it could be. I sold it to Jock when I upgraded. All those dudes—Jock, McKelvie, the 2000 *AD* artists—most of them, if not all of them, got into the Wacom stuff after me, partially I think down to my evangelizing. I sold a few tablets to some of them when I upgraded each time. It's so weird now seeing that almost everyone uses the computer to draw now, and I remember when I was one of the rare few who were regarded with suspicion for doing so. God bless Wacom and their fuzzy, little socks. I converted a fair few to Mac, as well.

MM: What about your workspace? Did you have a traditional studio space within your home where you went to work?

25

FRAZER: I worked in my bedroom/living room. Man, it was cramped, like, tiny.

MM: Was this your own place, the former place you lived with your brother, or something new?

FRAZER: This was the rented family home, the bottom floor flat where I grew up, lost my virginity, and smoked loads of weed, which is directly below me right now, in fact, having upgraded to the rented flat above some years ago.

MM: So you had moved back home with your family, or were they no longer there at the time?

FRAZER: My mum was; she's the only one left in the flat. I have sort of by default become the keeper of mother's security since the other two buggered off. Makes it hard to leave until I make millions and buy a mansion. I tried to escape, but I got magicked back.

MM: Well, working in those confined spaces, did you have a specific and established work schedule and routine that you followed every day to build discipline?

FRAZER: Yes. I woke up around 11:00, drank coffee and possibly smoked a joint, then I surfed the Internet for porn until I was hungry, at which point I ate microwaved meals or pizza, then I surfed the net some more, got high until the panic set in, and I started to draw until the wee hours of the next morning. [laughter] I'm amazed I ever got a rep for being fast.

Nowadays I'm way better. I get up at 6:00, I get coffee outside, then I draw until I rouse the missus at lunchtime, make lunch, then continue to draw. No more late nights.

MM: How did assignments work at 2000 AD? How did you get your first assignment?

FRAZER: Andy called me up after the festival meeting and asked me if I wanted a series. I calmly said yeah, and then he said until the script is ready he would send me some "Future Shocks" so I could earn some money.

He would then mail me hardcopy scripts, I would email roughs, then I'd make the pilgrimage into town with a CD-R of the art all labeled nicely, hoping that each time I showed up they'd take me for a free lunch. I miss those treks into the office. I met Chris Achilleos there on one of those trips.

MM: So the waiting script was "Necronauts" then? I was confused originally, because in the introduction for *Storming Heaven: The Frazer Irving Collection*, you say "Necronauts" was your first gig, but "The Last Supper" came before that.

FRAZER: Yeah, "Necronauts" was my first proper gig. The other fill-ins were just warm-ups as far as I was concerned. I was also dead chuffed that Andy gave me the cover to my second "Future Shock." He sort of fast-tracked me in the biz. I have a lot of time for Andy when he isn't arguing.

MM: [laughs] What were your other thoughts upon receiving your first script work?

FRAZER: The first script was such a validation. I wasn't that into it, but I was determined to

Previous Page: Frazer's first professional comics work was this "Tharg's Future Shocks" story, "The Last Supper," written by Steve Moore, which appeared in *2000 AD* #1205. Looking back at it now, Frazer says, "I can still remember making those pages, and it makes me very glad to have a Cintiq now."
Above: A panel from Frazer's first "Necronauts" strip. Frazer worked with series creator and writer Gordon Rennie throughout his entire run. In regards to Rennie's scripts, Frazer had this to say: "They were lean and mean. Very succinct in conveying the important information required to communicate the action and the character of the story, and also very fast-paced, with little or no decompression—my favorite type of script. Gordon's scripts are among the best I've ever worked on."

Future Shocks, Necronauts ™ and © Rebellion A/S.

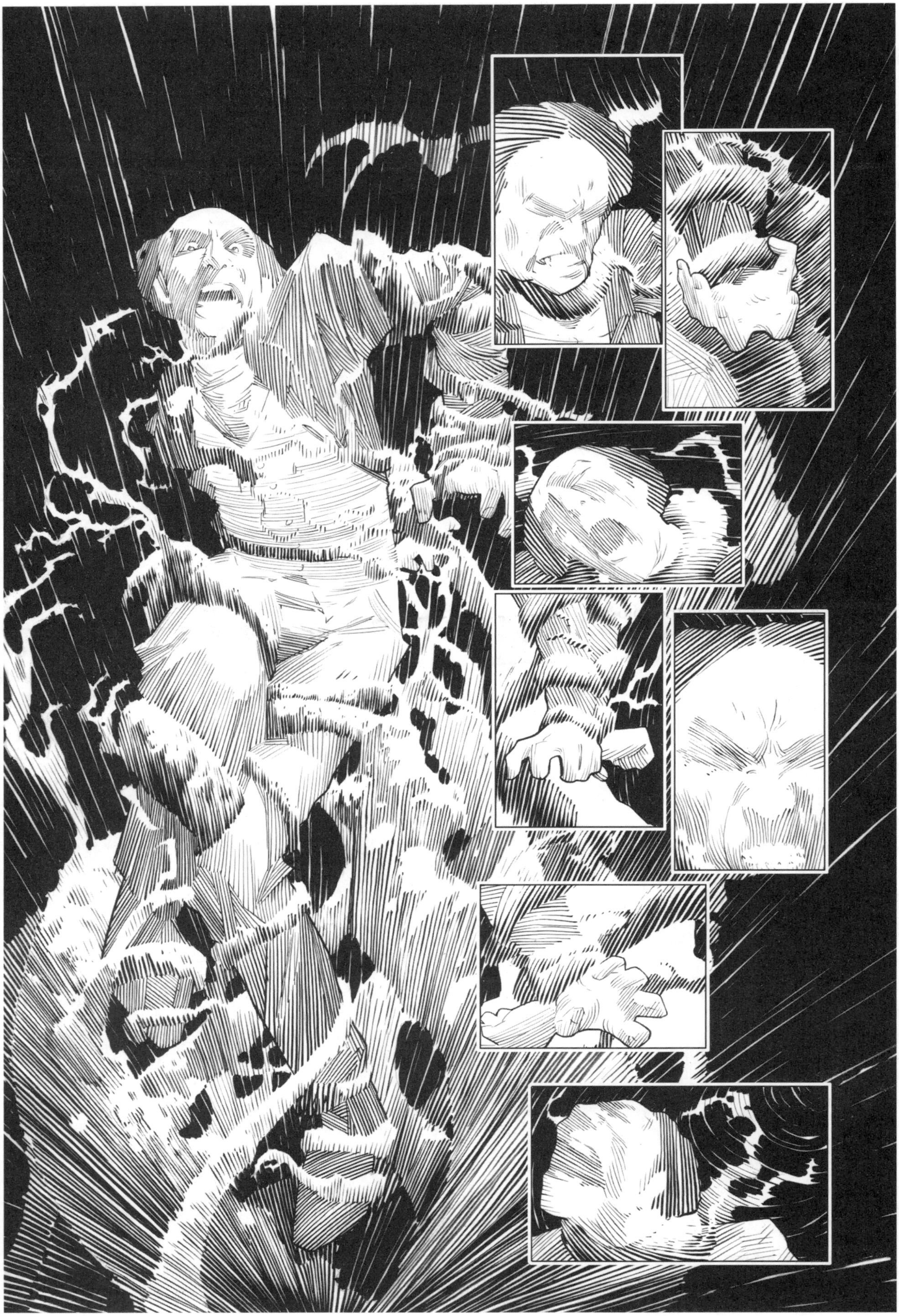

prove I was professional and do it as best I could. I didn't get really excited, though, until I got the "Necronauts" scripts, because that was more of an actual story, as opposed to a five-page gag strip.

MM: Andy told me you passed the entry stages of these "Future Shock" test stories faster than most artists. Were you aware at the time that these assignments were designed to gauge not only your artwork and technique, but also your commitment and professionalism?

FRAZER: Oh, yeah. It seemed obvious to me that newbies would be given try-outs before proper work, which was why it was odd he offered me the "Necronauts" before I'd been tested, but I expected it and was ready for it.

MM: Although I haven't seen your work in Prog #1206, "The Island," it was a "Judge Dredd" story with color, correct? Was this your first professional experience working with a colorist? Do you recall your impression at the time seeing your art transformed from black-&-white line art and into color?

FRAZER: Well, Andy offered me the coloring gig down the pub one day, and I was wary of failing the challenge, so I declined. When I did see the colors, I realized I should have done it myself after all, and besides, I think, two gigs since then, I've made it a rule to always do the colors myself. I don't think Len really knew how to deal with the utter lack of holding lines on my "Dredd" pages, and thus it all became muddy and vague. Plus, the lines were lowered in resolution, so they became more jaggy than when I color myself.

MM: When did you officially begin working on "Necronauts"?

FRAZER: I think I began "Necronauts" in the summer of 2000—July, in fact.

MM: One of the most fascinating aspects of the special features section in the *Necronauts* collection is the figure where you use yourself as a photo reference in the design. Is this something you often do? What constituted your reference library at the time?

FRAZER: I used to use reference a lot, so much so that Rich Johnston could have a field day finding swipes in my early work. At college we were encouraged to use found images as reference, and it was the norm for

me. I tried to use myself as a model as often as I could, especially when the pose was tricky, but these days it's very rare, and I don't swipe anymore.

MM: Reading *Necronauts* in the context of your earlier work with your later black-&-white work, the book stands out as a bridge between the efforts and experiments in *The Man Who Learnt to Fly* and your "Judge Death" pieces. Can you recall this transformation in your style and what steps you took to refine and hone your skills between *The Man Who Learnt to Fly* and what audiences see in "Necronauts"?

FRAZER: It was a natural thing. I just kept drawing and solving problems the same way.

Previous Page: Page 3 of Frazer's first "Necronauts" strip. You can really see the Charles Dana Gibson influence at work here. **Above:** You know you've reached the big time in the British comic book industry when you get to draw a "Judge Dredd" story, as Frazer did with "The Island," in *2000 AD* #1209.

Judge Dredd, Necronauts ™ and © Rebellion A/S.

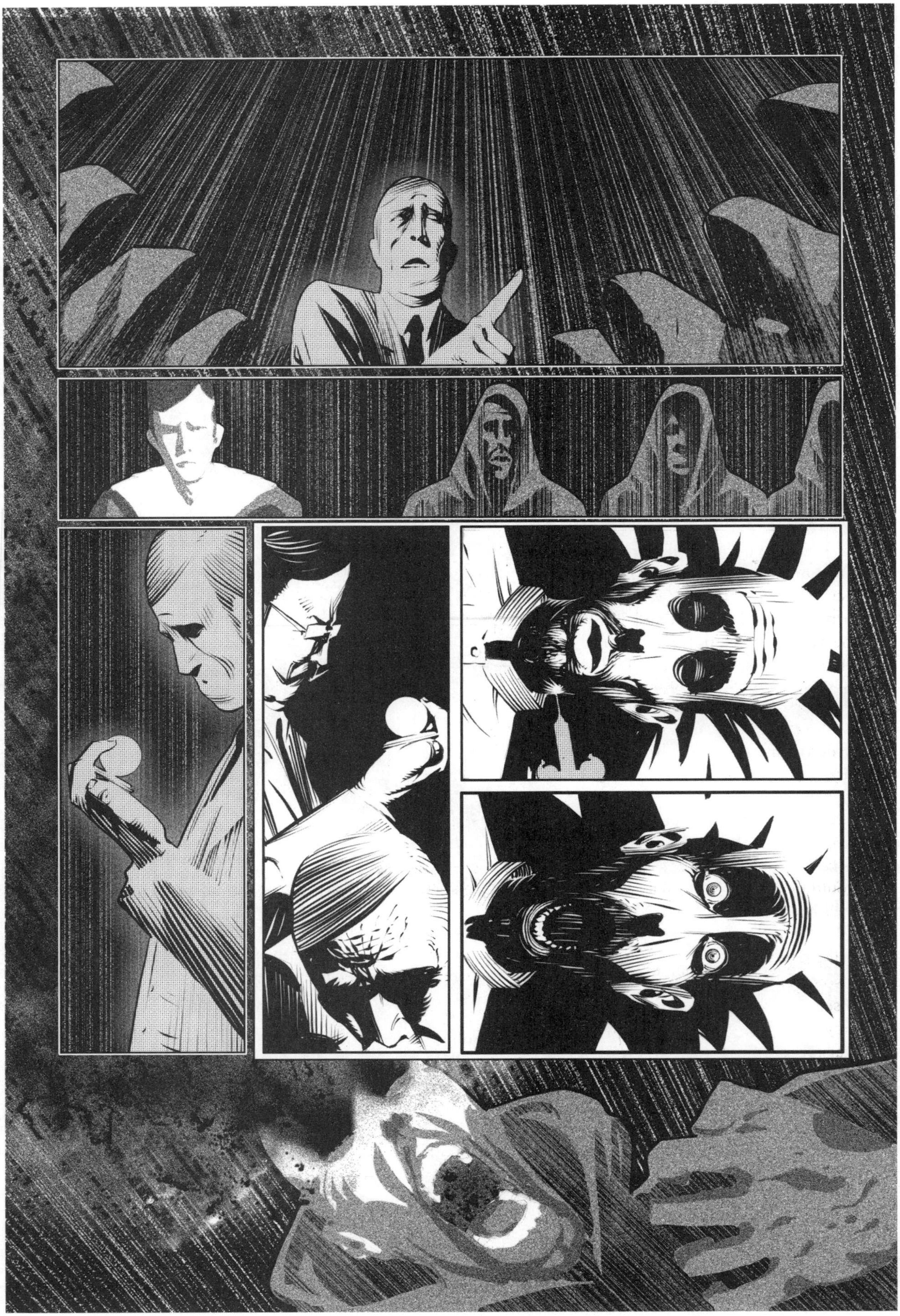

There was no conscious decision to change anything, beyond perhaps adding a few extra lines in the backgrounds and maybe looking at some Charles Dana Gibson art to see if I could pilfer anything for context in the "Necronauts," but the process was pretty much what I'd been using all along, which was pencil it, ink it, and wonder where the light sources are. The only real thing that I did between those two projects was to draw lots. All other considerations were there to serve the solving of problems as quickly as possible, and this still happens today on every pages, every cover, every doodle.

MM: There appears to be an evolution in the sharpness of your figures and characters as you move from *The Man Who Learnt to Fly* into later black-&-white work, and "Necronauts," I think, stands out as a significant sign post in this evolution. Would you agree?

FRAZER: That would be the sable brush at work.

MM: There are some really interesting effects in "Necronauts," particularly the graininess of the airplane with Lovecraft and Houdini or the aviator later on. It's far different than anything you had produced before. How was that achieved—traditionally or digitally?

FRAZER: Well, I knew, having read the synopsis, that there would be two distinct locations in the story; one was reality, the other was this strange netherworld. I instantly saw this as an opportunity to define the two by utilizing very different rendering methods. The reality would be drawn as normal, whilst the netherworld would be made of static-esque fills and figures drawn with hatching instead of shadows. When it came to inventing this, I did some experiments in Photoshop to see if I could make something dirty and staticy, yet also not too distracting, so like a regular repeated pattern with grain. Once I found my solution, I made one JPEG of it and cut-and-pasted it whenever I needed. I had also developed my own method of reproducing the classic Zip-a-tone effect and decided that would also feature, as it would allow another level to the illustrative depth and also fit in nicely with the static. The plane was really tricky to make, as it was all done with cut and paste in Photoshop over a picture I nabbed from the net.

MM: Your work on "Necronauts" earned you two back-to-back Best New Talent awards from the National Comics Awards in the U.K. in both 2001 and 2002 and a nomination for Best Artist in 2002. How did "Necronauts" and these awards benefit you with your assignments?

FRAZER: The first year I won it, I tied with Jock. It made sense, really, as we were both the most visibly new artists on the scene and we had distinctive styles, though I was surprised we both won it. Looking back, those nine votes we each got didn't make it that tight a race really. The second year, I think, was the more vindicating win, as it meant I won twice, and Jock didn't. [*laughter*] I think I

Previous Page: With "Necronauts," Frazer created and extensively used his own Zip-a-tone patterns.
Below: The first page of "A Love Like Blood" from *2000 AD* #1243.

A Love Like Blood, Necronauts ™ and © Rebellion A/S.

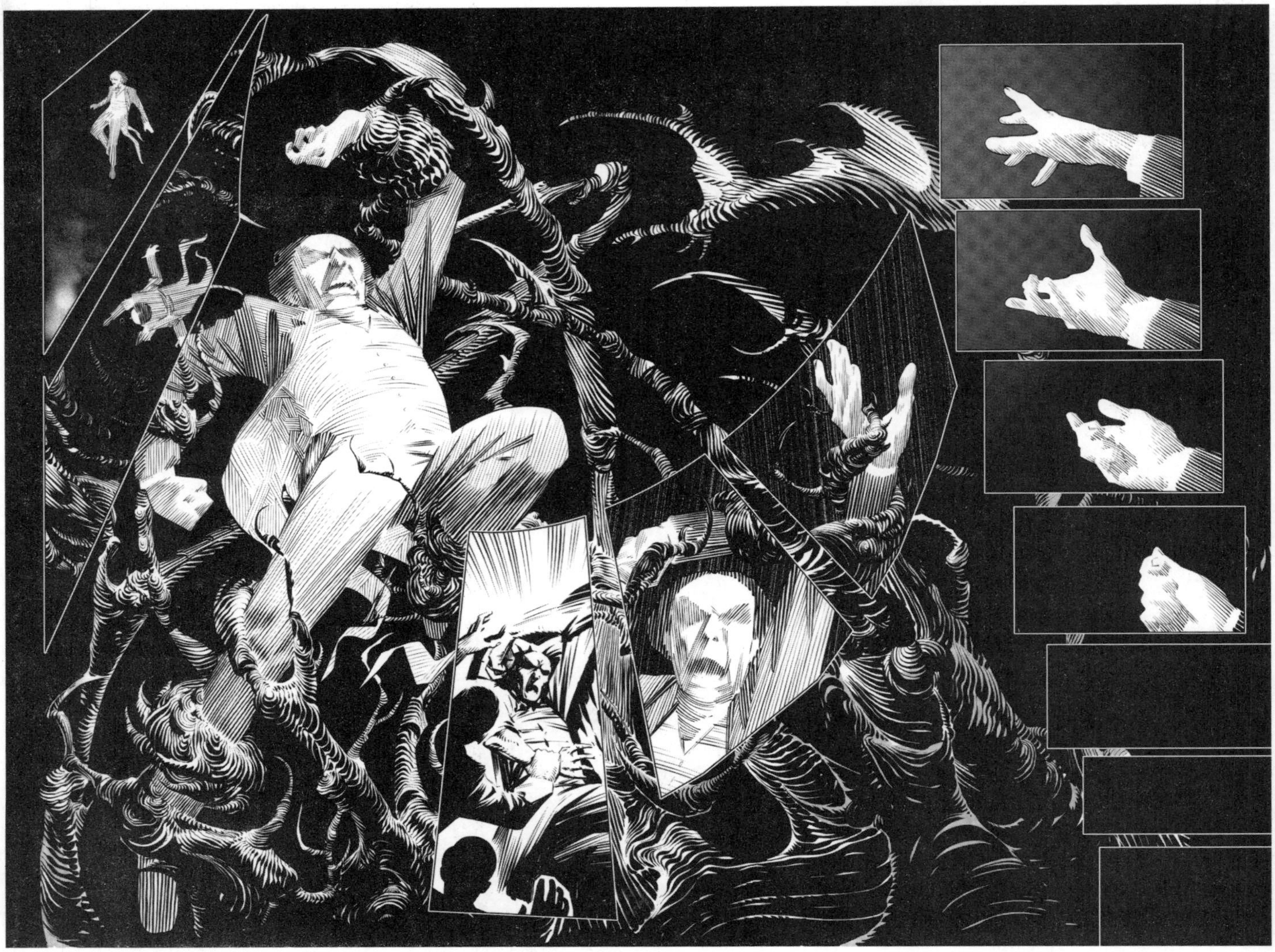

Above: A "Necronauts" two-page spread from *2000 AD* #1231. The Gibson-inspired spirit figures of Houdini and the woodcut-esque figures of the Sleepers blend together in a way that gives the story a sense of ancient, Gothic gloom and horror.
Next Page: It's vampires versus werewolves in this page from "A Love Like Blood." Will love prevail? Who cares? It's vampires versus werewolves!

had done some wildly different work by then, and that had pushed me back into the minds of the readers, maybe even confusing them into thinking there were two of me, but however I won it, I was chuffed. The awards didn't make a lick of difference to finding work, I must say.

MM: Following "Necronauts," you moved into "A Love Like Blood," a strip where readers see your first efforts at self-coloring your own work. Did you find that your approach to the black-&-white line art differed between producing work for another colorist and that which you would color yourself?

FRAZER: I left out some areas that I knew would be painted with color, but other than that it was pretty much the same sort of line work I would do normally.

MM: Was it your choice to go with color?

FRAZER: Oh, yeah. I was super-excited when Andy said it was going to be color, and I insisted he let me do it.

MM: What was your art process with "A Love Like Blood," since you were doing all the art duties?

FRAZER: Same as before, with small roughs enlarged and lightboxed, then inked, scanned, arranged, etc., but now I had the extra duty to paint on the Photoshop document on layers above and below the art. What evolved out of this was my least favorite hack, which is where, if I'm running late, I leave out detail in the ink art thinking I can fill it with some wizard color trick at the end, which very rarely works. The last episode has lots of that, though looking at it now it's way less of a problem than I initially thought.

MM: How did using color differ for you in conveying emotion and establishing atmosphere between "A Love Like Blood" and "Necronauts"?

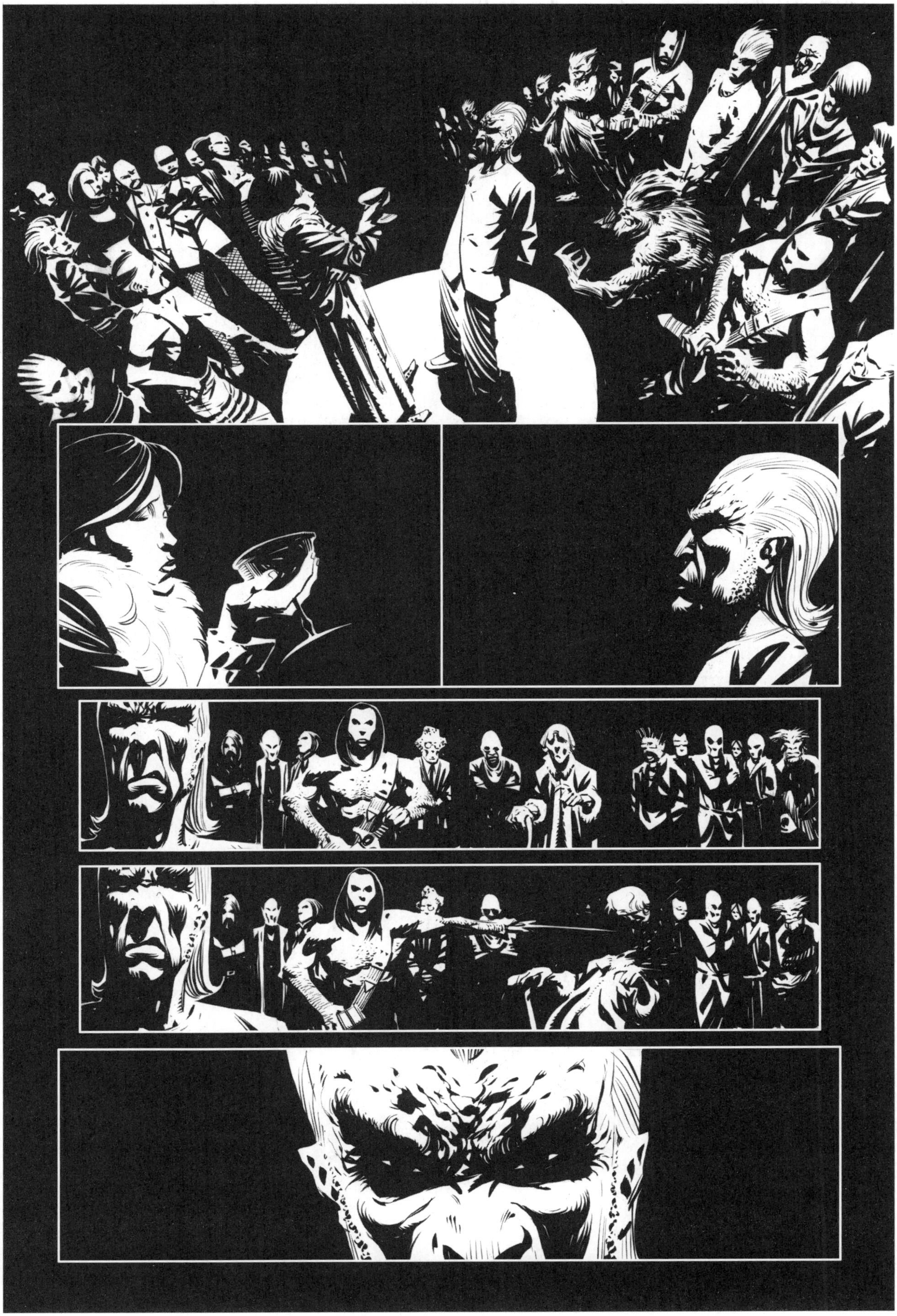

FRAZER: It made it easier to convey emotion. The linework is rather cold, and it takes an intellectualizing process to digest the art into an emotive response, whereas color is instant and instinctive. I could draw horrid lines but smother them with warm colors and create a weird uncomfortable vibe, or as I did with "A Love Like Blood," I could use slightly tainted hues to offset everything with a hint of menace.

MM: What aspects of comic storytelling did you learn from Gordon Rennie and John Smith that stuck with you into your next projects? Since you started alongside Jock, did you also draw upon him or other artists in the 2000 *AD* stable for influence, advice, or feedback on comic pacing? How about your editors?

FRAZER: From Gordon I guess I learned about brevity of action. Not that I've applied it yet, as I'm always working to other people's scripts, but I do bear that in mind when I think of my own stuff, about how one can say so much by leaving out so many other things. The odd thing about Gordon is that his ideas about storytelling were so very similar to mine already that it was like working with my better read and slightly grumpier clone.

John's stuff didn't really make much impact beyond taking care to consider the effect of emotional and succinct dialogue, again something I won't draw upon 'til I write my own projects.

As for Jock, well, I am always competing with him, even if he doesn't know it. I like his work, and I have stolen many, many ideas from him without anyone noticing.

As for editors, Diggle was the most influential, mainly due to his "first speaker on the left" bit and his many rants about boiling story down to rocket fuel, though I don't go 100% with that. It's the essence of that rant that is useful.

MM: I've read that "Necronauts" and "A Love Like Blood" may have tagged you as a horror artist. Do you feel this is a label you've had to work against or that limited your opportunities at the time?

FRAZER: It was a useful label at the time, and it's never bothered me, as it sort of gave me something to fight against, a challenge to overcome. It may well be that many editors passed me over for gigs because of this tag, but it hasn't made any difference to me getting here doing what I'm doing, so I guess it's not a problem. One always gets

Below: A seance gone wrong in these panels from "Necronauts."
Next Page: Tharg just says "yes" to "Reefer Madness," the *2000 AD* #1263 installment of "Tharg's Terror Tales." This time Frazer uses the woodcut style of the zombies as a stark contrast to the clean, open pencil lines of their would-be victim.

Necronauts, Tharg's Terror Tales ™ and © Rebellion A/S.

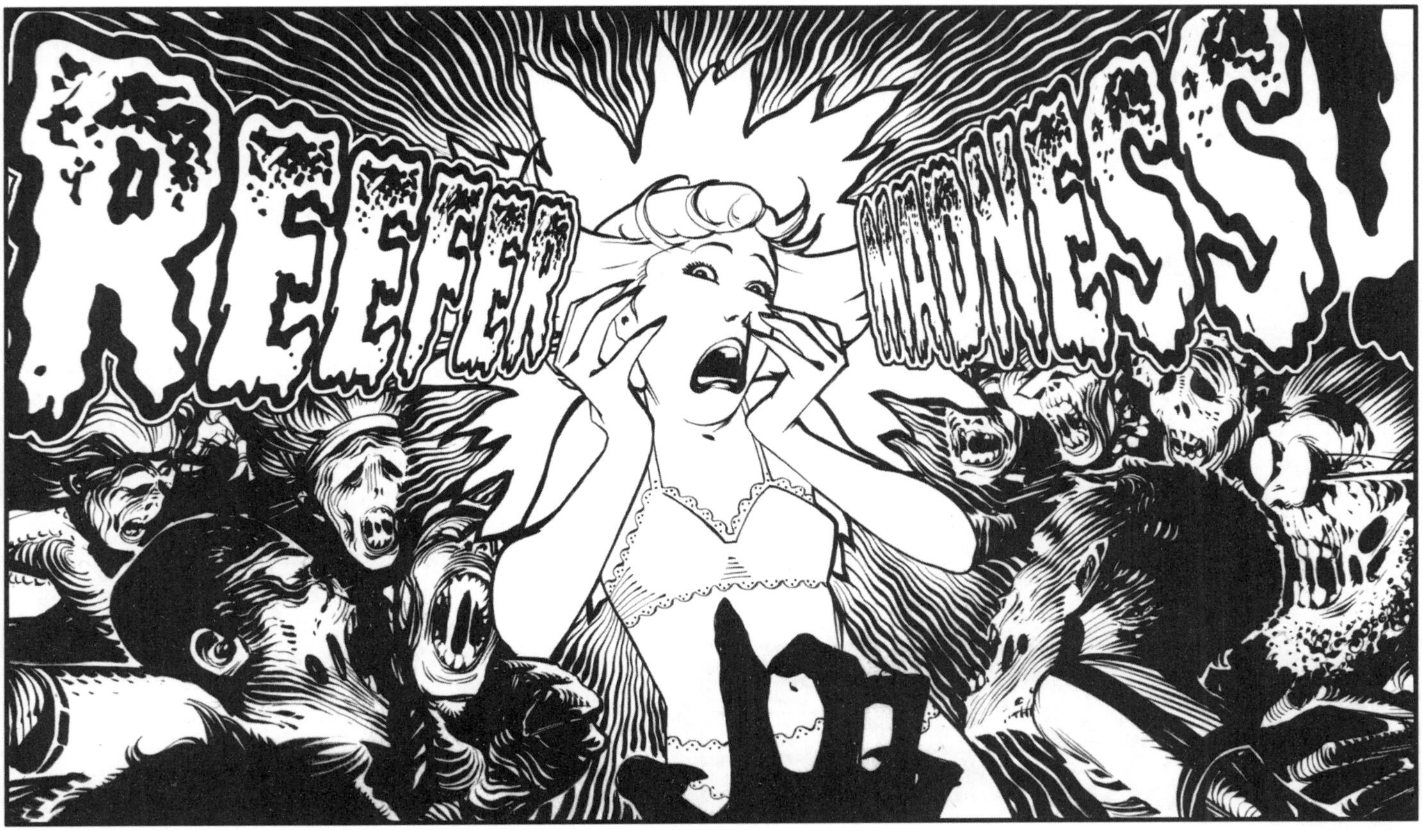
REEFER MADNESS!

pigeonholed no matter how hard one tries. If anything, my diversity has worked against me more, because some editors even said to me that they didn't know what they could put me to work on, and my obvious reply was always, "A good story."

MM: Reuniting with Gordon Rennie, you drew "Reefer Madness" in Prog #1263. In a 2002 interview, you mentioned that the story reflected a new artistic discovery for you of including "pencil art in the same image as a fully inked page." How did you come upon this discovery and can you explain its relevance for the story?

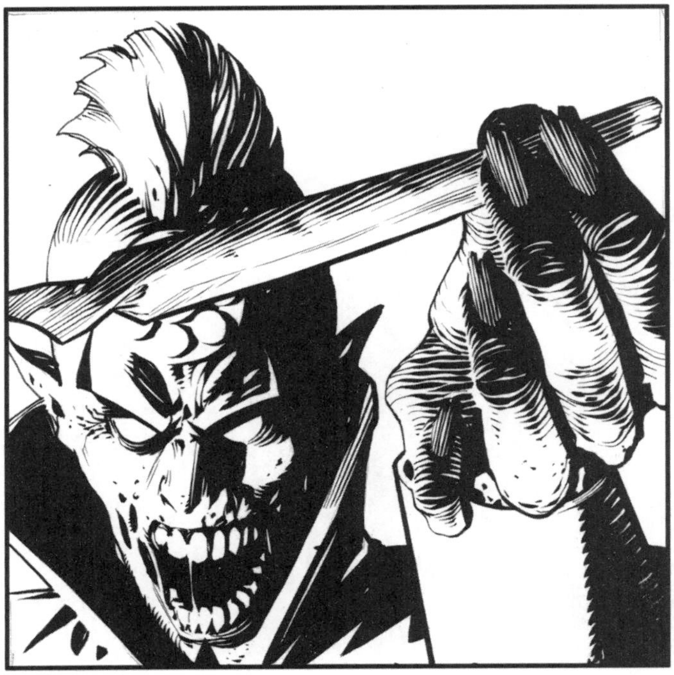

FRAZER: I was getting tired of doing the same sort of inking. It had its limits, and I was keen to explore other ways to render imagery without jarring it too much. At the time I made that page, I scanned the pencil art for inking, but during the preparation for the inks I noticed the pencil work had a fair bit of character itself, and that it was tight enough that it could stand on its own merits. Then I had the idea of including it amongst the inked zombies in order to create a warm, fleshy contrast with the cold, hard inks, thus expanding the dynamic range of that one panel. It was a bit risky for me, as I didn't want to rock the boat too much in terms of delivering work the editor wasn't expecting, but it blended well enough that they accepted it and effectively gave me justification for doing loads more weird things like that.

MM: From Rennie's script directions of a "big, busy panel" and "lots of flesh-crazed hophead maniacs" in the vein of a Roger Corman film, readers see what I contend as one of the first of your more modern female figure drawings that is much more familiar today. What, for you, explains this more polished rendering?

FRAZER: I was just going for contrast between the zombies and the girl. She had to have smoother and curvier lines to jar with the jagged shapes around her, and the pencil helped with that, as it offered up some delicate gray tones that translated into colored shades later on.

Below: The opening page of "Storming Heaven," with cameos by Cary Grant and The Beatles. **Next Page:** Page 3 of "Storming Heaven." Throughout the story, the only blacks used on the main character, Dr. Trips, are very basic holding lines. The rest of the figure is defined solely in the coloring.

MM: Did any of your coloring efforts in "Reefer Madness" reflect lessons or experiences you had obtained during "A Love Like Blood"? Did the coloring work in "Reefer Madness" hold any new approaches or techniques as a result?

FRAZER: I colored "Reefer Madness" pretty fast, I must say. After "A Love Like Blood," I decided to reduce the palette a bit, as that had become too busy in places and that confused the reading. So for "Reefer Madness," I went with two colors only, except for the blues on the last page, I think. It certainly made the strip distinctive and allowed me to explore subtleties within a simple color range. The only real concrete discovery here, though, was realizing that I could apply color to grays and make them vibrant enough so that they didn't look like colored gray, and that was on page one.

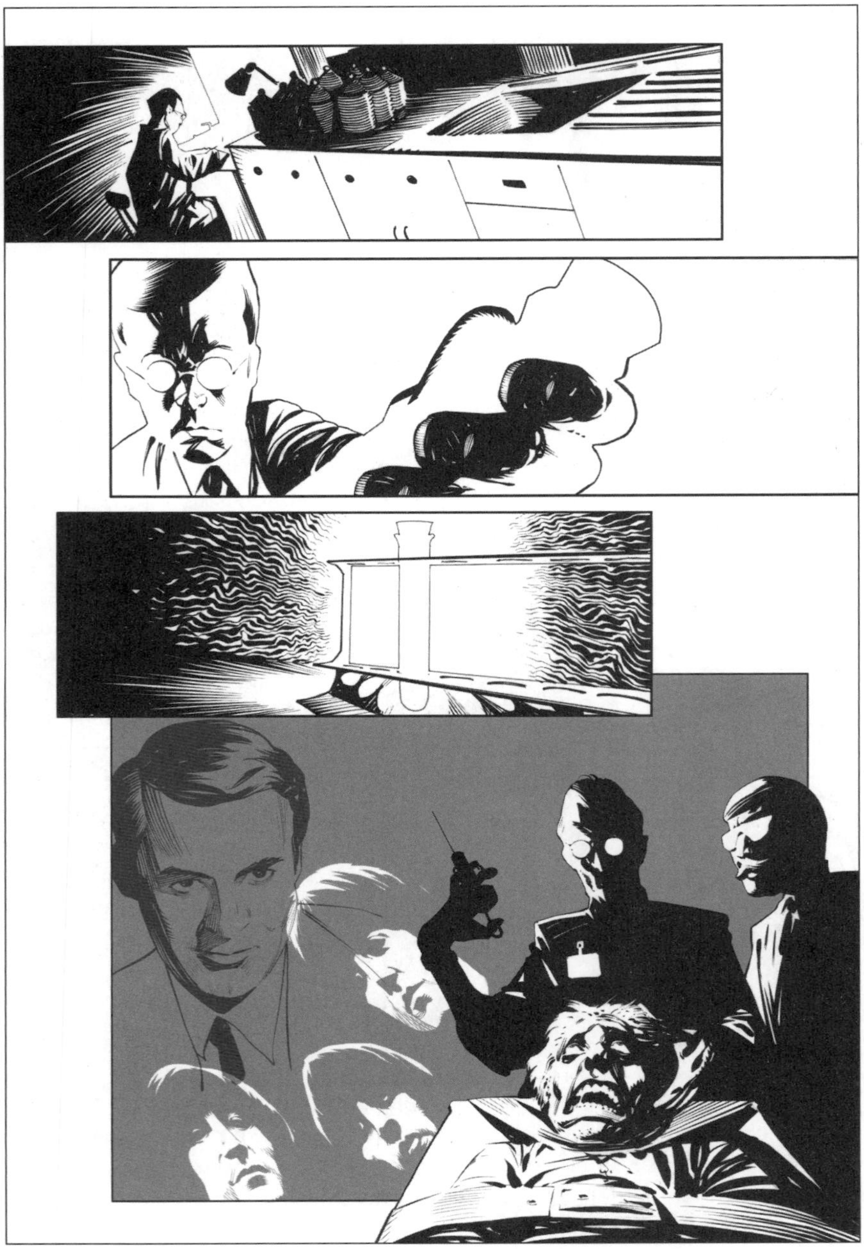

MM: In early 2002. before "Storming Heaven" came out, you started to move away from the coloring style you'd been using in order to focus on color in terms of mood and design. Why did you feel that you needed to break away?

FRAZER: I was bored doing the same thing. The same art style applied to different stories is such a wasted opportunity to me. Each time I got a script I saw it rendered in dozens of different ways, yet I was fearful that I would lose favor with the boss if I started changing aspects too much. After all, in comics then it was the case where an artist developed a "style," and that was what they were selling. I didn't want to be stuck doing horror stories or gaudy coloring on EC comic pastiches.

MM: Can you explain what you meant by color being more integral to the mood and design? In your opinion, how was this overlooked in the contemporary books of the time?

FRAZER: A lot of comics' coloring back then and even now is realistic in design. It has the sort of lighting that one finds in a generic situation, where flesh is flesh colored, red capes are red, green grass is green, etc. I know from looking around me that reflected light changes everything, that colors change depending on the colors around them, and, more importantly, in storytelling color isn't just there to represent an illusion of reality. It is there to enhance the story by adding and creating mood, drawing attention to details, flavoring outlandish elements in the art, etc. Comics coloring went through a nasty phase for a while where everything was airbrushed and shiny, with gradient fills obscuring line work and adding intrusive modeling to faces. Most comics I looked at didn't have color that told the story, they had color that patronized the reader by saying, "This is skin," which annoyed me. Coloring that really broke away from that stuff would be epitomized by John Higgins' work on *Watchmen* and *Killing Joke*, because it really became a dominant part of the story. Of course, there were comics that had some very left-field coloring and some were extremely inventive, often done by artists who would color other books with the standard reality tones, but these were in the minority, as far as I could tell.

MM: Was your creation and use of custom brushes, fills, layers, and effects self-taught, or did you rely on more experienced assistance from other artists?

FRAZER: All self-taught, or picked up from reading little tutorials posted online by other artists. I would say it's about 50% experimentation in a vacuum, 30% online tutorials, 15% tips from other artists and 5% dumb luck that I found my way to this point. We all knew our own little tricks, and it was good to share little things, but the application and processing of it was all done on the page, and often I found I used these tips in different ways than the person who suggested them. I see us early comic book computer people as pioneers in that respect. The only books on the subject sucked at the time, and we were the ones using the tools in the field, making it up as we went along.

MM: You once said your aim was to create art that looked as if it had been done completely traditionally, but upon a closer look, raised a series of questions about its creation. What for you convinced you to go digital as opposed to doing everything traditionally?

FRAZER: Digital has Undo and Layers. That's enough to swing it for me. The aim was to create art where I had ultimate control over everything. Paint dries and hardens, and one loses control after that point. On the computer, the paint is always up for modification, and great fruit has grown from this fertile ground.

MM: "Storming Heaven" is an amazing tale. What explains the transition to more realistic line art here?

FRAZER: I made a conscious choice to clean up the line work to allow the color room to breathe, and that was great because I was at the stage with my inking where I was

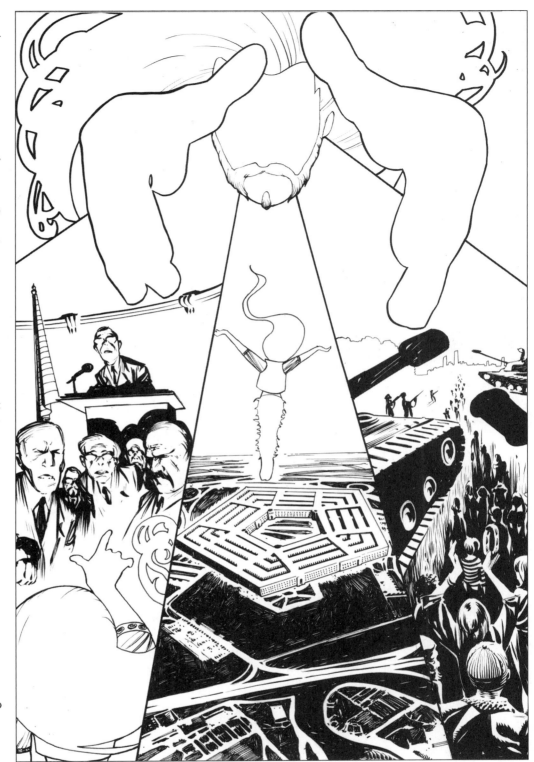

just filling in lines to cover up gaps in my understanding of the form.

MM: "Storming Heaven" seems to be an experiment in panel layout and design. You have the Davis and Lloyd fractured panels alongside cracked or torn paper-looking panels, curved panels, and panels that are inverted and break the fourth wall. Was this a conscious effort on your part or something that was generated by Rennie's script?

Above: A panel from the Rennie-scribed "Asylum," from *Judge Dredd Megazine* vol. 4, #5.
Next Page: The opening page of "My Name Is Death" [*2000 AD* #1289]. In regards to working with legendary *2000 AD* writer, John Wagner, on two Judge Death stories Frazer says, "Wagner is the king of succinct scripts...Working with John was like drawing my own stories in many respects, mainly because I never, ever had a moment where I felt I had to change a panel sequence to clarify the storytelling."

FRAZER: This was my thing. I wanted to use panel shapes and borders to draw the line between the real world and the dream world, the evil places and the good places. There were a lot of scene changes, and it is essential to communicate to the reader using all the tools available that we are in a different place with a different vibe, and in "Storming Heaven" I had the opportunity to experiment with a lot of those ideas.

MM: You returned to Judge Dredd in 2002 with "Judge Death." First off, what is the "round helmet" debate, and did this originate with your earlier Dredd stories or your work on "Judge Death"?

FRAZER: Dredd always had a bucket helmet when I read him, but during my research for the earlier "Judge Death" stories, I discovered that the very first few Dredd stories illustrated by Mick McMahon had him wearing a rounder helmet. I liked this difference in design and decided that since the rules on rendering Dredd varied from artist to artist,

that I would have round helmets in my first "Death" strip. Some readers took objection to this, and even Wagner wasn't so keen on it, so that was the only time I used it, though I still prefer it to the bucket. [*laughs*]

MM: In working on such a dark story, with such sinister themes, how do you invest yourself in the characters to make them believable, as Death is beyond redemption?

FRAZER: I always saw Judge Death as a comedy character. The world of Judge Dredd is so twisted and warped anyway, so full of satire and absurdity that Judge Death is just the headline comedy act. Even with his dark, sick deeds, when Wagner writes him, it's almost funny. So whenever I drew him, it was with a great dose of understanding between me and him that this is all one great big, dark joke, and that's how we got on.

MM: Talk about your approach to the linework you employed in "Judge Death." With it being a black-&-white strip, does the

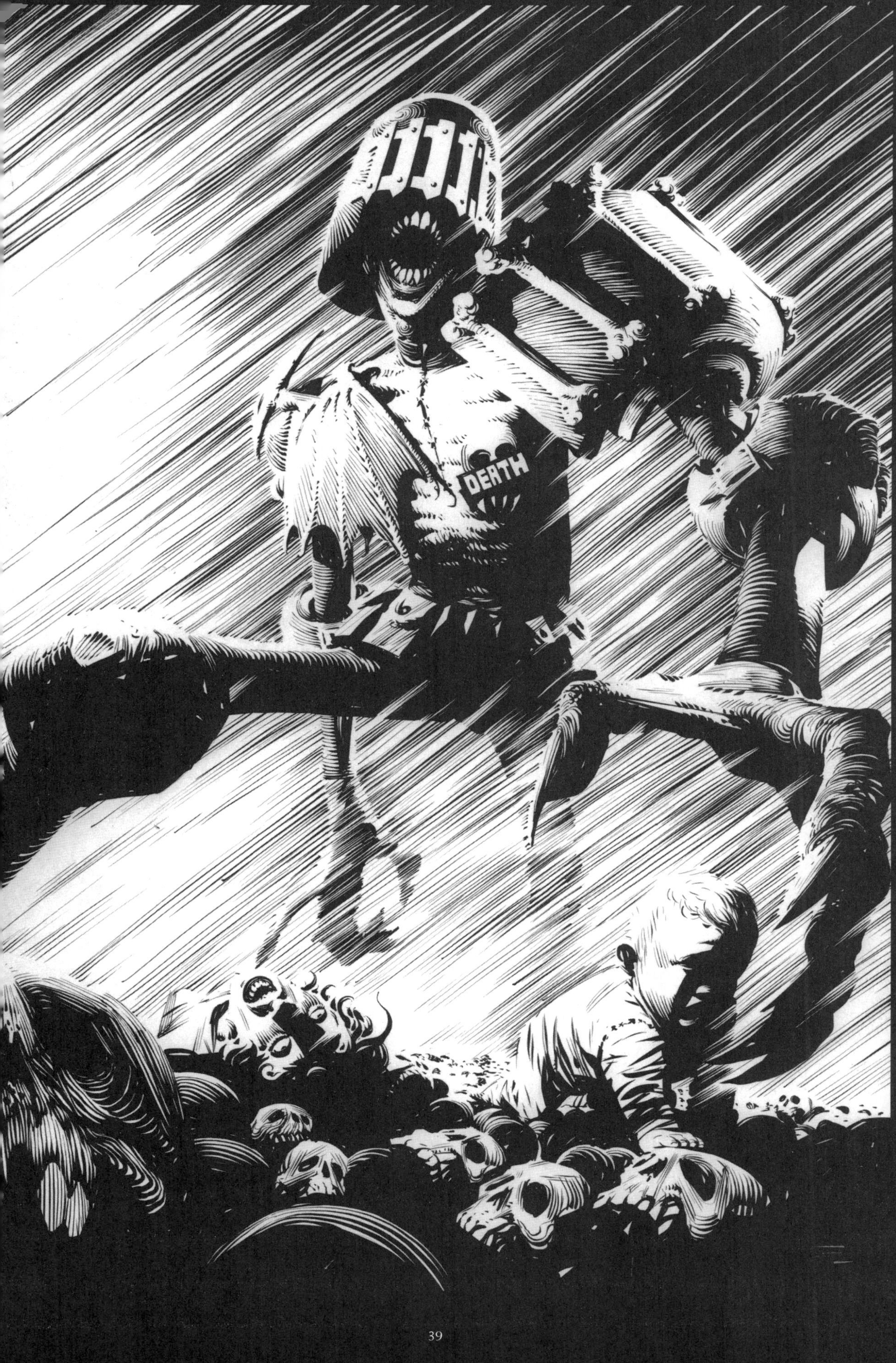
DEATH

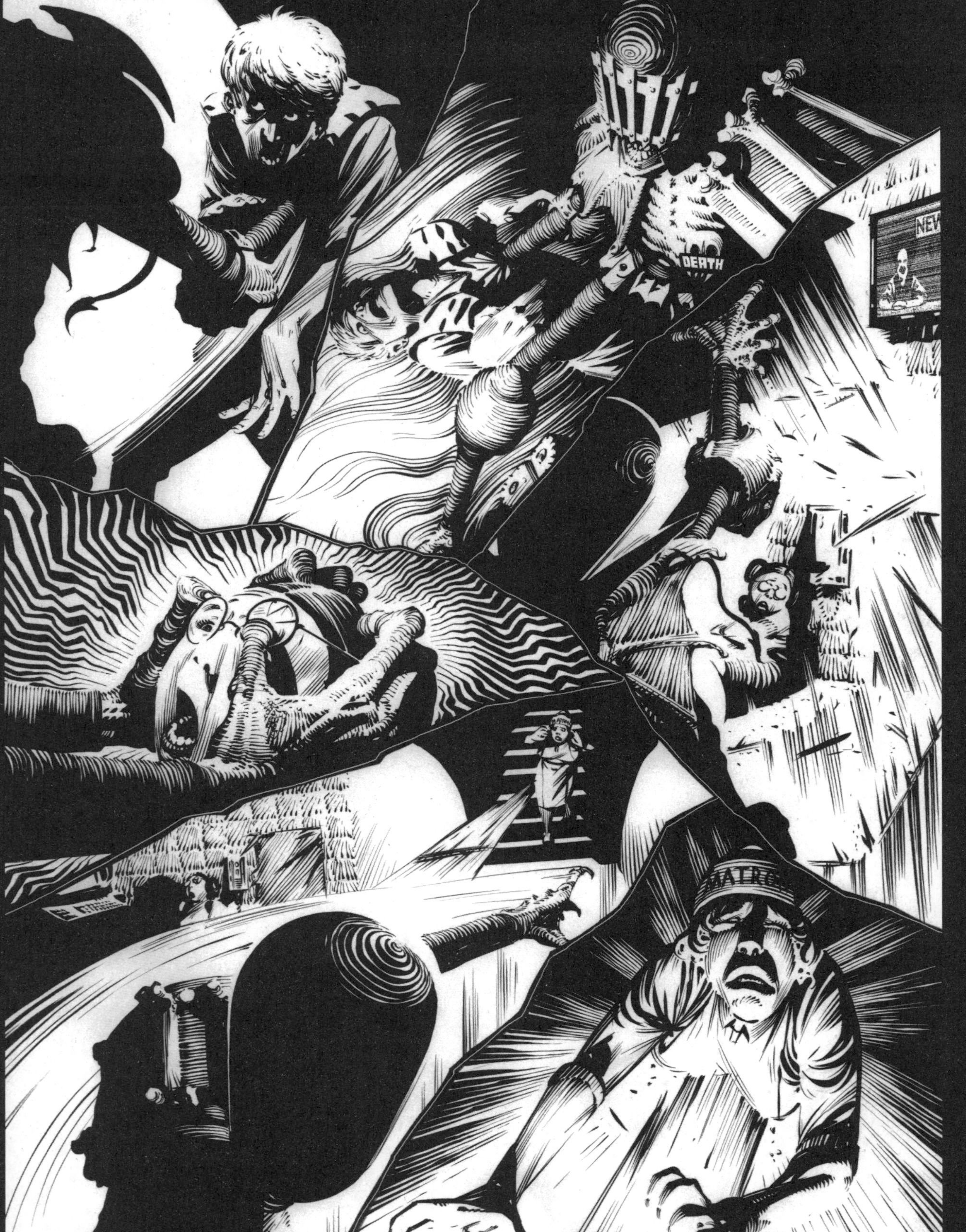
DEATH

linework become that much more important to the storytelling? What role does it play, versus the subject matter or composition?

FRAZER: Well, they all play a part, but the line is the bit that the eye responds to with the most immediacy. A smooth, curved line will have calm vibes associated with it, like smooth surfaces or warm curves on a body, etc. Jagged lines will remind the reader of knives, or rough edges that scrape, etc. One can do the same drawing with the same composition and achieve completely different effects just by altering the types of lines used. *Garfield* is seen as far more friendly because of those lines, and *From Hell* is colder due to the lines Eddie Campbell used. In work where the color is absent or muted, the line takes on the additional role of doing the mood enhancing that the color normally would.

MM: That's probably the best explanation of line work and its power that I've heard. Shortly after "Judge Death," you broke into the American scene through the Dark Horse mini-series *Fort: Prophet of the Unknown*. I read that Peter Lenkov saw an image from "Necronauts" and asked for you. Even though you are still working in black-&-white and returning to the Charles Fort character, the book has a very different look and feel than anything previously. How did your approach to the *Fort* project differ in regard to these earlier experiments?

FRAZER: *Fort* was a 20-page story padded out to make four issues. It looks different because it was like pulling teeth drawing so much padding. Going from the condensed 2000 *AD* format to 22-page comics was a huge jolt.

MM: Did you color the covers?

FRAZER: They wouldn't let me color the covers, and with all due respect to whoever did them, I thought the colors were awful. They did exactly what all comic colorists were doing back then, which was using gradient fills and effects to swamp the line work. The line work on those covers was solid on its own, and I was quite annoyed at how it all turned out.

MM: Did *Fort* employ any digital tools, particularly in the crafting of the alien character, or was it completely traditional pencil and inkwork?

FRAZER: Mainly traditional stuff, though a few little tricks probably sneaked in. The last few pages were all penciled on the computer, as well, as I was against the deadline, so that was interesting.

MM: How did your experience with Dark Horse and Lenkov differ from your experience at 2000 *AD*? What lessons did you take away from your first taste of American comics?

FRAZER: Firstly, if you are new to the American biz they will always offer you lower rates than everyone else. Also, there was less interest from the writer or editor's side on *Fort*. Even though 2000 *AD* never bugged me about anything, before we got into a story they were always very up for discussing the

Previous Page: A page from the second part of "My Name is Death." **Below:** Frazer revisited the character of Charles Fort in the Dark Horse four-issue mini-series *Fort: Prophet of the Unexplained*, written by Peter Lenkov.

Judge Death ™ and © Rebellion A/S. Fort: Prophet of the Unexplained © Dark Horse Comics.

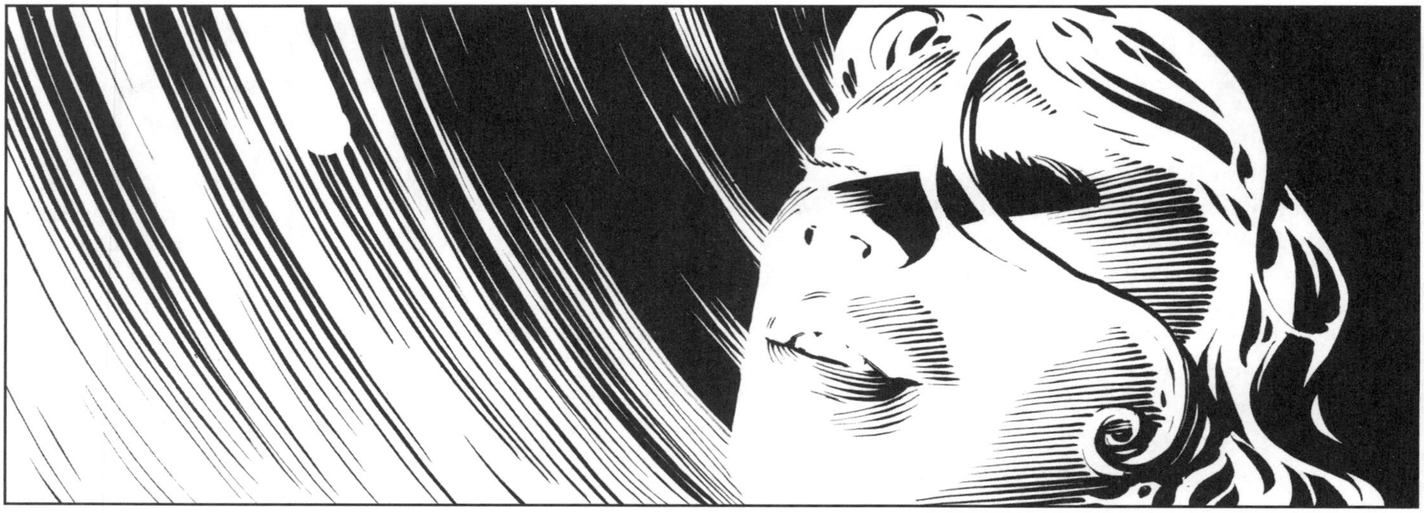

Above: A panel from page 2 of *The Authority: Scorched Earth* #1. With this job, Frazer employed a rather high-contrast style, with a different approach to the shading. **Next Page:** Page 3 of *The Authority: Scorched Earth* #1. It's a metaphor, kids! If you don't get, go ask your parents.

details and how I might go about it. On *Fort* it felt like I was just part of a machine.

MM: Was there any connection between your four-issue mini-series with Dark Horse and the subsequent one-shot, *The Authority: Scorched Earth* #1 in early 2003?

FRAZER: I think Scott Dunbier saw my art for *Fort* in *Previews*, and he said to me that he wanted to go with a different style for *The Authority* relaunch. Initially I was going to do a six-part series, but I think they suddenly realized they should test me out first, hence the one-shot. I failed that test remarkably.

MM: You were working on *The Authority* after a move to Croatia. What is the story behind this move?

FRAZER: I was finishing it after I moved there, working with a MacBook and my brushes only. I moved out there pursuing a damsel I had a "complicated" relationship with. The romantic in me decided it would be a good idea to uproot and relocate myself instead of actually focusing on what I could do in the UK.

MM: There was some diplomatic situation with you in Zagreb that eventually landed you in court and expelled to Slovenia. You had an art exhibition in Zagreb, though? What was the exhibition?

FRAZER: They have a yearly comic con like everywhere does, and because I was an international artist living there at the time, they decided to milk it and make an exhibition of pages I drew for *The Authority*, "Judge Death," and *Fort*. I got deported because I failed to observe certain rules about registering my stay-on time, and I put this down to the large number of people I encountered during my first visit who all gave me incorrect info, including the people at the police station who arrested me later. I got tried and kicked out in one afternoon. Sadly, I was wearing a "genius" T-shirt at the time, and I was pleasant and smiled when the judge asked me questions, which I was later told was a bad move, as the judges like to see humble, penitent, and groveling people.

MM: Were you able to return to Croatia? How long did you live there?

FRAZER: After three weeks, we managed to pull strings so that I could go back and have my record erased, then they re-tried me and found me innocent of all "charges." It was a ridiculous display of corrupt politics and crushed the dreams of at least one friend of mine who had planned to enter the legal sphere as a career. When they asked my profession, I said "freelancer," and they translated that as "unemployed," because they couldn't or wouldn't understand how someone can have a job that isn't in the city they live in. Still, I fought the law and I won, although it did take the steam out of it for me, and I left soon after anyway. My record was already deleted before the second trial. The second time they just sat there and read the info again and said that they had decided in their mercy to withdraw the sentence as long as I behaved myself, which got the job done, but it was a load of hogwash, it really was. In all, I lived in Croatia for about two years, though a portion of that was spent in the UK taking a week or two to deal with home stuff. And no, beyond swearing and asking for coffee I didn't learn the language.

MM: Getting back to *The Authority*, it is another Frazer Irving penciled piece, but colored by another artist. Was this your choice, or were you not allowed to color your own work?

FRAZER: This was their choice. Again, I wasn't happy about it, and it may well have infected the enthusiasm I had for the work, but I think it may have been best, as I wasn't really focused on the art during that period.

MM: You state in the 2008 interview that the work became a "travesty." Was this because of the Croatia situation? How did this affect your relationship with American comics?

FRAZER: It was 90% my headspace in Croatia and 10% dull story, really. I wasn't that into the gig once I got the script, and even Robbie said so later on that he thought it was bollocks, but the overriding factor would have been me chasing Croatian tail all over the place. That really derailed my career, but I think it was a good thing. After the job, my editor, Ben Abernathy, called me up and asked if I wanted to do a series working with Micah Wright, and I turned it down, because I needed to get my act together. He then laughed and joked that I had blown it, and then reassured me that they would have an open door when I'm back in the driving seat. Needless to say, that never happened. I think turning down that follow-up gig was what got me scratched off the DC list for some time.

MM: It was around this time that you attended the 2003 San Diego Comic-Con. Was this your first trip to San Diego and the U.S.?

FRAZER: Yup, first time. [*laughs*]

MM: Did it live up to your expectations of what you'd grown up reading about the U.S.?

FRAZER: It was hotter. [*laughs*] Aside from that, America was all I imagined. Oh, the sandwiches were as tall as trees. [*Nathan laughs*] I liked SDCC; it's still referred to as my yearly vacation. It's a madhouse at that con. I was more into the whole networking side than anything. I still can't remember why I decided to go. I think Jock and Diggle were going, and they suggested I go along as a mascot.

MM: In terms of professional development for you, what transpired at Comic-Con?

FRAZER: Well, it was nice to meet a lot of the folks whose work I knew, though they were all business and not very social towards the scruffy Brit. Also, I learned that comics people smoke and drink loads more than I expected. As for what happened there, well, nothing for me until Andy got me into the DC party and I met Grant. That was the big bonus for me at that con.

MM: Was this where you broached *Klarion*, or did that come next year in 2004?

FRAZER: It was just social. I didn't hear anything more from Grant 'til a year later when he emailed me saying he had a Marvel project in the works, but that my email had bounced and so I was out of the running.

MM: Did you come away with any American assignments or other projects that helped you professionally, or was it all about connections and contacts?

FRAZER: It was all networking. I left there with zilch, but I sort of expected that. I knew the Dark Horse guys out there, but they were hard to track down, and when I did, they were all nice and everything, but totally not interested in giving me more work.

MM: Even though you had expected that, was it still disappointing?

FRAZER: No, I did what I set out to do, which was show my face and be a nuisance.

MM: After San Diego, you did more work for *2000 AD*. Was it awkward to shift between the traditional black-&-white line art and heavily inked style of "Judge Death" and the polished, digital realm you explore in "From Grace"?

Below and Next Page:
With "From Grace," Frazer began exploring "penciling" digitally, as shown in these examples from the first and fourth installments of the series, written by Simon Spurrier.

From Grace ™ and © Rebellion A/S.

FRAZER: No. I was beginning to tire of the inks anyway and needed a way out. I think I was doing them both at the same time at one point, and the freshness of "From Grace" was really harshing the inks on "Judge Death." The problem with inking is that there's only black and white, no grays, and I like a bit of gray. Even making the grays with lines is still black-&-white, and it takes ages to do stippling or hatching.

"For all his many talents, Frazer's greatest flaw is a complete inability to say 'no.' And not just with work, either. I've seen the photos. That otter didn't deserve that. Seriously, his greatest strength? His unending capacity for humility. [laughs] Sorry. No, it's his inventiveness. His ability to take a

script and—without openly ignoring the writer's direction—to find unexpected ways to stage panels and scenes which make them better than the sum of their parts. He's a consummate storyteller. And a delightful weirdo."
— **Simon Spurrier**

FRAZER: That's correct. It's hard, but I'm learning.

MM: I have to ask. What is the otter story, because Spurrier mentions this in the introduction for *The Simping Detective* collection?

FRAZER: It's a fantasy he has and keeps banging on about. I let him because I know it makes him happy. I would never inappropriately touch such a creature. Simon, however... Ask him about the yaks.

MM: [*laughs*] I'm not sure I want to know about that one. Seriously, though, in an article you wrote about digital comic art in 2003, you said that "From Grace" was your first totally digital project. Did you have any concerns having worked so long with natural tools and media to going completely digital for "From Grace"? Since you were doing the two projects at the same time and employing two different techniques, was it all awkward?

FRAZER: I was more concerned about losing the touch for the brush, if anything. I took to drawing in Photoshop like a duck to water, so there were no problems there.

MM: So drawing in Photoshop came naturally, but how about digital brushwork that would have been done traditionally?

FRAZER: I didn't do any of that until very recently. Doing the traditional brush work on a Wacom tablet was too difficult for me. I know many did get into it, like Brian Bolland, but I needed the Cintiq before I dared emulate my brush marks digitally. I didn't abandon the brush for ages, in fact. What I did was develop two distinct camps of art: one was 100% digital and emulated painterly styles, and the other was traditional inked art then scanned and colored, such as *Klarion*. I didn't ditch the brushes fully until the start of *Silent War* and *Gutsville*.

MM: What do you mean in your 2003 authored article on digital comic art by a "kick back at the glut of shiny Bryce and Poser figures polluting the world of illustration" when discussing your process in "From Grace"?

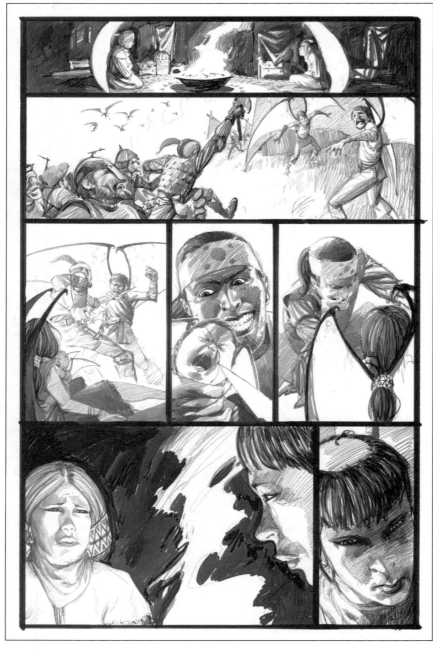

44

FRAZER: Oh, I was aware of a lot of digital art back then being mainly 3-D based software models, which were dumped into Photoshop instead of using drawing methods. It was common to use the tools in a totally different way to traditional art methods, but what I wanted was to bring them closer together. I am an art curmudgeon. "From Grace" was very low-fi in that respect, and my plan was to mimic paint as closely as I could to show that the computer can continue these age-old methods; it doesn't have to be space age and shiny 3-D bollocks.

MM: Is that still a concern for you today as you've moved into completely digital realms, the continuation of the age-old methods and avoiding the overly rendered look that digital art can sometimes have?

FRAZER: Well, what I'm aiming for now is something different but the same, sort of like finding new ways to make marks not so distant from brushes and pencils, but that offer a freaky new quality to them. I want the inherent qualities of digital brushes to speak out the same way the bristle marks on old paintings do. I'm not trying to make the viewer believe I used actual paint. I want them to look at it and see that I used the Mac, but in a non-obvious way.

MM: If I didn't know you worked digitally, I don't think I would immediately think, "Oh, he must be a digital artist." I would think, "How did he do that?" but my mind wouldn't immediately go to "digital."

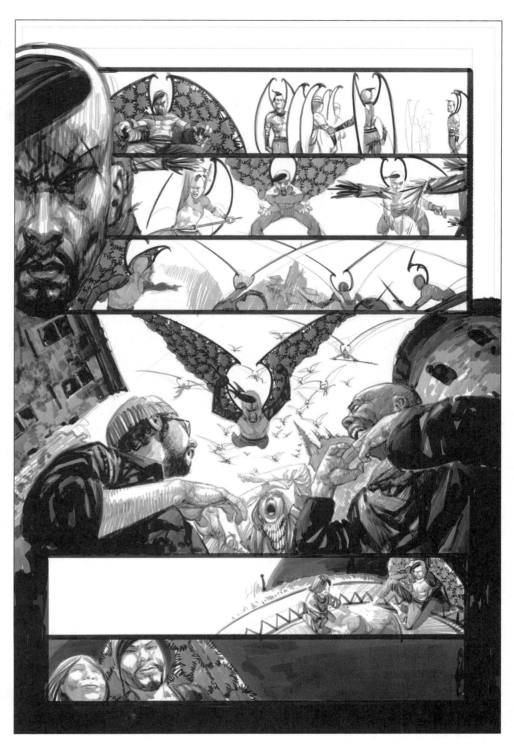

FRAZER: This is good. It's the more artistically aware ones that I suspect will see through my digi-ruse. If everyone could see it, then I would be too obvious. I was evangelizing back then.

MM: The digital prophet?

FRAZER: The Mac was my sword, Photoshop my book. I would tell everyone who would listen that they should get into digital painting, and since then it's sort of exploded and become the norm for almost all new artists I see working out there. But that wasn't my doing.

MM: What was it about "From Grace" that convinced you to go digital?

FRAZER: It was an accident. I was using my new Wacom tablet and big monitor in Croatia to do some pencils for the story. I had decided to pencil it on the Mac and then ink it with pens for some stupid reason, but during the sketch stage of page one, I noticed it looked kind of interesting, so I played about with the other brushes adding white paint, etc., until it formed. I had that nervous excitement of the new, but I needed to test it on an actual page to see if it was actually possible for me to do this. It seems silly looking

Above: More digital penciling for "From Grace."

Next Page: If Jack Point looks a bit familiar, it may be because you saw his prototype a few pages back among the sample pages Frazer was submitting to *2000 AD* in the hopes of getting work. He may have traded in his clown suit for a trenchcoat and fedora, but the nose and dour attitude remain.

From Grace, The Simping Detective ™ and © Rebellion A/S.

back now, but back then it was almost unheard of to do all the art on the Mac like this, and certainly not in the pencil-and-paint way I was doing it. But it worked, and I emailed Matt asking if it was okay and he didn't seem fussed. When I was doing those first pencils on the screen, what I noticed was that the grays I was getting would be hard to ink up cleanly, yet I liked the grays, I didn't want to reduce it to simple lines again. It was that moment that my river of art changed its course. In my bedroom, on Radiceva Avenue, Zagreb, Earth.

MM: That thrill of something new but slightly scary must have been a great and terrifying experience, but when it paid off, I bet it was all the more sensational.

FRAZER: Well, it kind of had aftershocks, because the same thing happened when I did "The Simping Detective," *Silent War*, and more recently *Xombi*. I try one method and then notice that this new way of doing it could happen instead, changing the entire vibe. It's a nice feeling, but is also very much like being ill or scared of public shame. Back in the Zagreb days it was almost as if my career depended on each gig being reliable, hence the

extra fear. Nowadays, I sort of tell the editors in advance, "It may look a little different."

MM: How strange was it to rough sketch digitally versus using traditional pencil tools?

FRAZER: It was liberating.

MM: No hesitation?

FRAZER: Nope. I could always undo it, and erasing was way easier than with standard tools.

MM: What about the tension and pressure on the screen tablet versus that of paper and art board?

FRAZER: The tablets are smoother, so the pen glides more. You adjust pretty quickly. Using real pencils is a hassle if you need to move stuff around, too. Photoshop allows all manner of tweaks without redrawing everything. Tracing is easier, too, no more taping the page to the window.

MM: Did you also create custom brushes and pencils? Is that a very intensive process?

FRAZER: It's pretty easy to make them, though it takes a bit of trial and error to get the effect one wants. But I didn't start making my own brushes 'til "The Simping Detective," mainly because I didn't know how.

MM: You color coded everything in "From Grace." The one that stands out is your use of magenta for the scenes of Kaith's father. How did that come about and what were your theories on coloring at that point for the story?

FRAZER: The idea was simple. The further back in time we go, the hotter the colors, so his conception is red hot, his youth is summer warm, then the later adulthood is almost gray, until he dies and it all turns to full color to show that we are viewing the scene objectively and not from his point of view.

MM: That's pretty cool actually.

FRAZER: I still claim it was my idea.

MM: I think Si said it was his.

FRAZER: He can sue me. [laughter]

MM: Of your work, "From Grace" has the most traditional feel or look in terms of textures, lines, and tones. Was this a conscious effort on your part? Would you say that "From Grace" was the bridge between where you are now versus how you used to work?

FRAZER: It was Simon's idea to get that sort of rough pencil with wash look, as he'd seen Bisley do it on "Slaine" a fair bit, and I agreed with him. As a bridge it most certainly was the turning point between the old style of working and the new, and a lot of it still stands up to scrutiny for me today.

MM: In early 2004 you began work on "The Simping Detective." The layouts in "Gumshoe" and throughout the various stories in the "Simping Detective" series are simply amazing, especially between the panels and segments of narration. Spurrier told me that the text panel notions were his attempt at bringing the "tone-setting narrative voice"
from the detective noir genre into the series, but how did this translate for you as the artist designing the pages and constructing the flow and pacing?

So they kick us out after the ninth goon joins the med wagon queue. I love it when the bouncers say please. I figure we're going back to hers for synthicaff when she goes and gets curious.

They all do, sooner or later

FRAZER: It meant I had to make room for more panels, but they worked well as graphic shapes to guide and shape the other panels. It was fun. I did play around with a few placements in order to get a better effect, but I try to avoid that.

MM: Since you've explained the power of lines before, can you address how the look and feel of "The Simping Detective" black-&-white

Below: Though "The Simping Detective" began as a black-&-white series with gray tones, with the second story, "Crystal Blue," a third color was added. The blue tint in the second panel of this page reflects the eponymous drug taking effect. **Next Page:** The opening page of "Playing Futsie," from *Judge Dredd Megazine* #234.

work is decisively more modern and polished than, say, in the scratchier, more traditional feel from either "Necronauts" or "Judge Death"?

FRAZER: Well, "The Simping Detective" was painted using white-on-black instead of black-on-white, and this means the light is the star, not the shadow. Plus, I didn't use brushes on this, so the same vocabulary of brush-specific lines were not available. The lines you see in "The Simping Detective" are mostly carved out from the shadows with the light here. I don't know about it being modern, though, as I was emulating painting techniques dating from the '50s.

MM: Well, modern in the sense of how futuristic Mega City looks versus how the city looks in, say, your "Judge Death" work.

FRAZER: That was down to me using the street lights to craft the city, instead of the black lines. One can get very atmospheric with a few well placed windows, and I could also vary the brightness and that would possibly make it look different.

MM: Does the white-on-black and lighting relate to why the appearance of color—such as the vial of Crystal Blue, the drug's effects within the story, or the segments in "Playing Futsie"—is so shocking?

FRAZER: No, the idea, initially, was just to use one color for the "Blue" story, but after that we decided to milk it 'til it was dry and apply it to every story. I think that was a mistake, the same way *Sin City* did it too much. I liked it in "Crystal Blue," as it had a reason for being there.

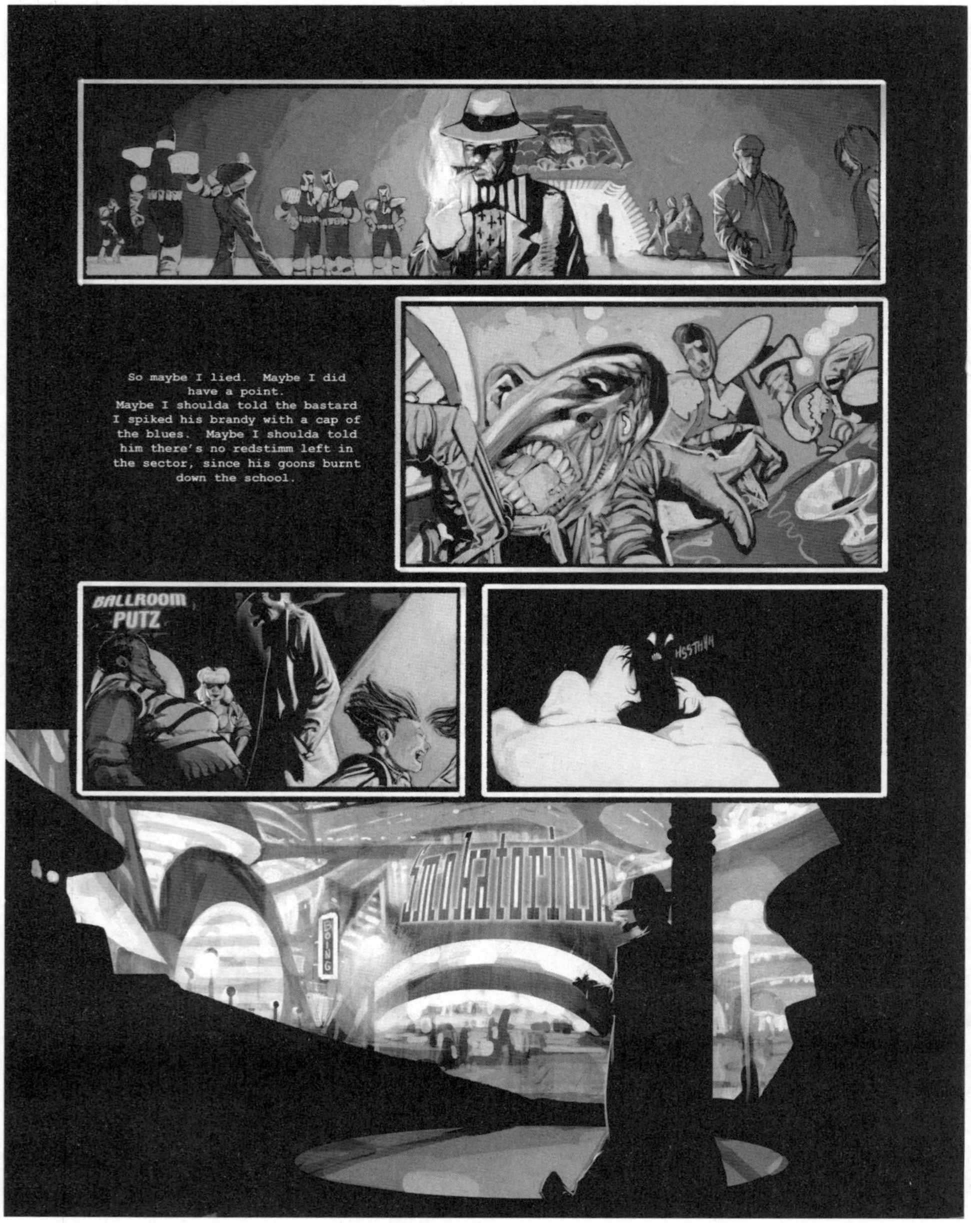
So maybe I lied. Maybe I did have a point.
Maybe I shoulda told the bastard I spiked his brandy with a cap of the blues. Maybe I shoulda told him there's no redstimm left in the sector, since his goons burnt down the school.
BALLROOM PUTZ
HSSTHH

MM: In reading the script for "Playing Futsie," I am immediately struck by the first image of Jack at the top, which isn't called for in Spurrier's notes. Can you tell me a little bit about your process of how you decide to create illustrations for segments that are not called for in the script? Or, when you eliminate them completely as in page one of part two? Do you have to consult with the writer or editor before making such changes?

FRAZER: That piece at the top was a nod to the old EC Comics where the story had a narrator. I figured it'd be nice to pop it in there for a laugh. At this point Alan [Barnes, editor] pretty much let us do whatever we wanted, and seeing as I was always handing in art on deadline day, they never got to say anything about changes I made. The way I see it, the buck stops with the artist, and whatever choices they make must be made for the good of the story within the artist's abilities. If everyone gets involved you get situations where writers or editors treat the artist as an extension of their own arms, trying to get us to draw things that we just suck at. I make these choices based upon what I think tells the story best using my voice, which is the one people see on the page.

With *Xombi* recently, I made some sweeping changes to the script, and

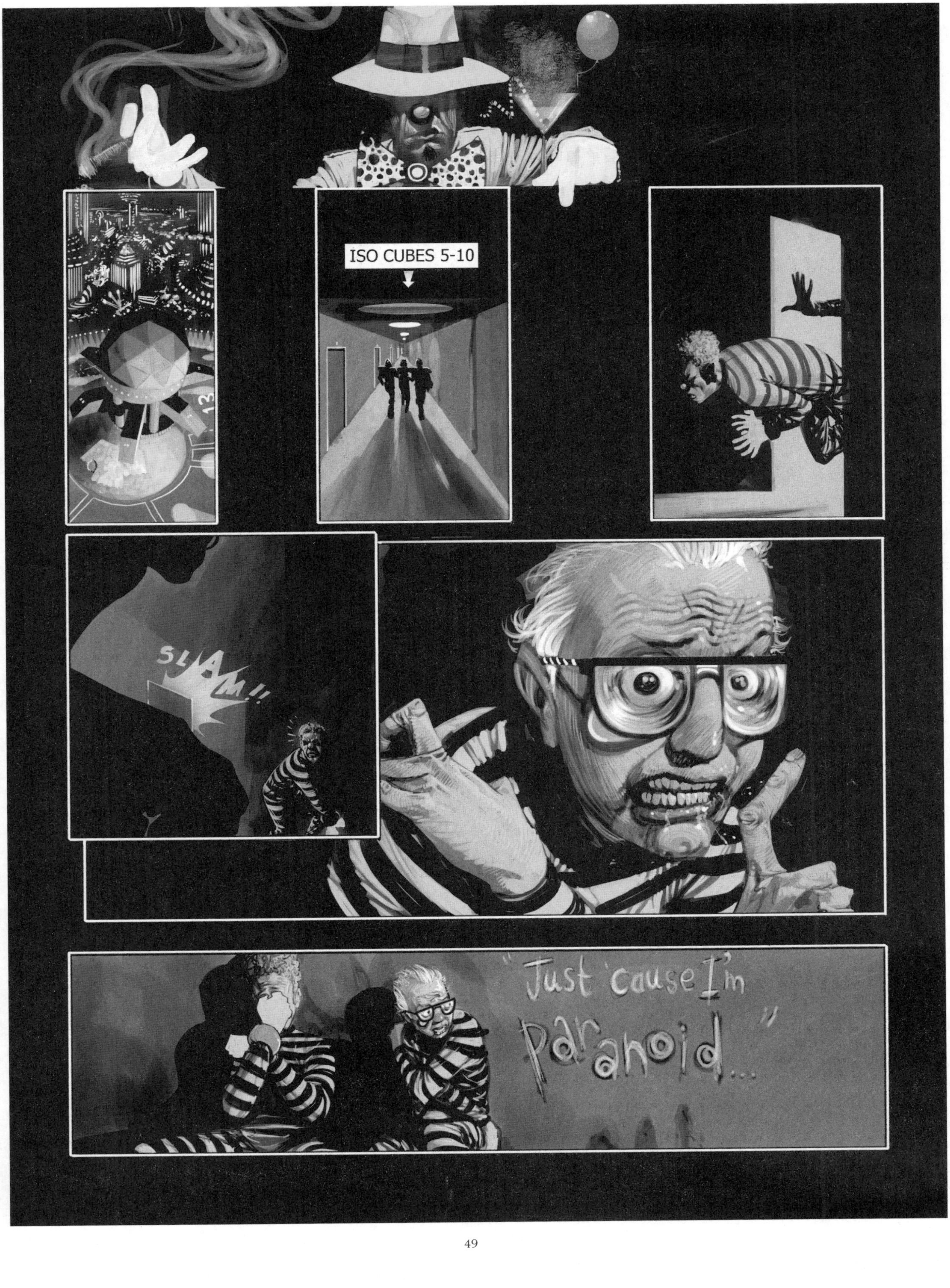
ISO CUBES 5-10
SLAM!!
"Just 'cause I'm paranoid..."

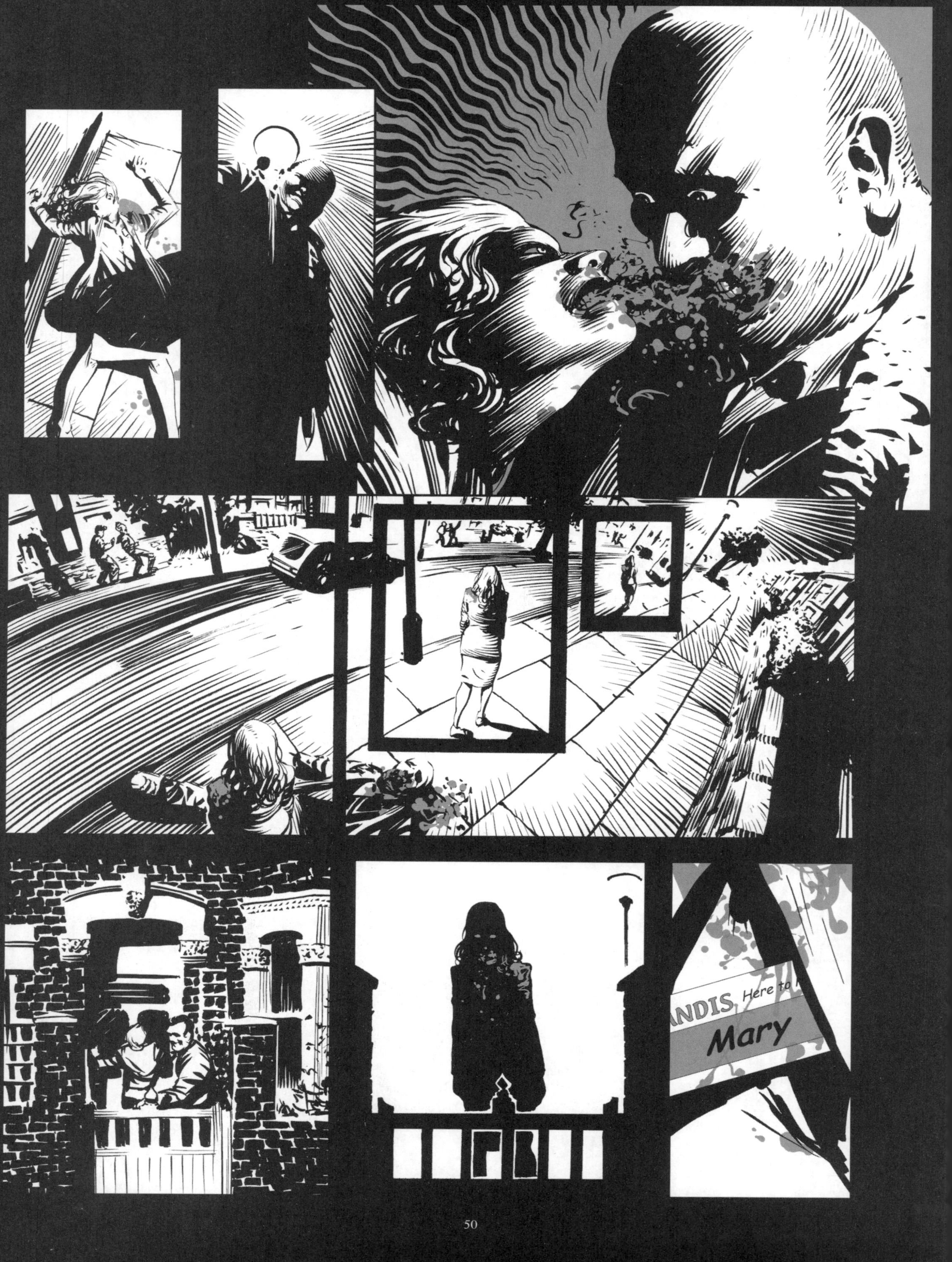
ANDIS Here to
Mary

I sent layouts to the editor and writer for their approval, but in my head they were the best choices and I would have been really annoyed if they'd asked for them to be changed. We all see it differently, but for my part I see my role as the storyteller. I'm the actors, the director, the lighting people, costume, etc. I have to do all the graft of making the marks on the page, so I get final say on matters. Writers tend to disagree with this, and I have heard many refer to us as mere engineers who trace their thoughts onto paper. The writers deliver the story, the themes, the feeling, the motivation, all the stuff that should inspire and move, but the acting is not theirs.

MM: Is that where a good editorial stance comes into play then?

FRAZER: Editors mainly match us up, throw us in a closet, and tell us not to get pregnant. They are nice people, but there's so much for them to do that we can't be managed in detail. I prefer to have an understanding with the writers, myself. If they know my stuff, I tell them I may well bend their scripts to suit my own brand of storytelling, and if they don't like the idea then let's not work together. Editors are there to make sure we don't show penises or swear words in the comics, and some fail magnificently at that. There are at least four penises in my mainstream work that no one ever spotted.

MM: Really?

FRAZER: And I'm not saying where they are.

MM: 2004 saw the release of the Simon Pegg *Shaun of the Dead* DVD with your strip "There's Something About Mary." What was your relationship with Pegg, and how did you become associated with the film?

FRAZER: I think it was the marketing guy, Dominic Preston, at 2000 *AD* who was dealing with that gig. Pegg and the boys had approached 2000 *AD* to do some sort of tie-in, I think, and Dom was charged with dealing with it, as it was outside the usual realms of what 2000 *AD* produced. In effect, it was like an advert, but posing as a comic. I don't know why they chose me. Possibly because I

Previous Page: A page from "There's Something About Mary," which ran in *2000 AD* to promote the film and was included as a special feature on the DVD release of *Shaun of the Dead.*
Below: The digitally drawn sketch—basically a thumbnail—and finished art for page 24 of *Mary Shelley's Frankenstein: The Graphic Novel.*

Shaun of the Dead ™ and © Universal Pictures. Mary Shelley's Frankenstein: The Graphic Novel © Byron Preiss Visual Publications.

could get it done quickly, and also possibly due to the zombie connection with all my horror art. However it originated, I said yes, shared an email or two with Simon about the script, spoke to Edgar on the phone a few times—I also ended up doing some art for his girlfriend's single "Bastardo" for the princely sum of a *Dawn of the Dead* DVD—and then waited for the scripts. They showed up quite late, and I ended up doing each strip over a weekend because the deadline was that tight.

MM: Ah. How did you become involved in *Frankenstein*?

FRAZER: I got a call out of the blue from the late Byron Preiss, and he just pitched it at me. "How would you feel about adapting *Frankenstein* for the kid's market?" was his pitch.

MM: Can you talk about the adaptation process? There was a script, correct?

FRAZER: No script. When I spoke with Byron at the very start I said that if I was going to do this for the outrageously low fee he was offering—the deal also included some tiny back-end royalties, which never materialized due to the unfortunate demise of Byron and subsequent liquidation of his company—then I wanted to adapt it myself, and then they could hire someone to add suitable text on top later, like the Marvel method. He agreed, and I went ahead to read the book and reduce it to key sections and beats so that we could fit it all into 144 pages. The structure in the novel is quite clear anyway, and that was a gift, as I could break it into three distinct stages. The rest of it was isolating key scenes and simplifying them into single panels. I drew 144 boxes, and once I had simplified the book into three stages, I then allocated a set number of boxes to each stage and set about scribbling in notes inside each box which covered each main beat of the story. There was trial and error involved, but it came quite easy.

MM: That seems intensive. How did your approach to the novel differ from comic scripts?

FRAZER: Well, I was effectively doing all but the text myself, so that was a major difference right there. I built in lots of mirrored panels where shots later on in the book echoed relevant shots from earlier on, such as where Frankenstein flees from the beast at the start mirrored how he runs to his wife's screams near the end. I figured something like that would work better if the imagery was almost the same, to hint at how his character had changed from coward to hero, sort of. There was lots of that, and that came from me doing all the pacing, etc., myself instead of translating another's script.

MM: In your sketches for *Frankenstein*, you have the very rough placement of objects and characters. Is this a throwaway or do you use this layer and then build upon it with the finished art?

FRAZER: It's a simple guide. The roughs have the most basic info needed to see if it reads okay when all the frills are absent. They also show me how much clutter I can have before it gets muddy. I do draw over them a lot of the time unless the original sketch is proving distracting, in which case I just turn the layer off.

MM: What did adapting a piece of classical literature teach you about storytelling that you had not learned from comics? In turn, what did your experience with comics bring to the adaptation of *Frankenstein* as a graphic novel?

FRAZER: What I took away from it was a vindication on the power of visual storytelling. I was pleased that I had managed to tell the story without running into space issues, and readers did come back to me with very favorable reviews stating that they were surprised how much story they could get from such a simple set of drawings. A lot of comics I had worked on were dependant on exposition, with talking heads everywhere, and *Frankenstein* demanded that it have less of that and make sure each image had a point to it.

What I brought to it was the variety of gimmicks I had played with on *The Man Who Learnt to Fly*, as well as the 2000 AD gigs, bending time in different ways, playing with borders to suggest different points of view, etc. I didn't want to do a boring, "straight" comic adaptation that was nothing more than a storyboard, I wanted the medium of the comics to add to the story whilst remaining faithful to the ideas and narrative. I'd seen some other adaptations, and lots of them had taken ridiculous liberties with the story and characters, and I decided that wasn't to be my plan at all.

Below and Next Page: Sketch and finished art for *Mary Shelley's Frankenstein: The Graphic Novel*, page 74. Instead of writing a script, Frazer broke down the novel into a detailed plot. As for scripts, Frazer says: "Verbosity is the great killer in the script... The drama and motive and feeling should already be set up and implied in the previous pages, so I don't need a panel saying, 'Steve grips the gun tightly, raising it with a nervous tremble as he takes careful aim at this evil that had stolen from him all that he cared for. He knew this bullet would end his suffering forever,' when what I really need is, "Steve points the gun at the evil dude," because I should already be in character for that part.

Mary Shelley's Frankenstein: The Graphic Novel © Byron Preiss Visual Publications.

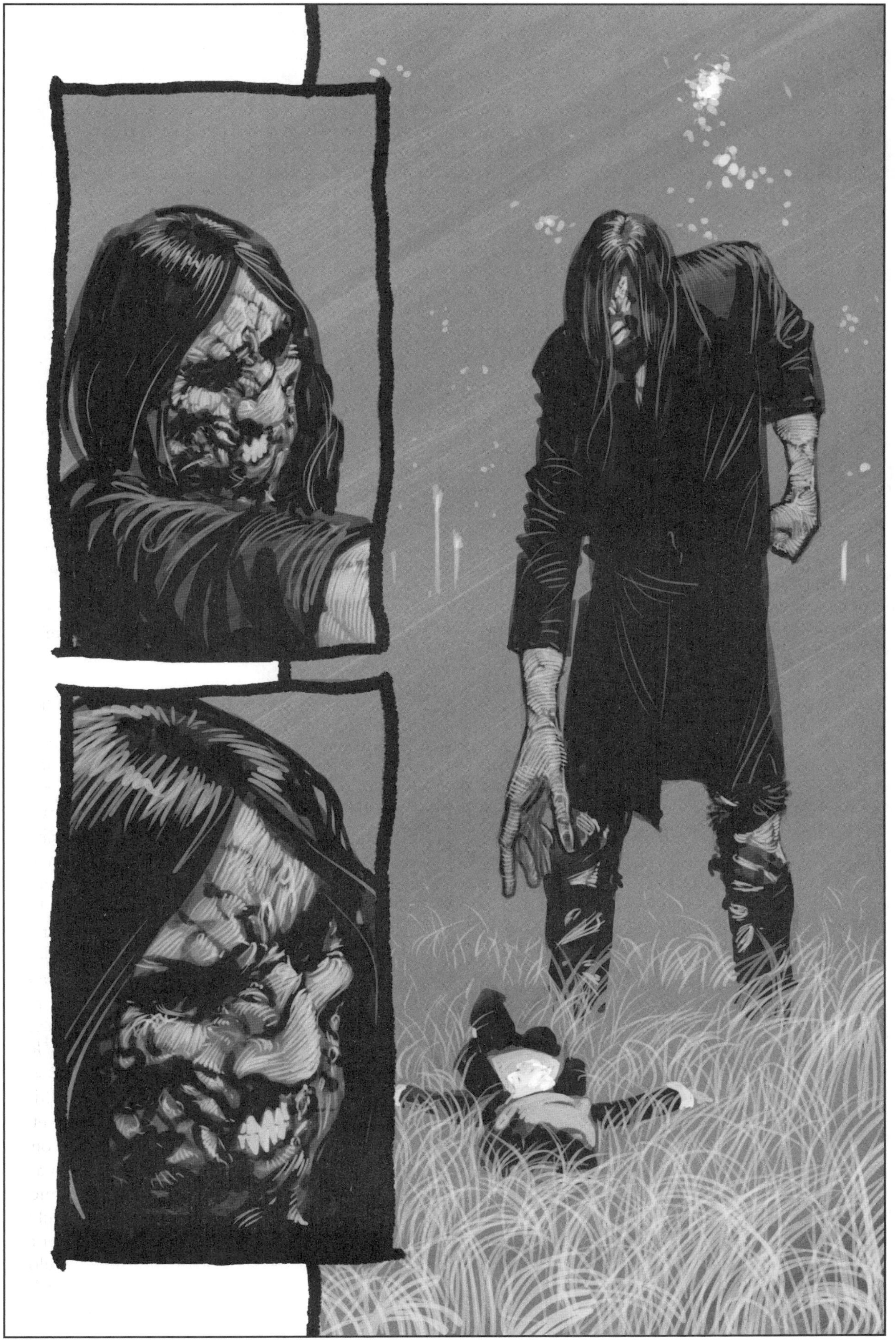

Part 4: The Season of the Witch Boy

MM: How did your involvement with *Seven Soldiers* come about?

FRAZER: *Klarion* happened because Grant emailed me and asked me if I was interested in working on a project, which I followed up at SDCC that year by asking the editor about it. He [Pete Tomasi] said they would prefer an A-lister to work on it, but they'll see what happens. The next thing I know a magazine prints an article by Grant where he states I will be drawing *Klarion*, so I figured the A-lister didn't show up and I got the gig. It's all Grant's fault.

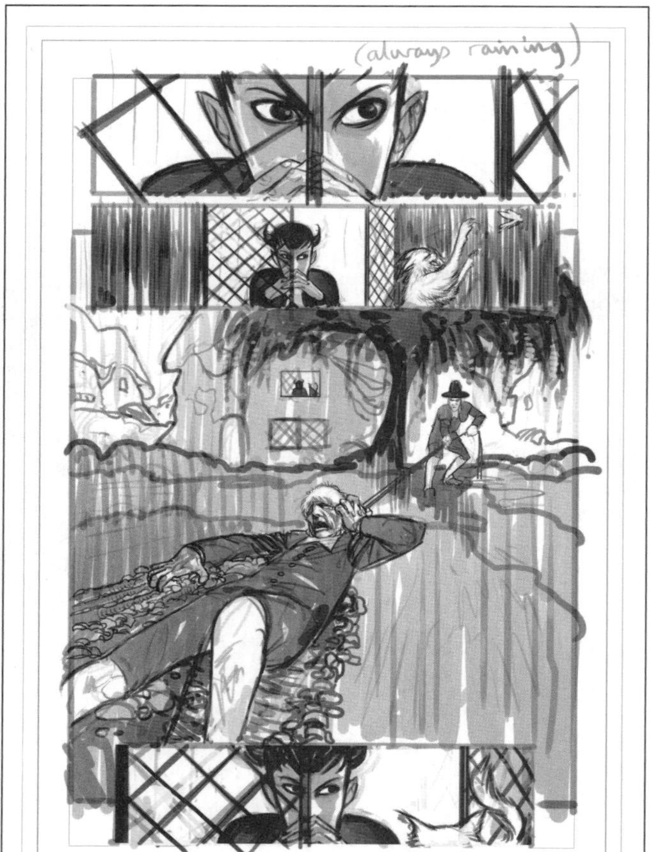
(always raining)

MM: In the notes for the collected trade version of *Seven Soldiers*, Morrison and J.H. Williams say they provided notes and designs on the Klarion character. How did these designs and guides affect and influence your audition piece for Klarion?

FRAZER: They showed me what he looked like. [*laughs*] That was all I needed really: the hair, the outfit, etc. I took that and ran it through the Irvingizor™ and what came out came out.

MM: The Irvingizor™, huh? You've said that the editor sent your rough thumbnails to Grant and the other artists involved on the associated titles. First, do you know why the editor would consider them finished pencils? Second, you mentioned that Grant was upset and you'd already finished the issue by then. Did you not talk with Grant about this misunderstanding?

FRAZER: Well, I don't know if Pete thought they were layouts or pencils, as I was new to him and he was probably used to folks sending in pencils instead of scribbles. I worked differently to a lot of guys back then due to the coloring and the digital aspect, so I guess they just didn't know what I was doing. As for Grant's comments, well that was a *faux pas* on behalf of Pete who sent an email to me that had all the correspondence about the entire series between him and Grant pasted in, and it was only when I snooped did I see the comments. Due to the timing of the email, I thought it was in reference to the final art I had sent in, so I emailed Pete to ask him—seeing as he was the editor—and he seemed as confused as I was. I didn't email Grant because not only does no one ever email Grant if they want a fast reply, it would have seemed a little petty of me to get all whiny and crappy about his opinions. The editor is the one paid to suffer that grief from us freelancers, so Pete had to take the brunt of it.

MM: [*laughs*] So in large part a simple misunderstanding of the digital age of email correspondence. Since your art was sent to others, did you also have an ongoing knowledge of the related *Seven Soldiers* titles as you were working on *Klarion*?

FRAZER: No. I was the only one *not* in the loop it seems. [*laughs*]

MM: It doesn't look entirely digital in its composition. What was your art process for *Klarion*?

FRAZER: I penciled in Photoshop, printed out blue line versions onto DC paper, inked them with borders, scanned that, and painted color on it.

MM: Why did you not select an entirely digital workflow for the title?

FRAZER: I wanted to use ink lines as well as paint because the audience was DCU people and the painty stuff wasn't so hot back then. I couldn't ink on the Mac back then because I didn't have a Cintiq yet.

MM: Was going back to a hybrid method frustrating for you?

FRAZER: It was, actually. By the end of the series I was keen to getting back into doing all digital art, as the gear changes between pencils, inks, scans, and colors was slowing me down too much and making the whole process a drag.

MM: How familiar with Grant and his work were you prior to the series?

FRAZER: I had read *Marvel Boy* and some "Zenith," as well as a bit of *The Invisibles* and *The Filth*. I wasn't a great follower of Grant's, mainly due to my not liking a lot of the art on the books he wrote. I couldn't look past the drawings, so it was only the ones that were well drawn that I read. It's the same with Alan Moore's work. But based on those few items that I did read I was aware of his style and unique flavor. It was weird, but it had intensity and depth, and I liked that.

MM: In terms of scripting and craft, how did Grant's writing and direction differ from your previous collaborations? Since it was your first time working with him, was it more organic to your style of storytelling or jarring because it was the first?

FRAZER: The first scripts had "text to be determined later" all over the place instead of dialogue. For issue #1 I was sort of waiting for the final scripts, but once I got issue #2 I figured this was what I was meant to work with. Prior to this all the scripts had been very tight, and I had followed them as faithfully as I could, but with this half-finished stuff I was a bit lost initially. Not having any guidance from anyone, I just decided to do my own thing, and it was around issue #3 that I discovered that that was what Grant was into. Once I knew that, it was awesome. In terms of compatibility, I liked Grant's way of working, as he clearly had an instinct for dramatic beats and he was very good at setting up sequences, but also free enough to allow for interpretation.

MM: Did he eventually write to your strengths as an artist as the series evolved?

FRAZER: I don't know what my strengths are! [*laughter*] He didn't ask for too many cars or horses though, so that's good.

MM: If you were selling or promoting yourself as an unknown entity to a new publisher

or writer, what would you consider as your strengths?

FRAZER: Variety? Independence? Unpredictability? I don't work in sales, fortunately. [*laughter*]

MM: Audiences see some of your trademark angular and inset panel layouts in *Klarion*. How much creative control did you have over the coloring and design of the book?

FRAZER: I think it was all on me. Issue #1 was all blue, intentionally, and I was surprised I didn't get told to mix it up a bit. Pete was relatively hands-off on this book, which was

Previous Page and Above: Frazer's digital "pencils" and finished, traditional inks for *Seven Soldiers: Klarion the Witch Boy* #1, page 2.

Klarion ™ and © DC Comics.

lovely. He was a good editor to work with, as when he did contribute he had good taste and a sense of what would work.

MM: Do you recall any of his specific contributions that aided you?

FRAZER: He suggested the idea for the cover to issue #4 before the script was ready, but beyond that I can't remember any specifics.

MM: *Klarion* was your big break in American comics—how was it received? Did you receive any feedback from Grant or the other artists involved or even DC on the project?

FRAZER: Initially the Internet hated me, but this is to be expected.

MM: It is the Internet after all. [*laughter*]

FRAZER: Yes. After a while they warmed to it, and now so many folks say it's the best thing I ever did. Ho hum. "It's a good record, but it's never as good as the first album." Grant did say some nice stuff at SDCC, I think. He was pleased with the character of Klarion, and that was enough for me. The other guys in the gang now had to acknowl-

edge me as a peer, whereas before I could quite easily be ignored in bars. Some of us are mates now, which is nice.

MM: Around the same time as *Klarion*, you were also working on a single issue of *Hellblazer* with Mike Carey. How did this assignment come about?

FRAZER: Not sure. I think Mike had said something to me at SDCC about wanting to work with me on it, and I had said yeah, but then I get an email from the editor out of the blue saying they had a one-issue script for me coming up and did I want to do it?

MM: Unlike your time on *The Authority*, "The Gift" seems to find a better balance between your line work and the coloring efforts of Lee Loughridge. Were you unable to color the issue because of your commitments with *Klarion* or was it another incident of a separate penciler and separate colorist mentality?

FRAZER: They just didn't want me to do it because it was Lee's gig, and if I colored it, it's like taking food out of his mouth.

MM: But the end product in *Hellblazer* appears to be much more conducive to your line art. How was this balance achieved versus, say, *The Authority*?

FRAZER: Lee had more time to color it perhaps? The *Authority* colors were done in a rush because I was late. But also the line work on *Hellblazer* was more suited to colors, as there were holding lines and stuff that serve an actual function.

MM: Looking back with the perspective allowed by time, what are your thoughts about your work on *Klarion* and the series itself?

FRAZER: I like it. It's weird and fun, and despite all the drawing errors, I think the character overcomes that and if anything adds to the weirdness, which is a plus for me. I can still see the bits that really suck, though, so I'll never be totally objective about it.

MM: You're always your own harshest critic? Did you see the errors at the time or is this the product of hindsight? Do you believe they were errors produced by the hybrid workflow that a completely digital environment has allowed you to correct?

FRAZER: I am indeed my harshest critic and greatest admirer. I see the errors as I make them, or more like just after the page is finished. Errors, or technical "wrongness," are a part of art. I expect them. It's only how badly they detract from the story and the focus of the art that is really important. Errors that really do make a real stink need correcting, others can be allowed to stay. The errors in *Klarion* were caused by my method of leaving stuff 'til the next stage. I had this thing where I would be in a rush and I'd say, "I can fix that in the colors," and then I'd get to the coloring stage and I'd be like, "Crap! I should have sorted that in the pencils!" It's taken ages for me to recondition myself to reverse that, making the main effort in the underlying structure, thus allowing the later stages to be freer and more experimental.

> *"Looking back, I'm not sure if the project would've existed at all if Frazer hadn't illustrated it. Feels that way to me, anyway. And, keep in mind, Frazer had never done that kind of material in comics before. Mainstream Marvel super-heroes, an extremely high-tech character and setting... it was fairly new to him. I don't know if he thought it was in his particular wheelhouse or not, but, as far as I can recall, he dove in headfirst and knocked it out of the park. I think Frazer can draw anything and make it look great. In the years since we did* Iron Man *together, he's just gotten better and better. His most recent work on* Batman and Robin *is some of my favorite work he's ever done. So few artists display that kind of artistic progression these days. But whatever he chooses to do, I know I'll be there."*
> — Joe Casey

FRAZER: Bless him. Writers are always so nice. This is the nice version of what police say when investigating a crime.

MM: So what's the naughty version of Casey's story?

FRAZER: There's nothing naughty about Joe. He's as pure as the driven snow. Although, he may have kissed a lady once. [*laughter*]

MM: You began work on *Iron Man: Inevitable*, with the first issue appearing in December 2005. How did you become associated with Casey and the mini-series?

FRAZER: He emailed me about it, I think, and asked if I was up for it, as he had put my name forward. I said yes, and then Tom Breevort emailed me making the offer official. I didn't know a lot about it, and I hadn't been following the current series, either, so it was a bit new to me.

MM: Had you pitched with Joe beforehand?

FRAZER: Not properly. He'd been talking about some pitches and said he'd do the hard bit and then let me know. There was one DC pitch which eventually got knocked back, and I was up for that. Back in those days, I assumed people like Joe could get any gig green lit. I know the reality now.

FRAZER IRVING LIMITED
BOOK
ISSUE
PAGE
DATE

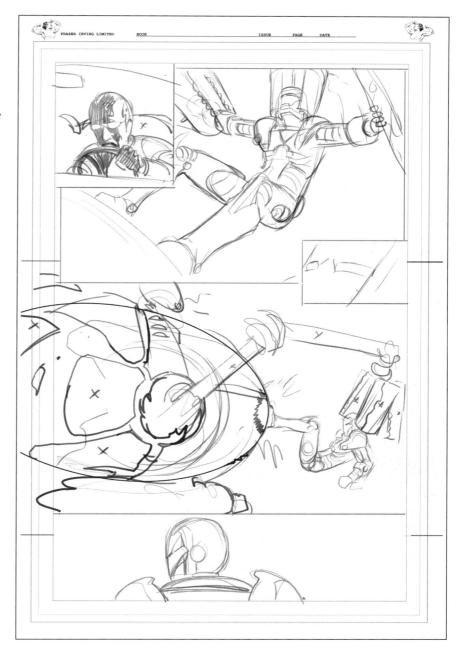

MM: Since you didn't follow the ongoing series, what attracted you to the project itself?

FRAZER: Money? [*laughter*] Joe was very polite when he asked me. I was also curious, but Joe has it right when he says that I didn't think it was my scene. I struggled with the art a lot, more the rendering and illustration than the storytelling, which was fine, as the script was tight and solid. I couldn't get the marks I wanted, and all my experiments cocked up during that series.

MM: What experiments?

FRAZER: Silly art things involving lines. I used the wrong pens. Looking back, the method is very similar to what I do now, but

Previous Page: While the line art for page 17 of *Hellblazer* #213 is heavy on the blacks, the art is actually quite open and leaves the shading up to the colorist.
Above: Pencils for *Iron Man: Inevitable* #1, page 12. Frazer used a mostly traditional process for this six-issue mini-series, only using the computer with the coloring.

Below: Cover art for *Iron Man: Inevitable* #5. Here, the line art is used merely as holding lines. The texture and lighting of the finished product was applied with digital painting.
Next Page: Your instructor for the evening, Miss Ivana B. Yoozd.

back then I didn't have the Cintiq or the chops to do the painting properly, so some line work tried to fill in, and it just looked empty to me. However, many folks—mainly French—have commented since then that they loved the bright, cosmic nature of it, so I accept this now and am glad that folks dug it.

MM: The wrong pens? You had abandoned your brushes for pens. Were these traditional pens or digital pens on the Wacom?

FRAZER: These were normal, traditional pens. I decided to revisit them for *Iron Man* as an experiment, but by page seven I realized my error and asked the editor, Aubrey Sitterson, if I should just do the rest with brushes, and he said they looked fine and just carry on. Looking at it now, a lot of the panels are quite confusing to read, although no one ever said anything.

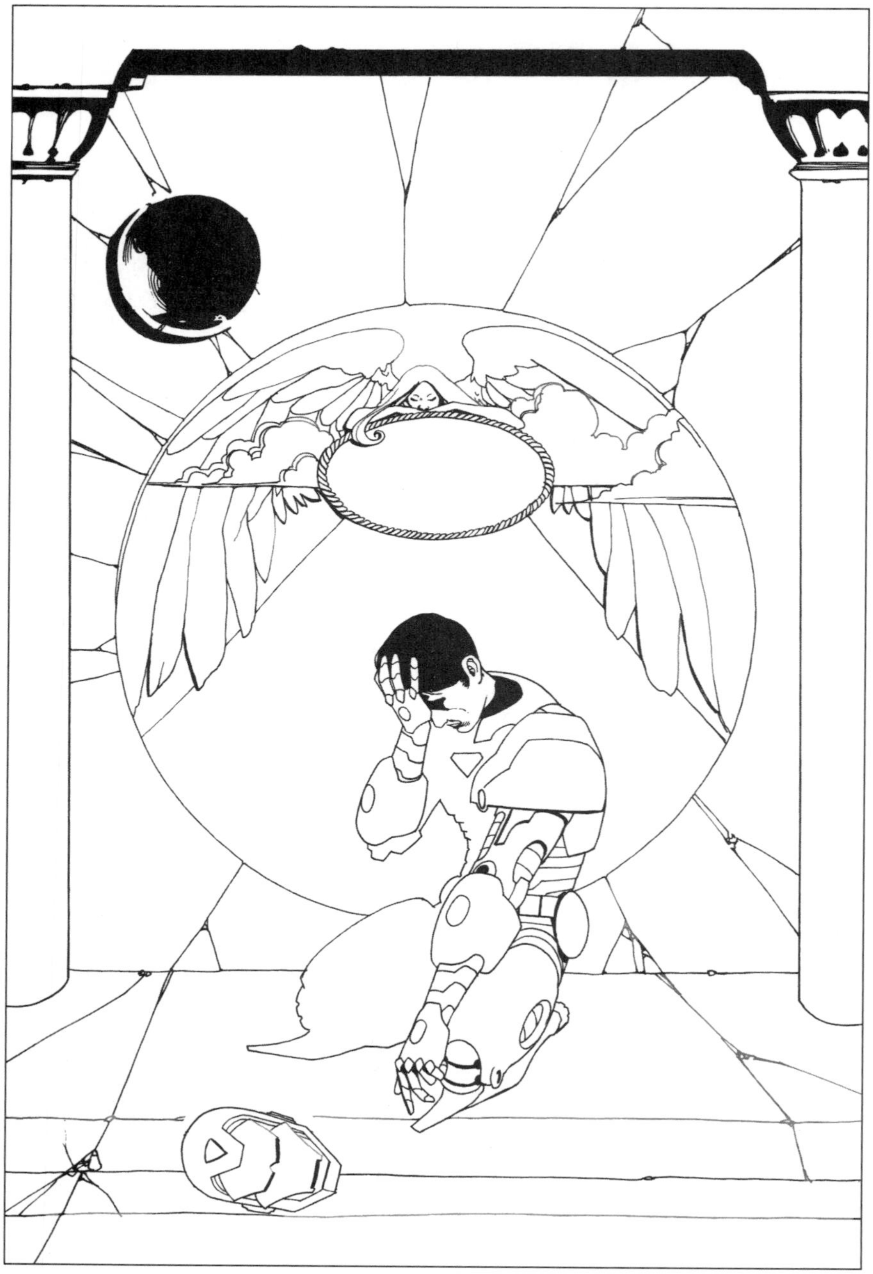

MM: If I am not mistaken, the last page of issue #1 has a college self-portrait of you on the wall, correct?

FRAZER: That picture, like so many others I sneak in from my personal folio, was there because the room needed art for the walls. I always figure, "Hey, why use someone else's art or spend ages making a new painting just for this when I can use all that stuff I did when I was at college," and this is why so many of my student pieces feature in backgrounds like that. With the page in question, I felt the style of the portrait was weird enough to suit the character who owned it as well. In comics, anyone who owns a genuine Frazer Irving painting is clearly either criminally insane or a genius.

MM: [*laughs*] Does that mean David Kim and his roommate Chet are geniuses or to-be-revealed criminal masterminds in *Xombi*?

FRAZER: Kim is totally a genius. He gave all the Frazer Irving art to Chet.

MM: [*laughs*] This was essentially your first super-hero book, since *Dredd* and *Klarion* are really not within the genre. Tell me what that experience was like dealing with a company-owned toy like Iron Man.

FRAZER: I felt like I had to make sure Iron Man looked heroic all the time. This wasn't handed down to me, it was just how I felt. Other than that, they pretty much left me alone to do my thing.

MM: Since he's a character with no visible facial expressions, what does that do to you as the artist to convey emotion, feeling, etc., in the pages? I mean, it's not even a soft mask to play with.

FRAZER: Well, that would all be angles on the helmet and lighting. One can do a lot with simple shadows using an inanimate object.

MM: So it forces you to be even more creative than, say, restrictive in what you can and can't do with his helmet design then?

FRAZER: Well, it cuts the choices down, which is nice, and this means I don't spend too long working out what his expression will be, as I use the same shapes and just light them differently.

MM: Since Casey was familiar with "Storming Heaven" and has praised it heavily himself, do you think he was writing the script for you with "Storming Heaven" in mind?

FRAZER: I think he was, yes. I was very far away from that, though, at the time. I didn't really see the connection, and if I had I may well have done something totally different.

MM: Since *Iron Man: Inevitable* signaled a shift in your art process, what was your attitude towards whether or not to return to traditional ink brush work following the series' conclusion?

FRAZER: I was keen to return to the safeness of brushes, but also drawn to the digital stuff. I think it was a case of getting the two issues on *Robin* that really made my mind up.

MM: You've said that you didn't like how *Iron Man* turned out because you knew what it could have been. Was this in relation to the art? Was it simply the reaction of the static super-hero genre audiences to the dramatic and innovative changes you implemented?

FRAZER: No, it's because it didn't look the way I wanted it to. The audience can love or hate it, it's all immaterial to me. If I don't think I achieved what I set out to achieve, then I feel disappointed. Boris Vallejo said in some book that even the finest artist can only ever realize 50% of the image in their head when they paint the canvas, and I agree with that in principle. For *Iron Man*, I got maybe 2% of what I was after.

MM: Do you do warm-ups when you work digitally?

FRAZER: A lot of artists will inflate their résumé or make doodles out to be prep work in order to improve their standing, but I have stopped that now, as it never did much for me. I dive in and warm up on stage like [jazz bassist] Jaco Pastorius used to.

MM: In your February, 2006, "Photoshop Penciling a Comic Figure" article in *ImagineFX*, you mentioned that you did not use pencils, but still inked with brushes. When did you fully abandon pencils in your workflow? Do you still use them at all for either sketching or sudden ideas or when traveling?

FRAZER: I think I stopped around the "Judge Death: The Wilderness Days," [2004]. I use pencils sometimes when not at the machine, but that's not often. I am glued here.

MM: Since it was something new for you, how did these opportunities to write instructional articles come about?

FRAZER: The first editor of the magazine emailed me to provide a back-up comic for the first six issues, and then it just kept coming until I started saying no.

MM: So, instead of a comic you chose to do an instructional guide?

FRAZER: No, I did both.

MM: I didn't find those.

FRAZER: Oh, dear, you haven't seen "Ivana B. Yoozd, the Meddlesome Muse"?

MM: [*laughs*] No.

FRAZER: Oh, God. I got Simon to help me with it by writing it. It was a travesty. It had a nice idea, but in the end it was just too difficult for me to pull off properly in one page.

MM: 2006 also sees Image put out *24Seven*, vol. 1, where you worked on a short strip by Matt Fraction. How did your association with Fraction begin and this project come about?

FRAZER: I knew the NYC Mech guys from all the SDCC evenings we got wasted together, and they were asking everyone to be a part, so I agreed. They then told me Matt had a script, and I just said yes, not really knowing him or his work. I knew he was mates with Jamie McKelvie, and that was good enough for me.

MM: "Static" shares quite a bit with *Iron Man: Inevitable* in terms of its color palette and warmer tones. Were you

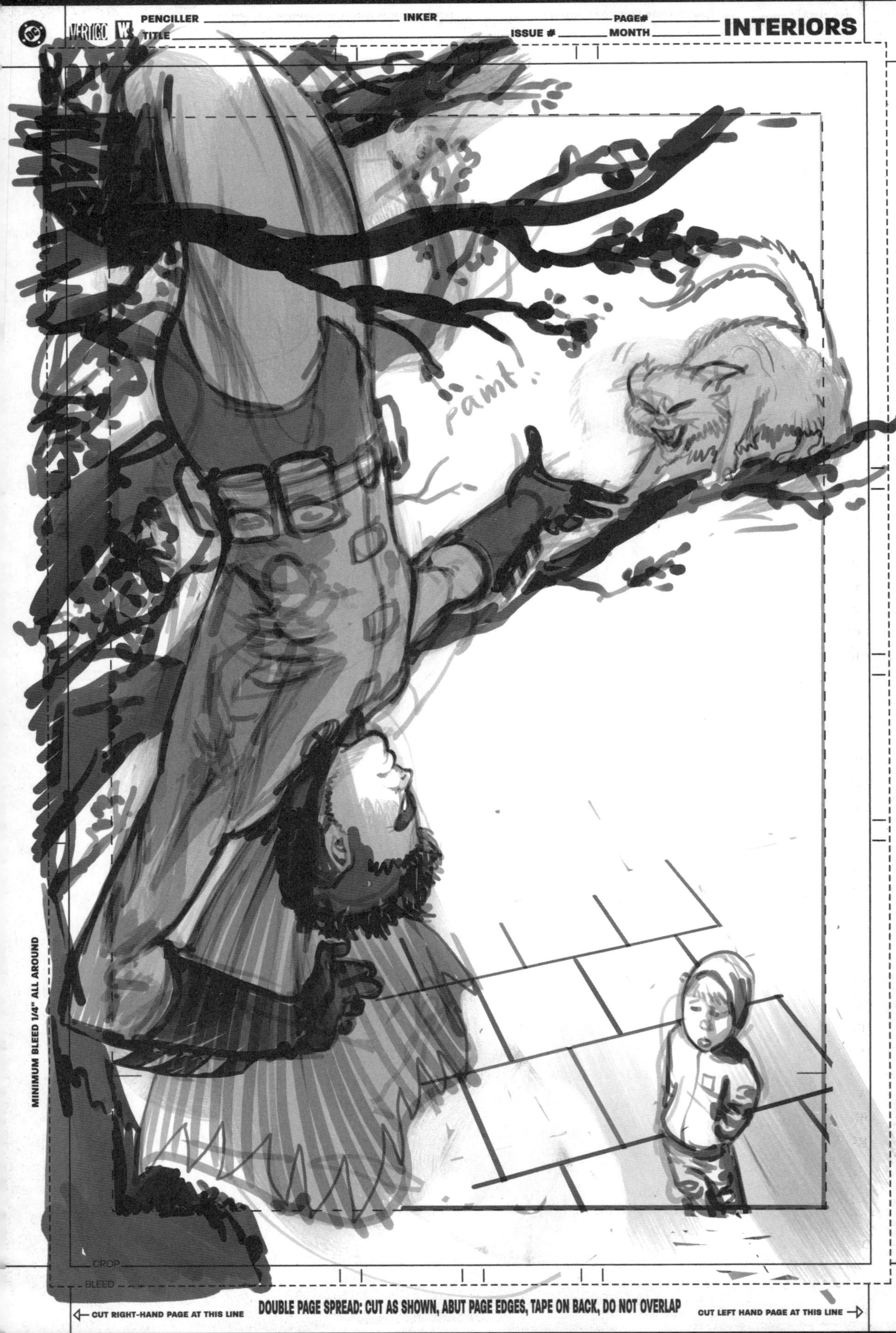
VERTIGO
PENCILLER
INKER
PAGE#
INTERIORS
TITLE
ISSUE #
MONTH
paint!
MINIMUM BLEED 1/4" ALL AROUND
CROP
BLEED
CUT RIGHT-HAND PAGE AT THIS LINE
DOUBLE PAGE SPREAD: CUT AS SHOWN, ABUT PAGE EDGES, TAPE ON BACK, DO NOT OVERLAP
CUT LEFT HAND PAGE AT THIS LINE
©TM DC COMICS©2002 DC COMICS. ALL RIGHTS RESERVED. Under no circumstances may this be reproduced without the permission of the copyright owner

working on the projects at the same time, or was it the similarity in techno-driven storylines?

FRAZER: It was just coincidence. By this time I was totally into doing the art digitally, but only brave enough to try it out in small doses such as with *24Seven*. I enjoyed that, though, and I realized I actually did like drawing robots, but only in my own way.

MM: There are moments in the yellow-toned panels that look as if they were created by traditional tools.

FRAZER: Naw, all digital. 100% pixels.

MM: You returned to work with Mike Carey on the *Ultimate Fantastic Four Annual* #2. Did this come about because of "The Gift" storyline in *Hellblazer*?

FRAZER: It may well have done. I knew Mike from back in the *2000 AD* days, so he was often keen to get me to do something.

MM: The *Fantastic Four* issue is a fascinating one in the juxtaposition between styles and stories. Did you have access to the complete script and Stuart Immonen's pencils, or did you work in solitude on only the Mole Man sequences?

FRAZER: No, I had both. I kind of needed the pencils so I could see what was happening.

MM: Is that method of working "in between" with another artist strange for you, or is the collaboration a challenge?

FRAZER: It was fun, but also a hassle, as we would ideally work together instead of just getting each other's pages and making what we would of it all. I had no contact with Stuart before, during, or since.

MM: The story is both tragic, yet humorous in its tone. Did you return to brush work since it was for Marvel, knowing that the brushes would better suit the mood of the book?

FRAZER: It was more a case of me never wanting to use pens again and being too scared to suggest full digital art at the time. I played it safe.

MM: So baby steps?

FRAZER: Fear.

MM: 2007—which if I'm not mistaken was your busiest year—sees you working on a two-issue stint on *Robin*, as Klarion was brought into Gotham. This was your first work for DC since the original *Klarion* series. What were your thoughts about returning to the character?

FRAZER: I was delighted they thought of me. It was nice to get more DC work, as I liked the guys I worked for—Pete Tomasi and Mike Siglain—and Adam [Beechen]'s script was light and fun.

MM: *Robin* was also one of your final attempts at a hybrid workflow that combined digital and traditional brush inking, correct? While you've admitted the difficulty in blending the two, what kept you coming back to brush inking? The fear?

PENCILLER
INKER
TITLE
ISSUE #
PAGE#
MONTH
INTERIORS
LIVE AREA
CROP
BLEED
MINIMUM BLEED 1/4" ALL AROUND
DOUBLE PAGE SPREAD: CUT AS SHOWN, ABUT PAGE EDGES, TAPE ON BACK, DO NOT OVERLAP

Previous Page and Above: Digital pencils for *Robin* #158, pages 2 and 9. Frazer's two-issue stint on *Robin* would mark his last time using the traditional brush and ink to finish his line art. Going forward, he would work completely digitally.

Robin ™ and © DC Comics.

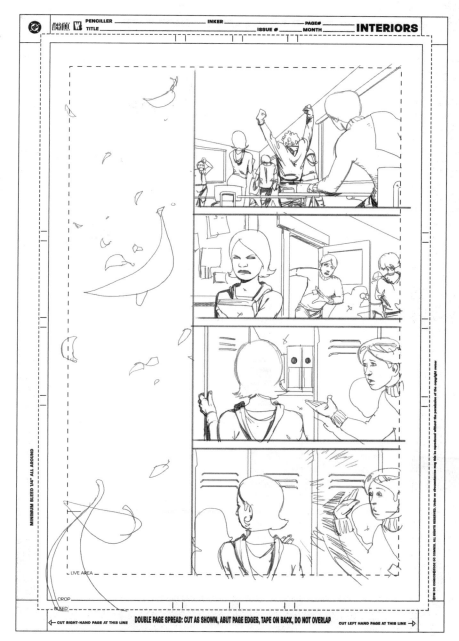

Below: In this preliminary for page 18 of *Silent War* #1, Frazer has already placed some of the tones as well as the red of Medusa's hair.
Next Page: A rejected sketch for a two-page spread intended for *Silent War* #6.

Inhumans and all related characters ™ and © Marvel Characters, Inc.

FRAZER: No, it was Klarion. He had to be rendered in the same style, so I was duty bound.

MM: Was that mandated?

FRAZER: Only by me.

MM: What was it about *Robin* that was the last straw for the brushes?

FRAZER: I was doing the pages in Canada, and without my usual set-up it was just so hard to get the right feel. Plus, I was tiring of the labor that went into it mixed with the issues of corrections if I cocked up, so I was itching to go all digital and free myself up.

MM: How did your mobile set-up differ from what you were used to back home?

FRAZER: I had a laptop, a Cintiq, and a small scanner, whereas back home I had all that plus a proper fast Mac, a big scanner, and a drawing board.

MM: So it was more about reworking than frustration over what you saw on the final pages?

FRAZER: Yeah, it was the method.

"I think the great thing about Frazer is that he doesn't always appeal to audiences. Crowd pleasers play safe. Frazer takes a lot of chances with his art. To make a comparison between comics and film, the scriptwriter is the director, while the artist is the actor. You just know that Frazer immerses himself in the art. I can imagine him cackling gleefully to himself as he works on a page like the infamous 'Medusa kneels before Maximus' scene, and he was probably wailing like a madman all the way through the Black Bolt primal scream scene. There are artists who are the Arnold Schwarzeneggers of comics. Their art is big and bold and impressive-looking, but essentially wooden and empty. Frazer is the Daniel Day-Lewis of comics. His characters are twisted and repressed and then, when they let it go, they turn the drama up to eleven. It's confrontational and demands a reaction from the audience. We definitely grew into each other's styles. We were probably a little wary of one another at the start. It's like a first date. You start out tentatively, finding out if you actually have anything in common, maybe not sure if this could actually work, and then by the third date you're shagging like lunatics. I'm not sure if Frazer would phrase it quite like that... actually, he probably would."
— **David Hine**

FRAZER: Yup, that's how I would phrase it. David and I are on similar wavelengths. He's a gem.

MM: How do you feel about being the Daniel Day-Lewis of comic art?

FRAZER: I like this, although I aspire to be the Orson Welles of comic art, before he had his falling out with Hollywood.

MM: Hine mentioned that you were not the original artist for *Silent War*, but that you stepped in and saved the project. Tell me about how the series came to your attention and what attracted you to it?

FRAZER: Well, I got an email from David at the same time as the editor, Steve Wacker, emailed me, both begging me to step in at the last minute and take over. I said yes, because it was just six issues, plus I figured I could do the art digitally, and David's pitch sounded, well, mature for want of a better word. It had gravity and depth. Sadly, I was doing *Gutsville* at the time, and this meant that I would have to do both, but this didn't happen and *Gutsville* suffered because of it. I just couldn't do two books a month, especially seeing as one of them involved doing lettering and layout as well.

MM: Does the six-issue format work better for you as an artist than, say, a three-issue mini in terms of connection with the story, the characters, and fleshing out the feel of the book?

FRAZER: It does, yes. Three issues is the first date and kiss, six issues includes the weekend of sex, the drugs, the fights, the fallout, and the make-up with another weekend of sex and drugs, etc.

MM: Since *Silent War* is tied into ongoing Marvel continuity, how much research did you have to conduct to familiarize

yourself with the major players? How much license and freedom did you have in designing the characters?

FRAZER: I could rework a few smaller players and I got to invent a bunch of Inhumans as supporting cast, but the main characters had to have a set look to tie in with the other stuff. The only research I did, though, was to read some of the other recent comics, as I had a pretty good knowledge of the designs from when I used to read Marvel comics as a kid.

MM: What was the experience like of creating the book completely digitally?

FRAZER: At first it was amazing, but then deadlines caught up and I had to invent new ways to make the time up, and that did strain things a bit. It was all a lot more painterly than now, and my method was very raw.

MM: Since it was the showcase for your new process, I would argue that *Silent War* #1 is really your first main-stream attempt at creating the Frazer Irving color palette, the coloring style that is immediately recognizable as your own. More than any other project, this issue seems to be a

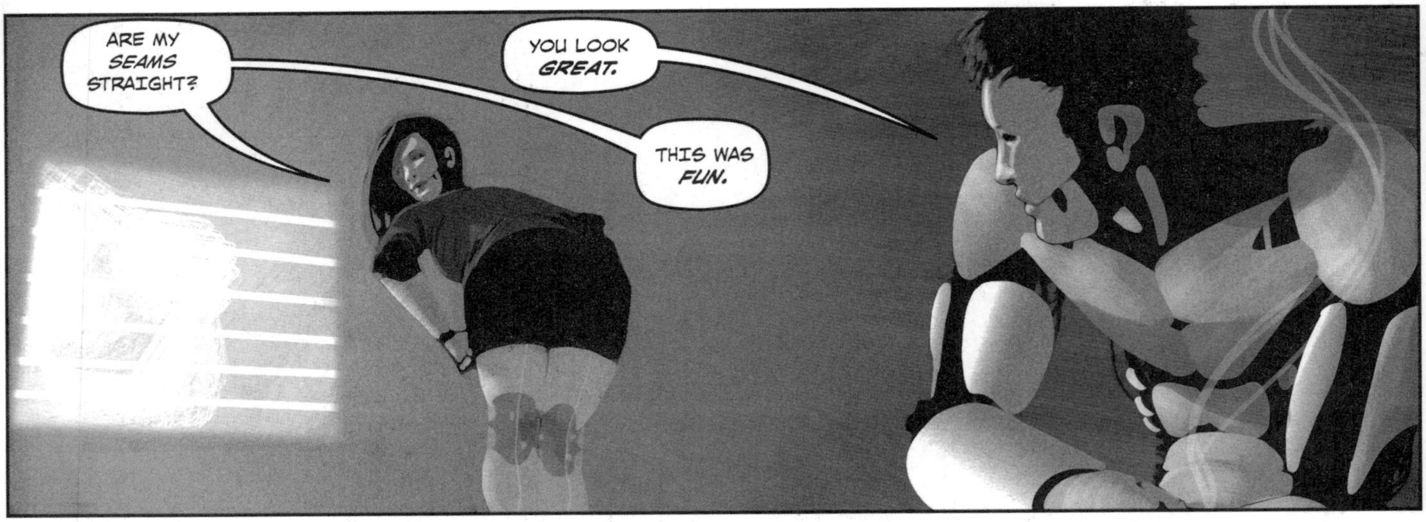
ARE MY SEAMS STRAIGHT?
YOU LOOK GREAT.
THIS WAS FUN.

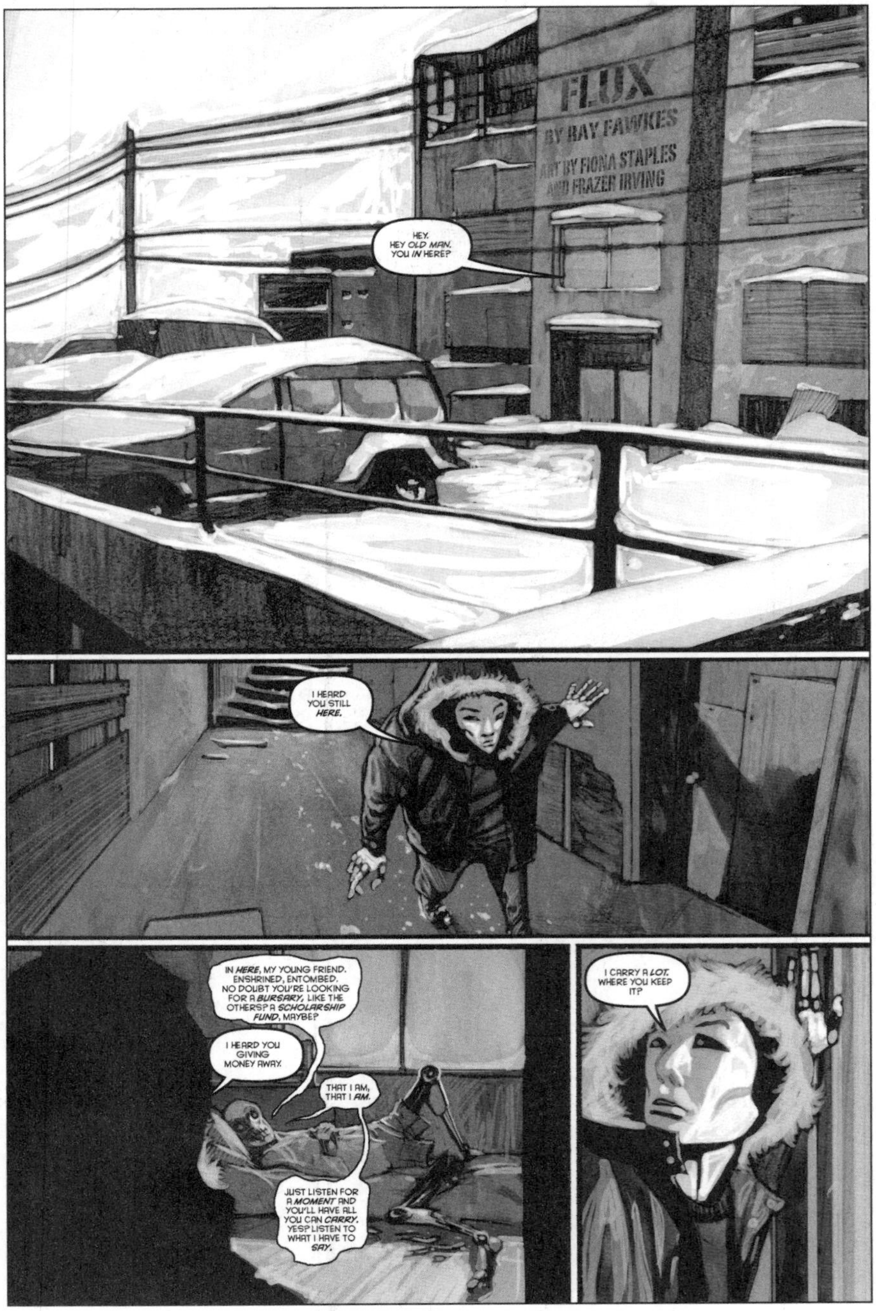
FLUX
BY RAY FAWKES
ART BY FIONA STAPLES
AND FRAZER IRVING
HEY. HEY OLD MAN. YOU IN HERE?
I HEARD YOU STILL HERE.
IN HERE, MY YOUNG FRIEND. ENSHRINED, ENTOMBED. NO DOUBT YOU'RE LOOKING FOR A BURSARY, LIKE THE OTHERS? A SCHOLARSHIP FUND, MAYBE?
I HEARD YOU GIVING MONEY AWAY.
THAT I AM, THAT I AM.
JUST LISTEN FOR A MOMENT AND YOU'LL HAVE ALL YOU CAN CARRY. YES? LISTEN TO WHAT I HAVE TO SAY.
I CARRY A LOT. WHERE YOU KEEP IT?

concerted effort at defining the breaks between warm and cool tones with colors shaping the emotions of the panels. Would that be an accurate assessment of your approach to the book, or something perhaps more indicative of the digital process?

FRAZER: If it was, I wasn't aware of it. I was doing what I had tried to do with the other books, but maybe the textures I was using made it more apparent? I didn't really get into color the way I am now until after I finished *Silent War*.

MM: It just seems to really showcase where you've been as a colorist and what makes you stand out in regards to your color choices at that stage.

FRAZER: The choices were all related to the environments as opposed to the mood, which is where I am now. I was deliberately color-coding the different scenes, but there's a lot of wishy-washy colors that mess it up in many places that I would never allow nowadays.

MM: Would the same be true in regards to how you approached the characters, because your panels with Black Bolt, Medusa, and Maximus are probably the strongest and most intense of any in the entire series, and you seem to be really investing yourself in them?

FRAZER: Well, the story was all about them. The other stuff was backdrop, and their conflict was what had the most resonance with me. When I drew the scenes with Bolt and Medusa, the aim was to capture the narrow range of emotions they were experiencing, both consumed by some marital discord or ideological conflict, and that was what made it easy. Those scenes just poured out of me. It helped that David really knew his stuff there and was adept at conveying it. When Maximus is on the scene, the drama steps up, and I have to relate to all three of them. The heartbreaking scene of Bolt witnessing Medusa kiss his mad brother was tapping into all that emotional crap I had felt as a younger man, and it was simple to act that stuff out on the page. Almost cathartic even.

MM: Oh, wow, so it was a very personal book for you. Would you say that the coloring you utilized in those scenes was more driven by their environment or, in fact, mood?

FRAZER: In those, it was mood-based, because they had to be distinct from the others, but even then it was pretty simple choices.

MM: You were also working on several other projects while completing *Silent War*, correct? Was there a lot of overlap between *Robin*, *Silent War*, the later "Simping Detective" stories in *Judge Dredd Megazine*, and "Button Man"? In addition to these, you were also doing another 24-Hour Comic Day and *24Seven* project for Image, yes?

FRAZER: Sort of. Some overlapped, others just printed around the same time. I finished *Robin* before *Silent War*, so it was mainly the *2000 AD* stuff and *Gutsville* that were happening around the same time. I think "Button Man" started just after *Silent War*, as I would have been mad to do three jobs at the same time, but there may have been a little overlap.

MM: Sounds like a crazy year.

FRAZER: It was. I was in Canada, and I took anything that was thrown at me. Freelancer's Disease.

MM: You did a follow-up strip to "Static" in *24Seven*, vol. 2 with Ray Fawkes' "Flux." This time, however, you shared the art duties with Fiona Staples. How did you meet Ray? You introduced Fiona to digital art, but how did this collaboration come about?

FRAZER: I met Ray at SDCC a few years before then, thanks to knowing Cameron Stewart. We kind of shared the same view on many things and became Internet buddies. Also, because he was Canadian, we had a connection there, and when it came time for him to pitch the story to Image, he asked me to sign up. Fiona and I had this thing going where we would send each other pencil drawings and get the other one to paint over it, like jamming, and when "Flux" happened it seemed like a fun idea to do the same gimmick for that. Plus, painting over Fiona's work is a lot easier than drawing it all myself.

MM: Did you meet her at SDCC as well?

FRAZER: I knew Fiona from just before SDCC 2006, thanks to the Internet, and we hooked up at that convention.

MM: Even though you've experienced others coloring your work, you were removed from that process. Was it at all difficult to share art duties with someone else in this regard?

Previous Page Top: A panel from *24Seven* vol. I's "Static," written by Matt Fraction. *24Seven* was conceived as an anthology book of sci-fi noir stories with robots serving as the characters. **Previous Page Bottom:** The first page of "Flux," written by Ray Fawkes and colored by Fiona Staples, which appeared in *24Seven* vol. 2. **Below:** A panel from page 2 of "Button Man IV: The Hitman's Daughter," *2000 AD* #1551. For this story, Frazer applied gray tones to the line art before handing off the pages to colorist Fiona Staples. This was in part to give her an idea of what he was looking for, but it also provided tone to the color as with a watercolor approach.

Button Man ™ and © John Wagner and Arthur Ranson. Static © Matt Fraction and Frazer Irving. Flux © Ray Fawkes, Frazer Irving, and Fiona Staples.

Above: In this sequence of panels from "Button Man IV: The Hitman's Daughter," Frazer used the story's colorist, Fiona Staples (pictured here), as photo reference for the lead character, Adele Cotter.

Next Page: Page 5 of the third "Button Man" installment, which ran in *2000 AD* #1553.

Button Man ™ and © John Wagner and Arthur Ranson.

FRAZER: No, we had a thing going with the jamming, and it was always fun to "improve" each other's work.

MM: So there was no protective nature, nothing like, "This is my art"? Was that level of comfort or acceptance strange to develop?

FRAZER: Not at all. We both operated on a similar wavelength with the art, and we both trusted each other not to damage anything, but more to improve it. At least, that's what I saw anyway. It was Lennon and McCartney.

MM: You mentioned before that you created a specific grayscale method of art. Was that something you designed back in "From Grace" and "The Simping Detective" that you tweaked for "Button Man," or was it something you designed specifically for this project, since Fiona was coloring your work?

FRAZER: It was specifically for "Button Man" so Fiona could color it. I had the idea for ages, but never found a good method to colorize the gray tones. It was Fiona's experimentation that unlocked that whole method for me and put me on the path I'm on now. I wanted to control the values and textures as much as possible, so that meant doing all the shades

of gray and just letting her choose the hues, with a few modifications in places. She used color layer combinations that I hadn't considered, however, and it was these revelations that set my mind ticking.

MM: Although you had worked with her previously, these were on pieces emailed back and forth. Did you have any concerns in handing over the coloring reins following your past experiences with separate colorists, since this was a big project for *2000 AD*?

FRAZER: No, it was all my idea, and I trusted her totally to make a good job of it, although I always checked the final files before sending them off. She was sort of subcontracted by me, so I also handled the payment and stuff. I was her boss, and I bet if she reads this she will gnash her teeth and mutter something about what a lousy boss I actually was.

MM: So in some ways, this was like a digital internship for her to learn the ropes of comic illustration, etc. That's a pretty cool arrangement.

FRAZER: It was part of my plan to get her more comics work and to be more a part of the comic scene, as she was just getting into it. Then WildStorm hired her, and I lost my employee. [*laughs*]

MM: Since you mentioned having control, one of the aspects of "Button Man" that stands out to me is that Fiona's color palette is both distinctively your own and yet subtly different. As a result, if I hadn't known you didn't do the coloring beforehand, I don't think I would have thought it was done by somebody else, but rather was a new experiment you took. Can you explain how the colors were chosen?

FRAZER: I would make suggestions, but they were quite broad. The pink section at the start may well have been one of my requests, but overall Fiona used her own judgments to pick the hues. I think a lot of the connection may be with the way the textures I used are the same today, and that forms a part of the color effect, because I know Fiona and I have very different coloring now. She totally has a better sense of natural color than me, that's for sure.

MM: Probably the most evocative image throughout the book is Adele, particularly in how she is colored. The scene where she is dressing and applying lipstick is very powerful, because it's a blend of your command of the female form with a decisive and recognizable shift in the warmth associated with the scene. How much of that power in the scene was your guidance versus Fiona's color decisions, and was she coloring the pages completely digitally or blending traditionally with paints?

FRAZER: It was all Photoshop. I think I suggested the basic colors, and she did them in her own way. Fiona is also the model for Adele, especially at the start when I could use her for photo references and stuff. Her acting helped define the character. I changed the hair and stuff, altered her features a little.

MM: Since your prior work with Wagner had been within the horror genre with "Judge Death," how did the project itself come to be? It seems atypical of your other 2000 *AD* work. Did you have to go back and read the older series, or were you familiar with "Button Man"?

FRAZER: I knew the first book quite well, and I think Wagner actually asked for me to do it after Arthur Ranson had declined. I don't know why he thought I would suit it, but I was more than happy to give it my shot. It was a welcome change to the usual routine.

MM: Looking at Wagner's script, the one feature that immediately stands out is just how sparse his panel descriptions are, leaving quite a bit of room for the artist to design

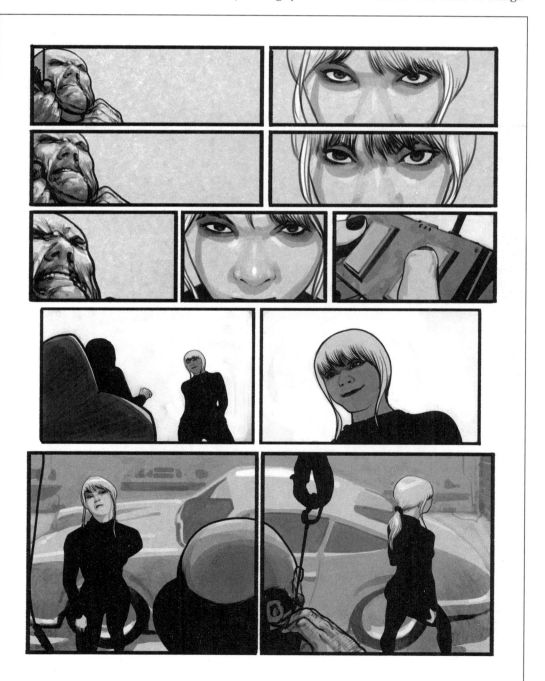

Right: Unused rough sketch for the cover of the creator-owned mini-series *Gutsville* #1.
Below: The alternate cover of *Gutsville* #1, which appeared on the two (!) reprintings of the first issue.
Next Page: Gray tones for *Gutsville* #1, page 8, in which Emelia's intentions are somewhat misinterpreted.

the look and atmosphere of the book. First, has this always been the case in your experience with Wagner? Second, since "Button Man" was originally serialized in *2000 AD* in six-page installments, how much of the script were you given at a time, and how did this in turn affect your ability to craft the story progression?

FRAZER: Yeah, John always writes like that, in my experience. I like it. I had 16 episodes upfront, so plenty of time to get the feel of the piece. I tried to plan it out in advance, but eventually I slipped back and ended up doing it one episode at a time. I blame the extra jobs I was doing at the time.

MM: Did that in turn affect the pages you turned over to Fiona for coloring?

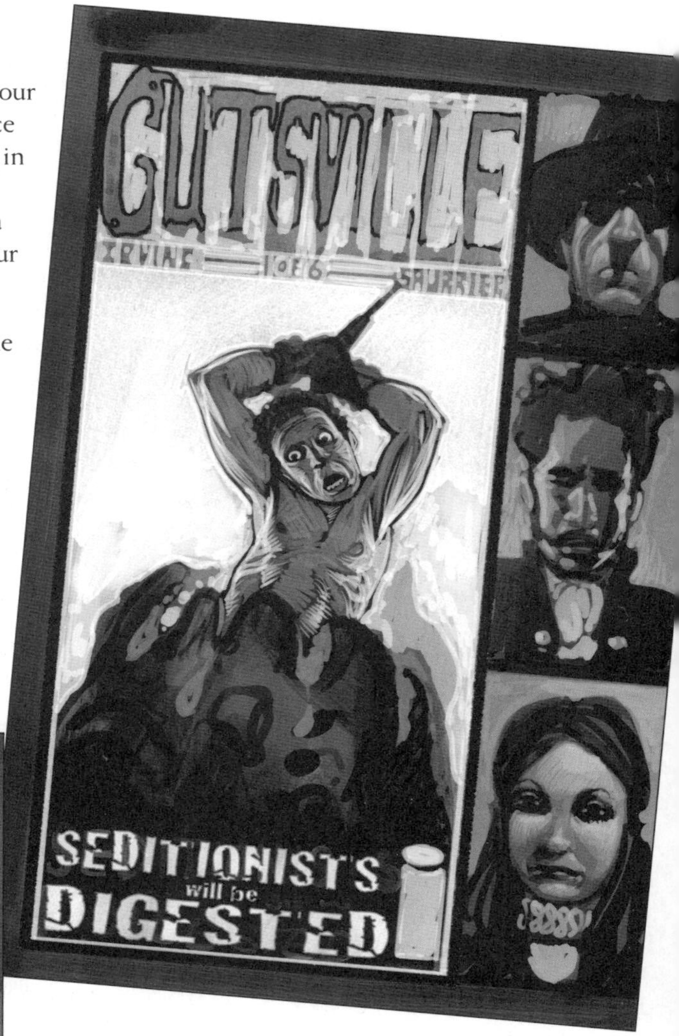
GUTSVILLE
IRVINE
1 of 6
SPURRIER
SEDITIONIST'S
will be
DIGESTED

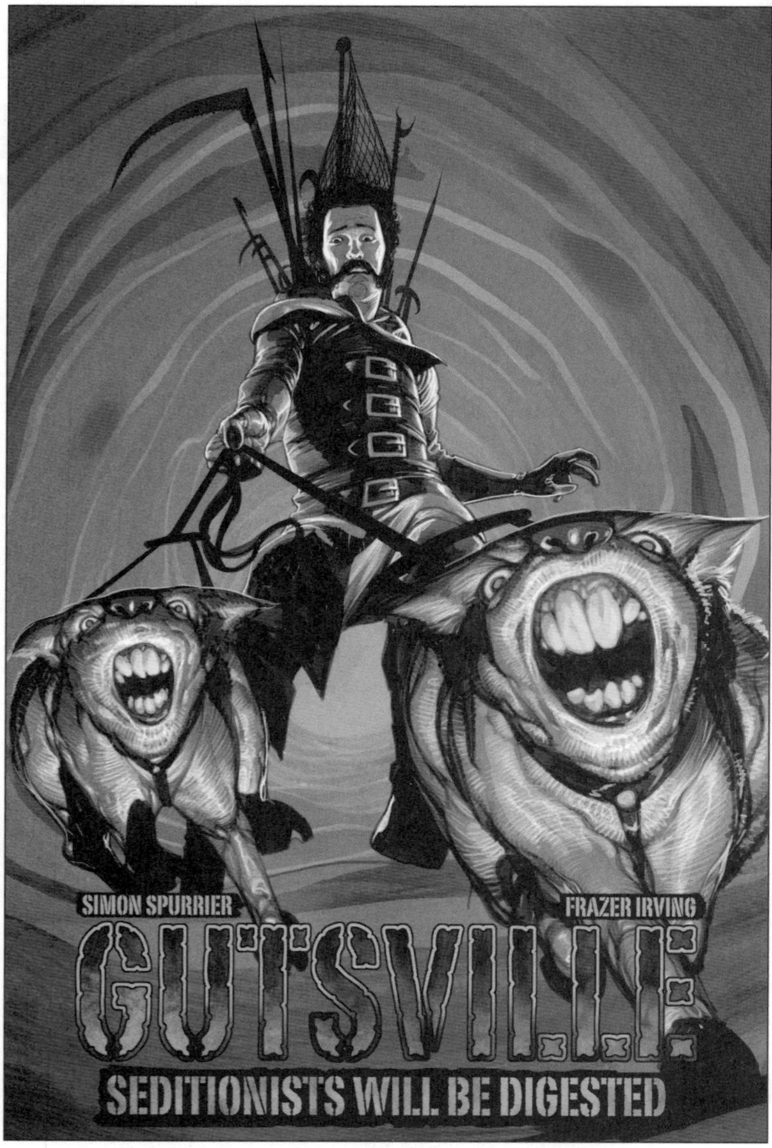
SIMON SPURRIER
FRAZER IRVING
GUTSVILLE
SEDITIONISTS WILL BE DIGESTED

FRAZER: Yeah, towards the end I was falling behind and she got real mad at me.

MM: Did you have to step in and do any coloring as a result?

FRAZER: I colored a couple of episodes myself, because I had left it so late, cramming through the night to hit the deadline. I would sometimes email her at four a.m. and expect pages by midday, even calling her to wake her up. I am a cruel boss, but a lovable person.

MM: While you're working on "Button Man," you've also embarked on *Gutsville* with Si Spurrier. How did this level of creative output and working on so many projects affect you both personally and professionally?

FRAZER: I think all things suffered. None of the projects really remained consistent, and there was a lot of strain on me to produce stuff whilst I also wanted to enjoy the success and have fun. I think I burnt out as a result of it, but it was also a serious workout that was essential to move up a level.

MM: Did you envision it at the time as an essential move to transition up a level?

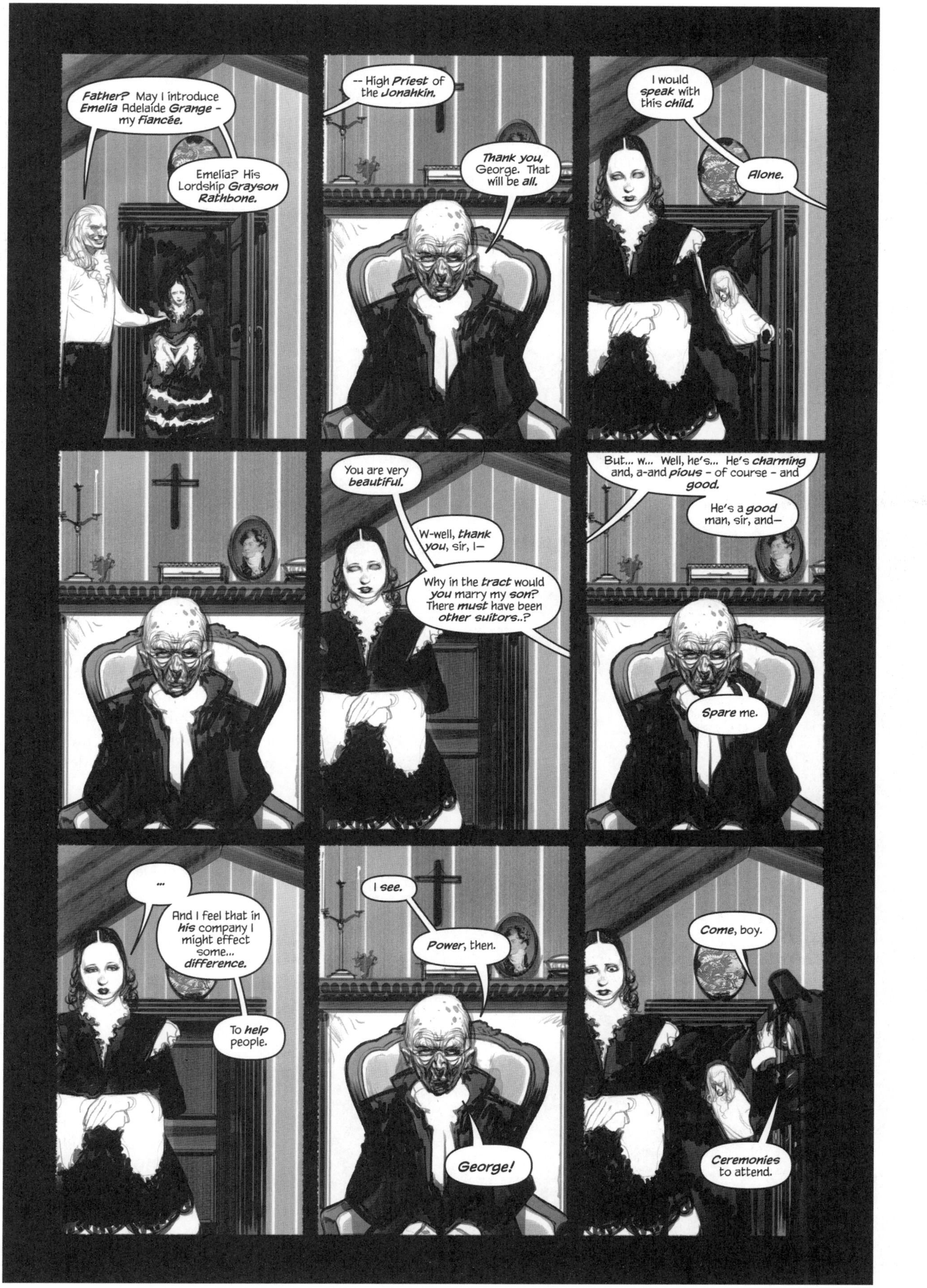
Father? May I introduce Emelia Adelaide Grange - my fiancée.
Emelia? His Lordship Grayson Rathbone.
-- High Priest of the Jonahkin.
Thank you, George. That will be all.
I would speak with this child.
Alone.
You are very beautiful.
W-well, thank you, sir, I—
Why in the tract would you marry my son? There must have been other suitors..?
But... w... Well, he's... He's charming and, a-and pious - of course - and good.
He's a good man, sir, and—
Spare me.
...
And I feel that in his company I might effect some... difference.
To help people.
I see.
Power, then.
George!
Come, boy.
Ceremonies to attend.

FRAZER: No, I was just so engrossed in churning out product.

MM: How much later then did the realization occur that the transition had occurred and paid off for you?

FRAZER: It was towards the end of 2008, when I made some *Gutsville* pages that looked way better than I thought they should have, and I realized that I was now drawing with more engagement even when not totally focused on the work. I drew a lot of stuff in a haze back then, and the final product was often far better than if I had tried that the year before. Some stuff still has charm from those days, but just before I started on *Azrael* I could see that the drawing had improved on a fundamental level.

MM: What convinced you to take on this creator-owned endeavor with *Gutsville*?

FRAZER: Well, Si and I had toyed with the idea of creator-owned stuff for a while, because we had heard the tales of great riches, and so we pitched it to Eric Stephenson at Image. During a visit to London, Eric told me that anything I pitched would be fine. I think it was partly due to the *Klarion* wave that I was still riding, but also because he trusted us. Sadly, I didn't heed his advice at the start, which was to get three issues completed before soliciting the first. I was overconfident that I could manage all this work. *Gutsville* was and is the most trying script I've ever worked on, so that made it even more difficult.

Ah - flesh reclaimed! A moving spectacle...
'S a wrigglin' one, sure enough. Eels, ain't they?
Aha. Very good. Albert Oliphant, yes? George Rathbone.
Emelia has told me so very much about you...
I do hope we shall be friends, Mr Oliphant.
In these troubled times such things are a... scarce commodity...
Much like, shall we say, meat. Much like safety from vermin.
Commodities a Ratcatcher may provide - selflessly, valiantly, uniquely, I say - for his city.
...Emelia tells me you're quite the artist, Mr Oliphant...
Eh? What's that got t—
Gutsville needs meat. Gutsville needs a Ratcatcher.
It does not need frivolity. It does not need art.
No more than any woman, shall we say, needs the company of chaps.
Beyond her own husband, of course.
Good day, Mr Oliphant.
Hurry home now.

MM: Because it's creator-owned and you're thus invested more in the process, or because of the nature of the script itself in terms of Spurrier?

FRAZER: It's the toughest script I've ever seen, in that the details are all laid out and the structure is so solidly built that in order to work it I need to bend myself to fit it totally, and that's not easy. It's extremely hard for me to let go and be slave to someone else's storytelling to that degree. I want it to get the attention it deserves, and that means that I need to do a lot of sketching layouts and staring into space to visualize how best to make certain panels work. Simon has put so much thought into it, that any attempt by me to change stuff structurally would destroy the rhythm, so I must just do that extra amount of work to get the art cooking.

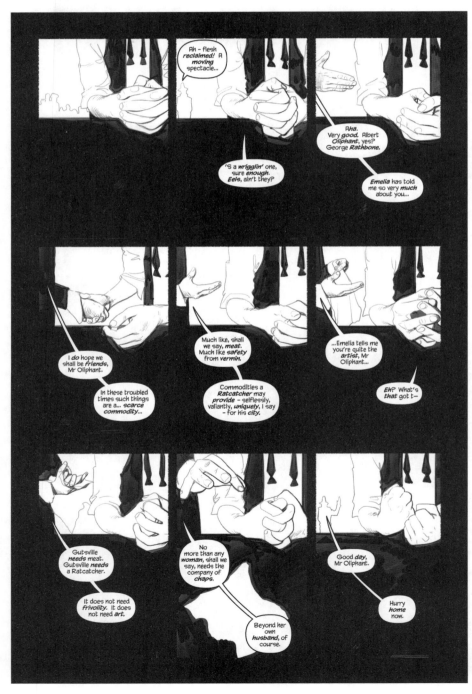

"Whenever I collaborate with Frazer, there tends to be an emphasis—for both of us, I think—on experimenting, pushing the envelope, doing something interesting. I like to think we both regard Gutsville *as something unique: an opportunity to play outside the box. There was a sequence in episode 1 in which a pair of characters are standing side-by-side talking. There are hidden agendas, veiled threats, weird things left unspoken. In the script I had one of them using a handkerchief—to clean himself after shaking hands—on the grounds that 'talking heads' pages should always be enlivened by a prop. Frazer took it one step further: fixing the camera entirely on the speaker's hands and nothing else. It takes a decent artist to express a range of subtle emotions using faces. It takes a major skill to do the same thing using only the positioning of characters' hands."*
— Simon Spurrier

FRAZER: That page was interesting.

MM: Why did you decide to focus on the hands for that sequence? Because it is truly powerful.

FRAZER: The script called for a level of detail that just wouldn't have worked with the art style I was using, and I was furious. I got so mad I decided to actually not follow the script and do something that I thought would be better. I was convinced he'd throw a fit and demand I do it the way he wrote it, but luckily that didn't happen. I chose the mitts because of the handkerchief. It was the most obvious prop in there, and the bit where he drops it over the side had so much power and revealed so much character that I felt the other stuff was just a distraction.

MM: You mentioned earlier that your process evolved with specific series. How did *Gutsville* alter your work flow and digital tools?

FRAZER: I refined the grayscale method from "Button Man" during issue #3 as well as developing new ways to alter the colors using different layers. Most of that was just refining stuff, as I had a brand new way of working and I needed to iron out the kinks.

MM: Throughout *Gutsville* #1, audiences see some of your trademark styles: the colder blues, the dread magenta, but there is also an inking style that harkens back to your brush days, as well as color tones that betray greater browns, blacks, grays, whites than before. For you, what explains this palette shift? Just something inherent in the script?

FRAZER: I wanted it to have a painterly feel from the start, one that would change as the story develops until the end, which will have a much clearer feel to it, and that was pretty much the reasoning behind it. I see Albert as the focus of the script, and so his state of mind sort of dominates the visual feel of the book, hence the very cluttered and messy opening issue.

MM: In issue #2, readers start to see more of the non-narration and non-dialogue panels. For you, how is creating a text-free image versus one guided by dialogue or narration in the script? Is it liberating, frustrating, more difficult, or easier? Is it part of the clearing up process?

FRAZER: It's easy if the writer knows what they're doing. Wagner was a master at it, and Si is pretty good, too. The cleaning up

process is all in the lines, not in the actual action, as Si never dictated that part of the art. In fact, he won't have heard me mention it until he reads this. [*laughs*]

MM: Can you tell me how the period of burn-out you went through in 2008 affected your work and your life? Had you ever experienced a dread of art before like this? Did your music provide any solace or outlet for you during this time?

FRAZER: Well, I was concerned that my health was suffering due to my lifestyle, and my social life had also become stale, so those took precedence over the art as I had begun to see the art as a weight crushing the life out

Previous Page: Besides the eyes and mouth, the hands are the most expressive part of the human body, and Frazer takes full advantage of that in this page from *Gutsville* #1.
Above: Gray tones for *Gutsville* #3, page 12.

Gutsville ™ and © Simon Spurrier and Frazer Irving.

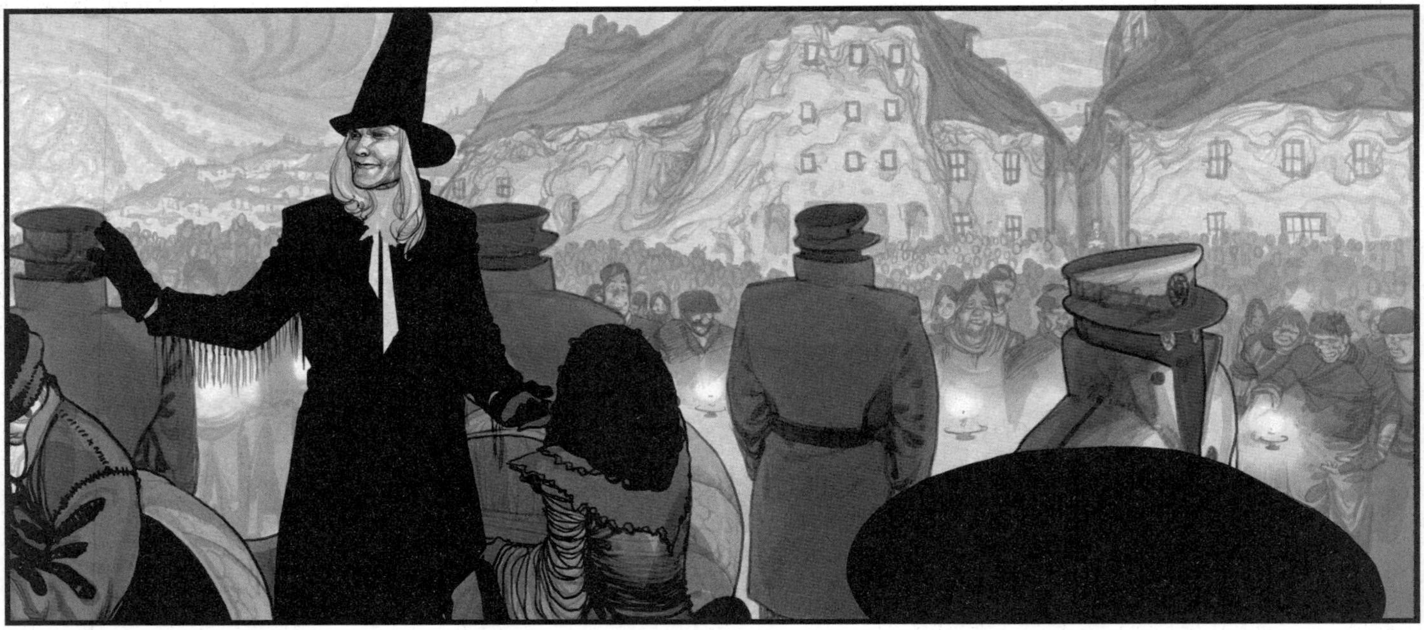

Above: Gray tones for a panel from the as yet unpublished *Gutsville* #4. **Next Page:** With the *X-Men: Divided We Stand* one-shot, Frazer further refined his technique of starting with gray tones before adding color. He also experimented with layout design, as can be seen in this page.

of me. Because it's so sedentary and isolated, drawing all day when one is going through a bit of a crisis is very unappealing in that one is left to one's thoughts for long periods, and this is not only bad for the state of mind but it also feeds into and infects the art being produced. I figured I needed to get my head together before doing any serious work, and that's why *Gutsville* just got put on the back-burner.

I hadn't had anything quite this intense before, not even during my Croatian odyssey, but back in Zagreb I had a lot of friends and a lively social group to distract me from that stuff and take the heat off the art. I did throw myself into the band at the time. That was my main social outlet, and playing music was very cathartic. The immediacy of playing music, the interaction with others during the jams, this was all very different to the solitary and slow-moving act of drawing comics, and that helped a lot. Around Autumn 2008 I got really into composing music, and it was then that I noticed that I was paying far more attention to my hobby than my career.

MM: If I'm not mistaken, is this in part why readers only saw *Gutsville* #3, your coloring of *Proof* #7, and *X-Men: Divided We Stand* #2 in 2008?

FRAZER: Yeah. *Gutsville* #3 was already done. I had started issue #4 at the beginning of 2008, but the *X-Men* story had interrupted that, and by the time that was done it all fell to bits. The coloring in *Proof* had been done a while before, I think, possibly during my last Canada visit.

MM: With the tables slightly turned in *Proof* #7, what was it like coloring someone else's pencils versus not only your own, but your previous experiences in having a separate colorist yourself?

FRAZER: It was awkward. [*laughs*] I wasn't sure what to do with it, because the art didn't really have all the right sorts of holding lines. A lot of it was roughed in and quite vague, so I couldn't read what was going on in places, so I was glad I only offered to do a couple of pages. Riley [Rossmo] has improved immensely since then.

MM: The eight-page strip you did in *X-Men: Divided We Stand* was interesting and very angry in its tone and feel. Tell me about how the project came to you and about designing the pages, particularly breaking the panels, the introspective and isolated "head" of Havok.

FRAZER: The editor, Nick Lowe, emailed me asking if I wanted to contribute. I figured it was one of those "test" pieces where they were trying out new people to see if they fit in with any potential upcoming projects. Even though I had already done loads of work for them, each editor is their own person and has their own ways of testing new artists and writers. I didn't mind that, as it was low commitment and a chance to try some new ideas out. Once I got the script, though, I didn't like the pacing of it at all. I couldn't find any structure. It was like a series of panels, and that was it. I asked if I could try fiddling with the script to structure it a bit better, and Nick was fine with that. So I broke it down into seven major beats,

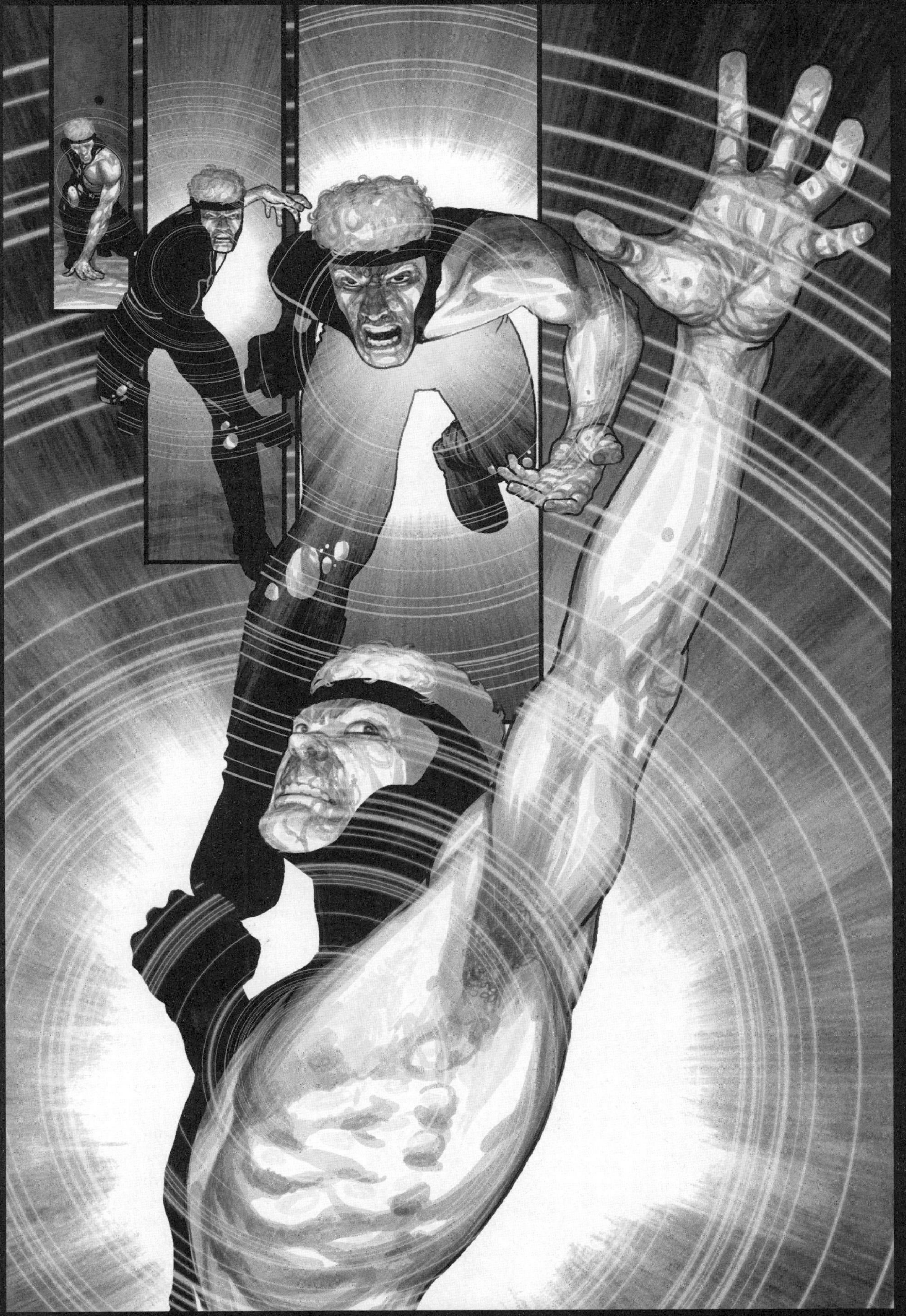

Right: Rough sketch for the cover of *The Darkness* vol. 3, #10.
Below: Cover sketch for *The Darkness* #76 (the series was renumbered with issue #75).
Next Page: Figure with gray tones added done for the cover of *The Darkness* #77.

The Darkness and all related characters ™ and © Top Cow Productions, Inc.

with no crossovers in terms of panel layouts, so that each page had its own message and contribution to the story. The simple color scheme was needed to create the tension and emotion, and I tried to vary the types of panel arrangements on each page as well. The head gimmick is one I no doubt lifted from old Marvel comics from the '70s, but I had used it a fair bit in *The Man Who Learnt to Fly*, so it was a sort of a Frazer Irving standard gimmick at this time. I was quite pleased with that job. It did what I wanted it to and refined the method I had used on "Button Man" further,

which led to me adopting it for *Gutsville* and ultimately everything else from then on.

MM: Can you tell me a little bit more about this new method and how it has affected your subsequent projects?

FRAZER: Basically it was using grays to model the forms in a more watercolor way, building up shades to have a greater range of tones and thus give the characters more form. I pulled back on that after the Batman gig, as it was becoming cluttered. It really suited the Havok story, but I felt it went a bit far into the muddy realms with more complex stories.

MM: Unless I'm mistaken, your first published work of 2009 was your cover work for *The Darkness* #10. Tell me about how you became involved with Top Cow and the project?

FRAZER: Rob Levin. I knew him from conventions and the Internet, and I had always teased him about being such an important editorial dude whilst being so young as well. He'd mentioned he liked my stuff and wanted to make something happen before, but it wasn't until this cropped up that we began our working relationship. Those covers were a godsend for me. They allowed me to really show off without putting in tons of effort, such as with interiors, and they looked good, too. I refined the method further with them and learned all manner of groovy tricks regarding color.

MM: What tricks, and have they shaped your current output?

FRAZER: Without going into too much detail, I started using more black lines in my work, as well as introducing new and different brushes into the mix for special effects. This has led onto me expanding on this ink line angle and introducing even more wacky brushes into my tin, which is kind of where I am at now, figuring what to do with them next.

MM: Were cover assignments for *The Darkness* something you took on because of the burnout in not wanting to commit to a full-interior comic?

FRAZER: Yeah, pretty much. That and no one was offering me stuff at that point. I did get some offers later from publishers I was unsure of—one of whom ceased trading shortly after and the other is in flux right now—but there was a period where no one came knocking on my door, which led me to begging for work at SDCC that year.

MM: At that point, having worked for several years in the industry, how did that lack of attention affect you considering your already burned-out feelings regarding art?

FRAZER: It was sort of what I expected. I never felt I was ever part of the American scene. Many of my mates had been snapped up for exclusive deals by the same people that had hired me, and others had been wined, dined, and wooed by editors who would have little to say to me, so to be left out in the cold wasn't such a shock. It was disappointing for sure, and when I did that run through SDCC asking for work pretty much everyone gave me that fobbing-off look saying they're all booked up, etc., which in quite a few cases I knew was bull.

I ended up talking to Mike Siglain, who I had worked with on *Klarion* and *Robin*, and he is such a good egg. He said there was nothing that he could think of but he would put the word out and let me know. Three or four months later I get the first email from Marts about *Azrael*, and then Mike Siglain followed that with an email congratulating me on getting the gig, so I quietly assumed he had done what he said he would and put my name out there, which Mike Marts then picked up and ran with. I've only ever asked for work once as a pro, and it took four months to get any feedback from that. It wasn't a pleasant experience, and I think it works better when editors are actively seeking the talent as opposed to the other way around, but I may just be spoiled. Hard to tell, really, but I appreciate how fortunate I've been the past eleven years.

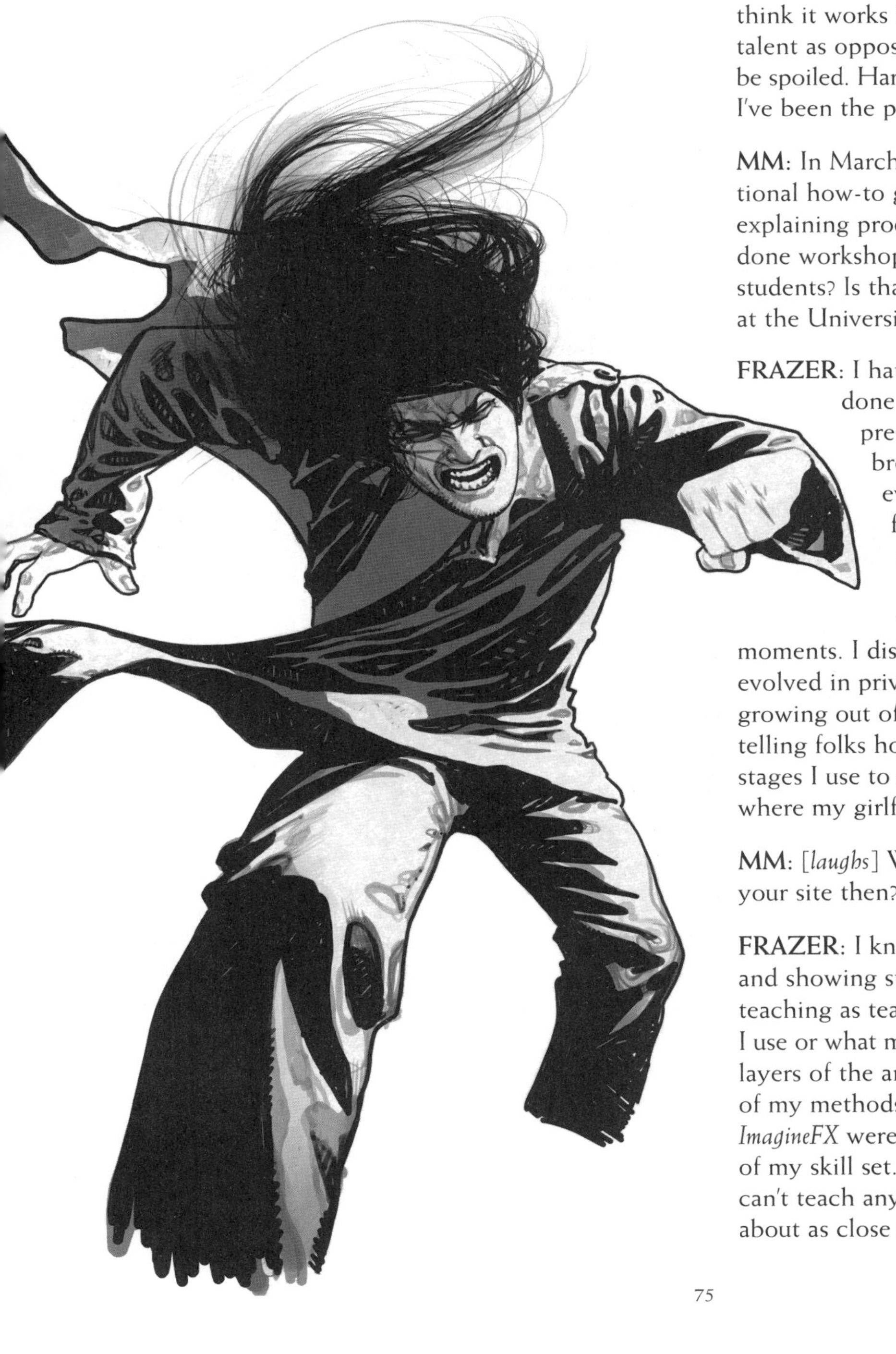

MM: In March or April 2009, you began posting instructional how-to guides for your cover work. Is teaching and explaining process something you enjoy? Have you ever done workshops or talks about your work and process for students? Is that what your February 2009 presentation was at the University of Leeds?

FRAZER: I hate teaching. The only workshops I have ever done have been at the request of others. I prefer presentations, where I talk about stuff in a broader manner, and then the discussion that evolves out of that. The Leeds thing was ideal for me, as they wanted me to give a talk about my life as an illustrator, and that is very easy to do, as it has many lessons contained within that extend beyond simplistic "how-to" moments. I dislike telling folks how I make my art, as it has evolved in private over the years with lots of hard work, growing out of ideas I invented myself, so it feels like telling folks how I arrange my layers and the sequence of stages I use to make cosmic effects is similar to telling them where my girlfriend's erogenous zones are.

MM: [*laughs*] What drove you to post "how-to" guides on your site then?

FRAZER: I know how fans like to peek behind the curtain, and showing stages of the art as I make it isn't so much teaching as teasing. After all, I don't tell anyone what layers I use or what my brushes are set at. I don't mind showing the layers of the art, it's the explaining and revealing of details of my methods that I dislike. That's why those tutorials in *ImagineFX* were so awkward for me, because it was so far out of my skill set. I can't teach anyone music, either. In fact, I can't teach anything. I try to teach by example, and that's about as close as I will ever get to being an educator.

Part 5: Batman and the Return of Frazer Irving

"A quirky eeriness. It sounds odd, but I wanted a bit of a disjointed, dysfunctional approach to the title and the character. I think people who read Frazer's super-hero work are drawn to it specifically because it is a different approach to the iconic characters they know. His storytelling is flawless, his camera moves around beautifully and he always creates a real sense of place and mood through his environmental drawing, and most specifically his washed-out color palette choices, that always bring, to me, a feeling like I'm watching a 1970s Scorcese film if all the players lived in the Victorian era."
— **Fabian Nicieza**

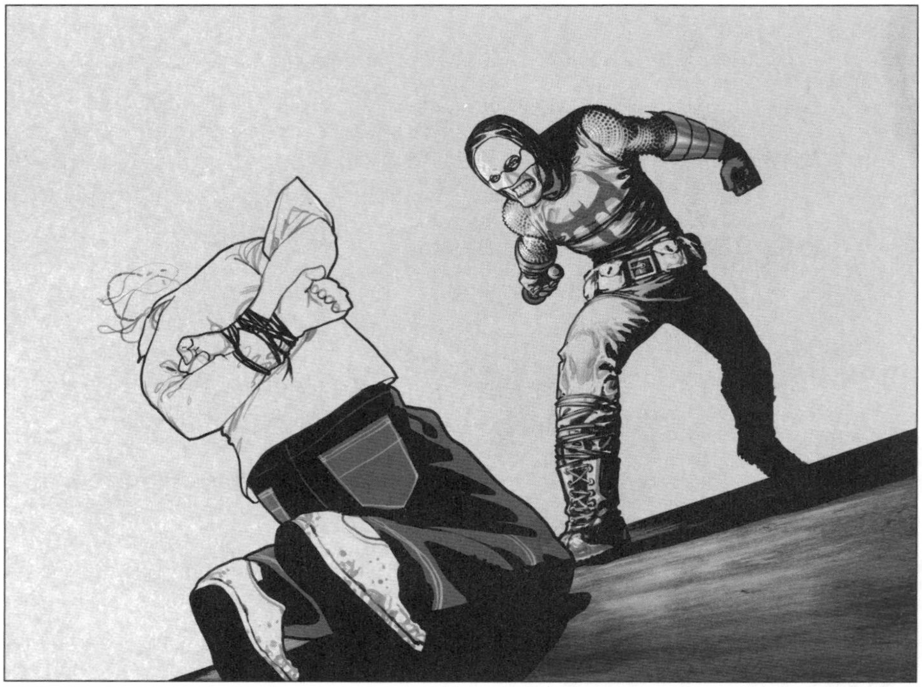

MM: How do you respond to Fabian's description of your work and approach to *Azrael*?

FRAZER: By blushing? [*laughter*]

MM: Tell me about how Mike Marts came to you with *Azrael: Death's Dark Knight* and what attracted you to the project?

FRAZER: First off, I was attracted to the gig because I was almost broke and I really needed a juicy gig. Marts was like the cavalry charging over the hill when he emailed me about this story, and even though I knew zilch about Azrael, I agreed. I got the synopsis, and despite most of it involving characters and events I knew nothing about, it clearly had an arc and there was emotion involved, so that was good.

MM: Even though you'd been in Gotham before, the colors resemble much more of your post-"Button Man" work. Can you tell me how you approached the costume and design of Azrael both in terms of the character and the environment?

FRAZER: In the script it sounded like the whole revival of Azrael was a bit ramshackle, so I figured his costume should be made of normal bits of clothing instead of sparkly super-hero stuff, hence the boots, the shoelaces, the sash, etc. Fabian made him sound like a wraith compared to a super-hero, and it was logic that dictated his appearance in that respect. As for the environment, even though it was Gotham, these places are all dependant on the point of view of the protagonist. Like, there is no set generic Gotham, but there's a Gotham seen through the eyes of however many main characters you can cook up. Azrael's Gotham was distorted, warped, and disturbed by his experiences, and it meant that I approached every aspect with that wishy-washy watercolor effect to make the details less sharp than you would expect.

MM: Did you also read the "Battle for the Cowl" and related *Batman: RIP* books at the time, or did you worry about any cross-contamination with the other titles influencing your style?

FRAZER: I read nothing that wasn't essential to the gig in hand. Generally that's what I do, otherwise I'd end up reading hundreds of comics which would do no more than to confuse me with continuity and conflicting styles. When I take on a job like this, I expect the script to be self-contained in terms of giving me the info I need. Fabian made the script self-contained and even mentioned this in the notes, which is excellent, as I really like to work in a vacuum in order to focus the mood and energies free from interference.

MM: We've joked about this before, but what is your obsession with sashes and the fevered pitch you felt at getting to use that on Azrael?

FRAZER: [*laughs*] Sashes are cool, dude. Why, don't you and your family all wear sashes? Oh, my God, sashes should be compulsory. I wear over 28 sashes on different parts of my body at all times of the day. I sleep in a giant sash. I eat sash soup. [*laughter*]

MM: Now there's an image for the book cover. [*laughter*]

"*He thinks about color the way guys from my generation think about black-&-white. I'm all about economy as an artist. I try to reduce things to stark icons. Frazer is the herald of a new paradigm. He uses color as an integral part of the storytelling process rather than an accent or afterthought. As I said earlier, his character acting and mise-en-scene authenticity are at a very high level. He's also a brilliant draftsman. The truly scary thing about all of this is that he's still in the early stages of his career. He's a sharp guy and has more than one magnum opus in him. I'd be lucky to work with him again.*"
— **Phil Hester**

MM: How do you feel being the "herald of a new paradigm"?

FRAZER: I feel like I want to hug Phil. But of course he's absolutely correct. A very wise man, indeed.

MM: [*laughs*] Rob Levin brought you onboard for *Days Missing*. Was this because of your prior association from *The Darkness*?

FRAZER: Yes, that would be through *The Darkness* stuff earlier. After I did that he kind of got hit by downsizing at Top Cow and was let go from what clearly seemed to be his dream job. I admit I felt a great deal of sympathy and pity for the little chap, especially when he wrote a rather heartbreaking entry on his blog the day it happened, and I lent some token support via email as did many others. He then latched onto this for later, and when he got the gig editing *Days Missing* he tugged at my ankle and asked me if I would want to do these two issues. I bet if he knew what a headache I was going to be he would have reconsidered.

MM: How so?

FRAZER: I made him wait for pages 'til the very end of the deadline. I didn't miss the

Previous Page and Above: First, look at Frazer's finished digital inking for a panel from *Azrael: Death's Dark Knight* #1. As part of his inking process, Frazer also lays down flat gray tones. Once the inking is complete, Frazer adds texture with more gray tones. From here Frazer will go into the coloring, using the gray tones basically as a wash underneath his colors.

Azrael ™ and © DC Comics.

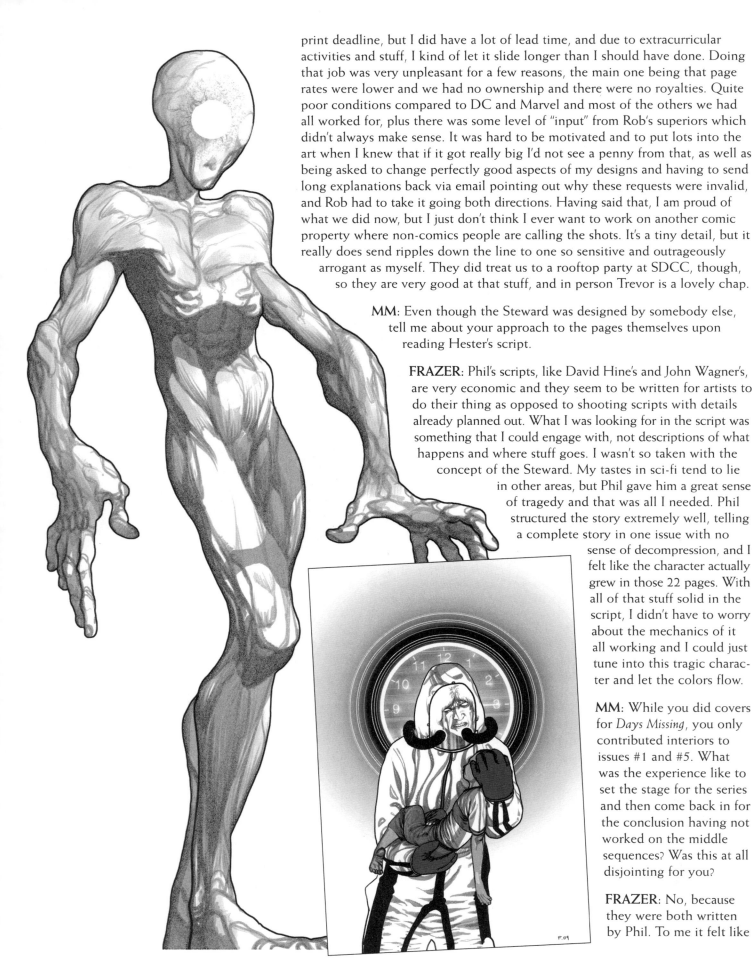

print deadline, but I did have a lot of lead time, and due to extracurricular activities and stuff, I kind of let it slide longer than I should have done. Doing that job was very unpleasant for a few reasons, the main one being that page rates were lower and we had no ownership and there were no royalties. Quite poor conditions compared to DC and Marvel and most of the others we had all worked for, plus there was some level of "input" from Rob's superiors which didn't always make sense. It was hard to be motivated and to put lots into the art when I knew that if it got really big I'd not see a penny from that, as well as being asked to change perfectly good aspects of my designs and having to send long explanations back via email pointing out why these requests were invalid, and Rob had to take it going both directions. Having said that, I am proud of what we did now, but I just don't think I ever want to work on another comic property where non-comics people are calling the shots. It's a tiny detail, but it really does send ripples down the line to one so sensitive and outrageously arrogant as myself. They did treat us to a rooftop party at SDCC, though, so they are very good at that stuff, and in person Trevor is a lovely chap.

MM: Even though the Steward was designed by somebody else, tell me about your approach to the pages themselves upon reading Hester's script.

FRAZER: Phil's scripts, like David Hine's and John Wagner's, are very economic and they seem to be written for artists to do their thing as opposed to shooting scripts with details already planned out. What I was looking for in the script was something that I could engage with, not descriptions of what happens and where stuff goes. I wasn't so taken with the concept of the Steward. My tastes in sci-fi tend to lie in other areas, but Phil gave him a great sense of tragedy and that was all I needed. Phil structured the story extremely well, telling a complete story in one issue with no sense of decompression, and I felt like the character actually grew in those 22 pages. With all of that stuff solid in the script, I didn't have to worry about the mechanics of it all working and I could just tune into this tragic character and let the colors flow.

MM: While you did covers for *Days Missing*, you only contributed interiors to issues #1 and #5. What was the experience like to set the stage for the series and then come back in for the conclusion having not worked on the middle sequences? Was this at all disjointing for you?

FRAZER: No, because they were both written by Phil. To me it felt like

just two issues that could have run side by side, one dealing with very human subject matter and the other going off into the wild realms of sci-fi/fantasy. I was very pleased with the way issue #5 ended, though, with Phil leaving it dangling like that and having the Steward left as a damaged person. This broke the status quo, and it was the right sort of vibe for me.

MM: You designed the characters on the pages themselves with no preliminary sketching. Was this a process you developed specifically for the series or something you had employed beforehand?

FRAZER: Dude, it's pretty much what I do all the time. It's like acting. I can't get into the character until I'm actually playing the role.

MM: That makes sense. From reading the script to *Days Missing #5*, it appears you played it pretty tightly to the script. Does this relate back to the art qualities you attributed to Hester?

FRAZER: Phil makes it easy. His pacing is simple and smooth, the dialogue—the most important part of any script for me—is economic and to the point, and the themes in the narrative are clearly identified, so I don't need to screw with it. He built in that nanobot critter and I reckon he knew I'd latch onto that as my window of expression. And he was right. I loved playing around with that thing, it was so easy and fun to make it contrast with all the other stuff around it.

MM: You returned to DC for cover work on David Hine's *Arkham Reborn*. Was this assignment via your previous work with Hine or through your work on *Azrael* with Mike Marts?

FRAZER: I think Mike was keen to keep me busy during this period. I know a lot of editors like to retain some talent on projects connected to their office in case they get poached by someone else, but that's all speculation on my part. I don't know if David had a hand in it, but we did discuss some details together at SDCC that year.

MM: Were you asked to do interiors for the book?

FRAZER: No, that was already set before I came onboard.

MM: Since the covers employ so many layers, did you actually design each of the figures' individual profiles and then alter them accordingly, or did you piece them together as you went?

FRAZER: It was halfway between. I sketched out entire heads, but I knew roughly which parts were to be exposed in the jigsaw, so I didn't do too much drawing that would be unused.

MM: How did the concept of the puzzle design originate and how many players were you dealing with in terms of faces to incorporate?

Previous Page: One of Frazer's nanobot creature designs for *Rodenberry Presents: Days Missing*, along with the gray tones for his cover to the first issue of the five-issue mini-series.
Above: The two sketches on the left are ideas for the cover of *Arkham Reborn #1*. The other sketch was an idea for the third issue of the series. Frazer proposed the jigsaw puzzle motif— fitting for a story involving mystery and madness— as a way to help unify the series.

Dr. Jeremiah Arkham, The Joker and all related characters ™ and © DC Comics.

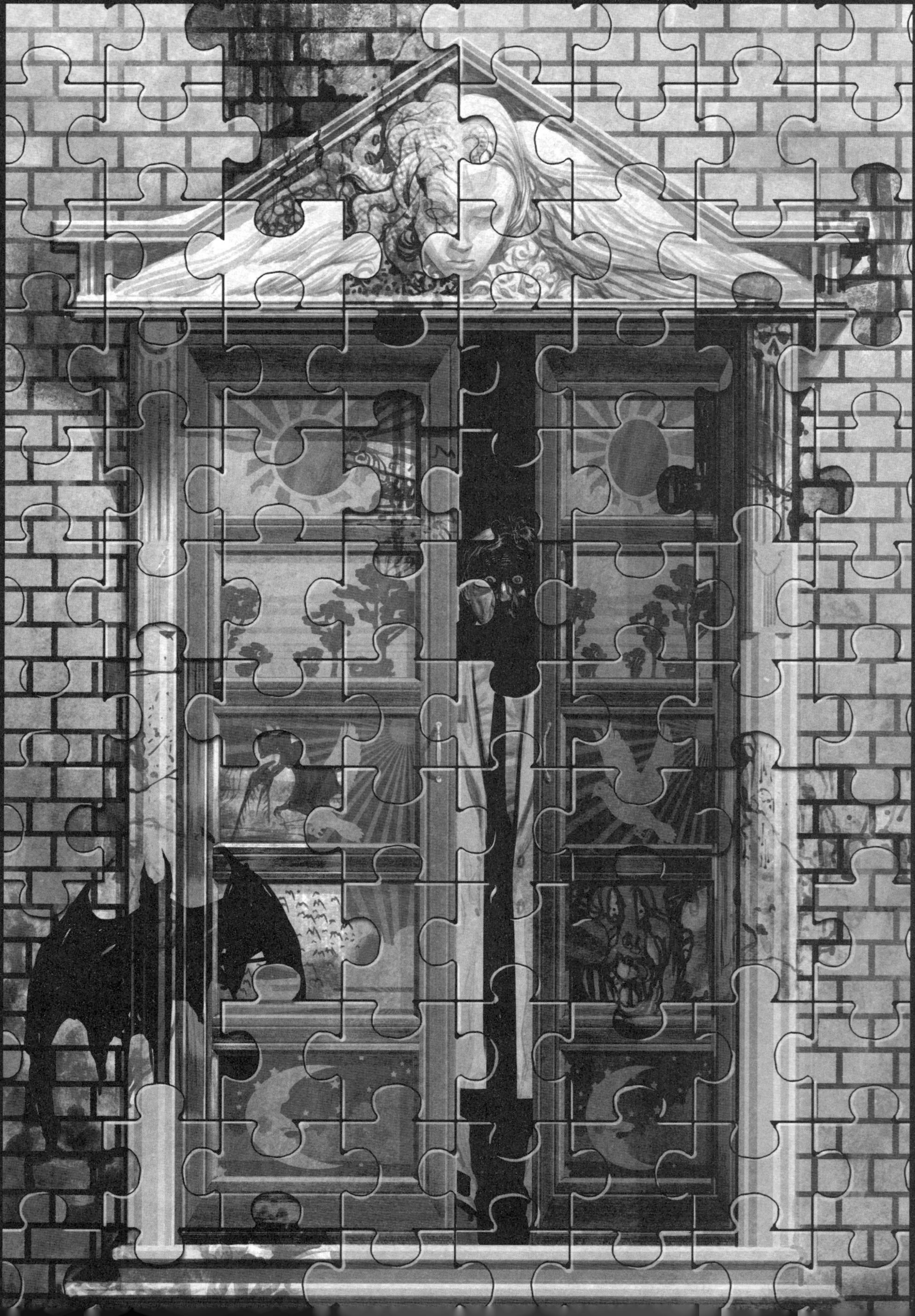

FRAZER: The puzzle idea was mine. I wanted a unifying theme to link the covers, and given that the story dealt with madness and figuring out a mystery, I thought the jigsaw gimmick could convey aspects of the characters I was told I could use on the first cover.

MM: Were you originally slated to do covers for all three *Arkham Reborn* issues? If so, what happened with the final installment?

FRAZER: Well, I drew three, but after they were all accepted it was decided that the second cover I did wasn't strong enough, so they bumped my third cover to the second spot and got another artist to do the cover to issue #3. I was a bit miffed at that, as I would have happily done a replacement cover, especially seeing as the cover was originally accepted at the time. I wasn't too keen on it myself, but that happens a lot in comics: one submits three sketches and it's almost always the one I like the least that gets chosen. It means that in the future I have to only submit sketches that I know I can really get into.

MM: You had a short strip in Marvel's *The Mystic Hands of Doctor Strange* with writer Kieron Gillen. How did the assignment come about?

FRAZER: Let me start that by explaining how important that Dr. Strange story was for me. As I explained before, 2008 had sucked and I really dropped the ball, torturing poor Simon over the delayed *Gutsville*, then giving Rob Levin gray hairs with *Days Missing*. I even got threatened with being taken off *Azrael* on the first issue due to my system of providing all the art at the end of the deadline instead of in weekly batches. After a year of that, I had

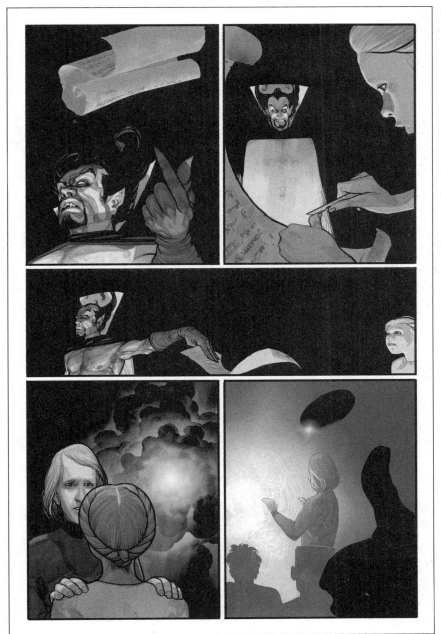

resolved to start sorting things out, not only to make the work happen, but to improve the quality—which I viewed as inferior to what I was capable of, another reason *Gutsville* was delayed, as it deserved better—and this meant changing my lifestyle and revising my system to enable me to make the work happen smoother and allow me greater control.

When I was offered the Strange story with Kieron, I knew it was a one-off and wouldn't amount to anything, but I had to treat it as if it was just as worthy as any grand opus I was engaged in, putting the story center stage in my life and viewing it not just as a way to pay the bills, but a way to explore art and story-telling, which is after all my main drive to do this. I figured it has my name on it, I should

Previous Page: Frazer's rejected cover intended for *Arkham Reborn #2*. **Above:** A panel and page from "The Cure," the lead story from *The Mystic Hands of Dr. Strange* black-&-white, 52-page one-shot, written by Kieron Gillen, in which Strange and Clea investigate an insane asylum.

Below: Gray tones for the cover of *Do Androids Dream of Electric Sheep?* #10, based on the Philip K. Dick novel. Can you spot Frazer's girlfriend? **Next Page :** Frazer gets his Puritan on in *Batman: The Return of Bruce Wayne* #2.

make it represent me the best it can. So when I started that strip I became more determined to work in a disciplined fashion. It was odd for me, as I was still very Bohemian at the time and my girlfriend was visiting twice a week, which soaked up a lot of time. But she was understanding of my need to sit and draw instead of spending all my time with her, which helped loads. Artists are not easy to live with, and teaching her that we could mix work and pleasure into a routine was part of that process of getting my act together. That was the first job I'd had in years where I didn't actually feel like I was rushing any part of it, and it felt awesome. I still like a lot of the art, and a lot of that has to do with the way I can see the confidence growing in the pages as it progresses.

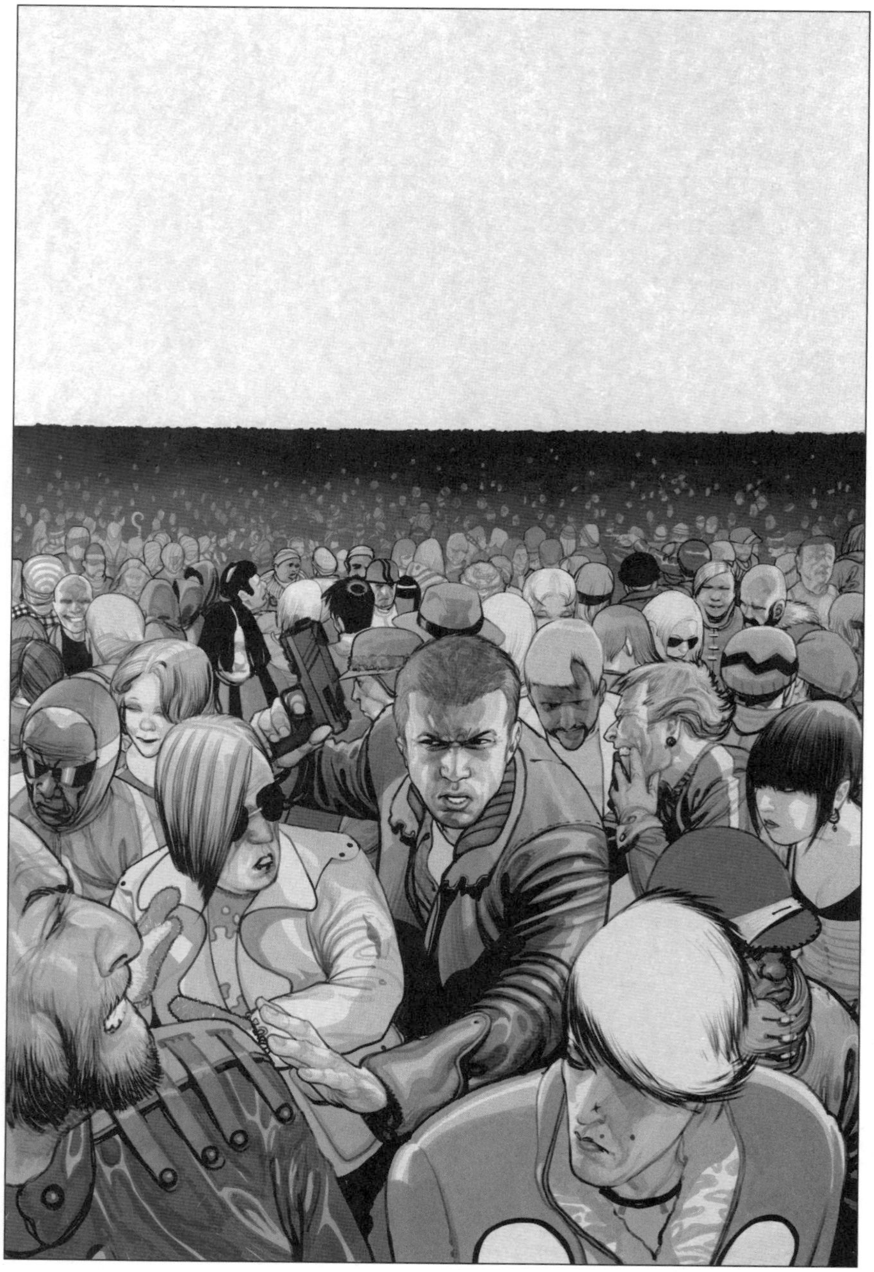

MM: Has that disciplined nature carried over to the present as well? Was any of this new attention on your part acknowledged by either Kieron or Marvel publicly or privately?

FRAZER: Oh, I'm very disciplined these days, relatively anyway. Some others like David Lloyd or Chris Weston may be like military machines compared to me, but compared to what I used to be like I'm a very efficient creative organism now. I draw in the morning, and this is unheard of. As for whether Marvel or Kieron noticed, I can't say they did, and it wasn't for them anyway. What my collaborators and clients think of me is kind of not important to some degree, because they always think something different to what the reality is. What's important is that I see the difference, because it's me that makes the art happen, it's me that peels off a small sliver of my soul each time I draw these twisted pages. I am my own motivator.

MM: Since the Strange strip is black-&-white, how does it differ in regards to your process from your earlier black-&-white digital work in "The Simping Detective"?

FRAZER: What you see in that strip is what I do before I add colors. I pretty much just left the color stage out, which is why it looks that way. I had toyed with changing the style to suit a more natural black-&-white look, but in the end it seemed contrived and I just drew it the way I normally do, in reaction to the mood and vibe of the story.

MM: With the cover for *Do Androids Dream of Electric Sheep?* #10, you'd mentioned that the crowd scene was difficult to approach. Was it simply constructing so many profiles or the amount of detail required?

FRAZER: It was, yes. I dislike crowd scenes because I've never had a method to deal with them. It scared me. But it was also my idea and so I figured it was the right choice, taking on something I'm not used to and learning ways to deal with them. I put my girlfriend on the cover as well, which humanized it a bit more for me. By the time I finished it, I was much more confident approaching crowd scenes, as I sort of began working out a method to deal with the composition issues. I kind of like the idea of crowds now. [*laughs*] It was also another watershed for me in terms of seeing the art as art and not a value-based freelance gig. The fee wasn't as high as what DC would pay, but

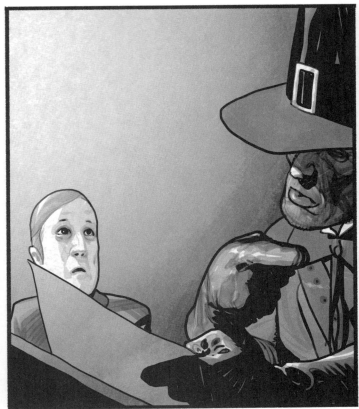

I couldn't allow myself to alter the quality level according to the fee. I accepted the job, and I treated it the same as any other.

MM: Were crowd scenes scary because there are so many different faces to compose, or is it fitting and arranging them all together? Had a value-based vision guided the majority of your work prior to this assignment? Would you say this new attitude has affected your contemporary output as well?

FRAZER: It was always a compositional issue, but the ever expanding roster of characters to invent also affected it. I could draw endless blank heads and still have issues with composing them. The trick is to slow down and have fun with it. Thinking about the crowd as lots of individual characters that I am inventing, imagining their thoughts, ticks, and ways does seem to paint the picture for me. Prior to this I had often seen cheaper or free work as being something I should put less effort into purely because of the logic that if clients see they get the same art for less money, they will just lower my rates for everything. Luckily, comics don't work like that, there is some stability in page rates, but as an illustrator one has to consider these things, because clients are like bloodthirsty sharks, always looking for easy pickings.

Since then I've just treated every gig the same, including the *Monsters* movie poster, the birthday print I drew for Si Spurrier's 30th birthday party, the charity piece I drew for this Chilean comic project which hasn't been printed and I'm actually wondering if it ever will and if the dude was actually conning me, because each artwork is innocent of these values placed on them by others; each image is an

exercise and a message in itself and should get the same treatment. The trick is to just start saying no to cheap gigs.

MM: You and I have joked before about being labeled by your art, particularly being the go-to "Puritan Dude" of comic illustration. I think you mentioned before turning down a Puritan-themed series at one point, correct? What was your first reaction then when offered Puritan Batman in the 2010 *Batman: Return of Bruce Wayne* series?

FRAZER: I turned down the *Solomon Kane* series from Dark Horse partially due to other commitments, but also I didn't fancy the idea of doing loads of Puritan stuff, as that would totally typecast me. The *Return of Bruce Wayne* issue, though, was okay, as it was just one issue and it was also part of a much larger story, and I liked that idea. My first reaction to getting the gig, though, was shock, as I figured I was too small fry to get a big, fancy Batman Grant Morrison gig. I was dead pleased and very flattered.

MM: You acknowledge a fear of being typecast as the Puritan artist, but you've also said there was no fear of being typecast as a horror artist earlier in your career. How do you reconcile this or is that even a consideration for you?

FRAZER: Horror is far broader. It covers any time period, fits into any genre, and can be considered a "feel" as opposed to Puritans, which is quite specific. I could do space Puritans, I suppose, but that's about as far and wide as that gets. It's like "Horror" is to "Puritans" what "Jazz" is to "Songs about Fish in the Key of A Lasting No More Than Two Minutes."

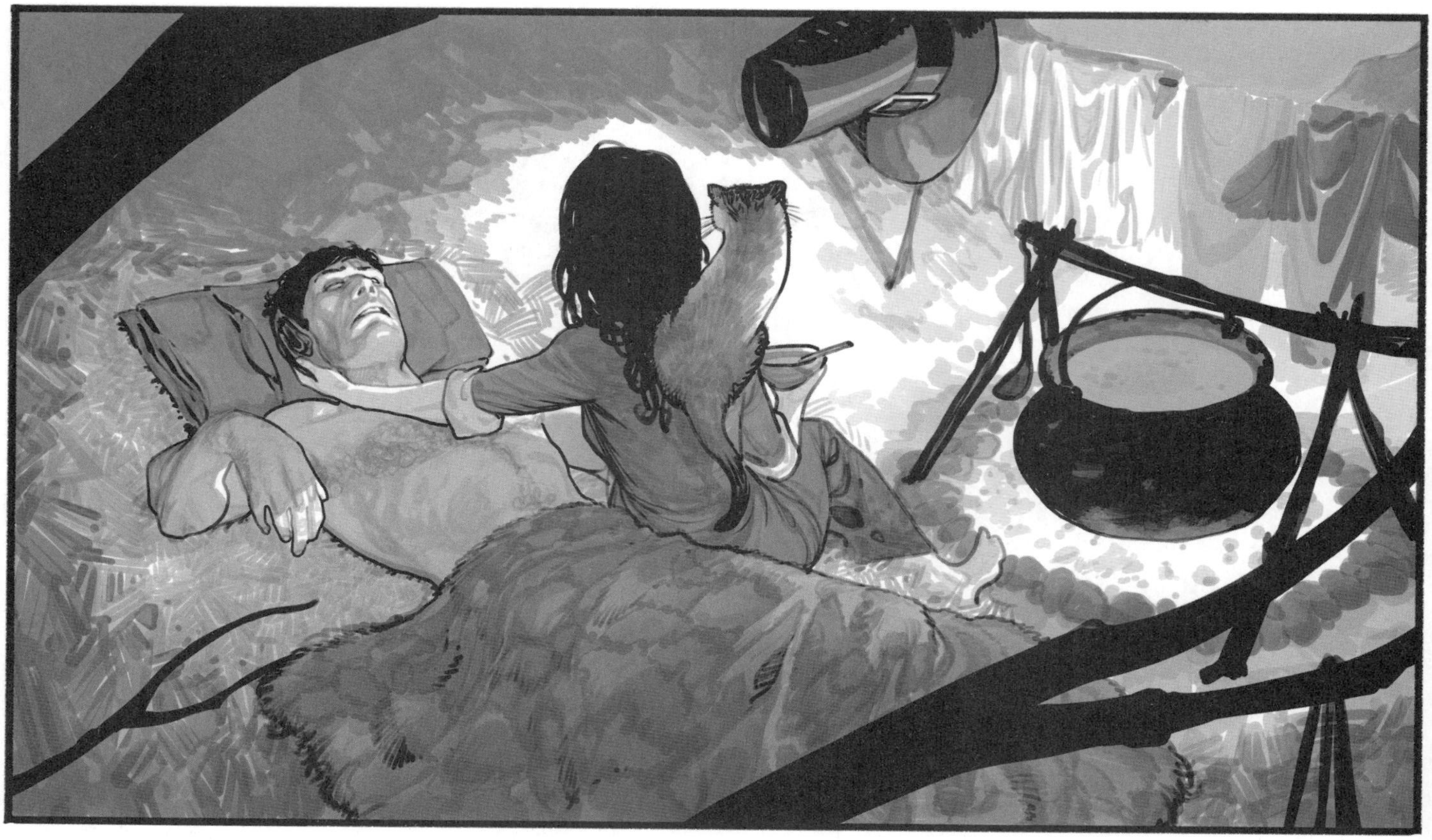

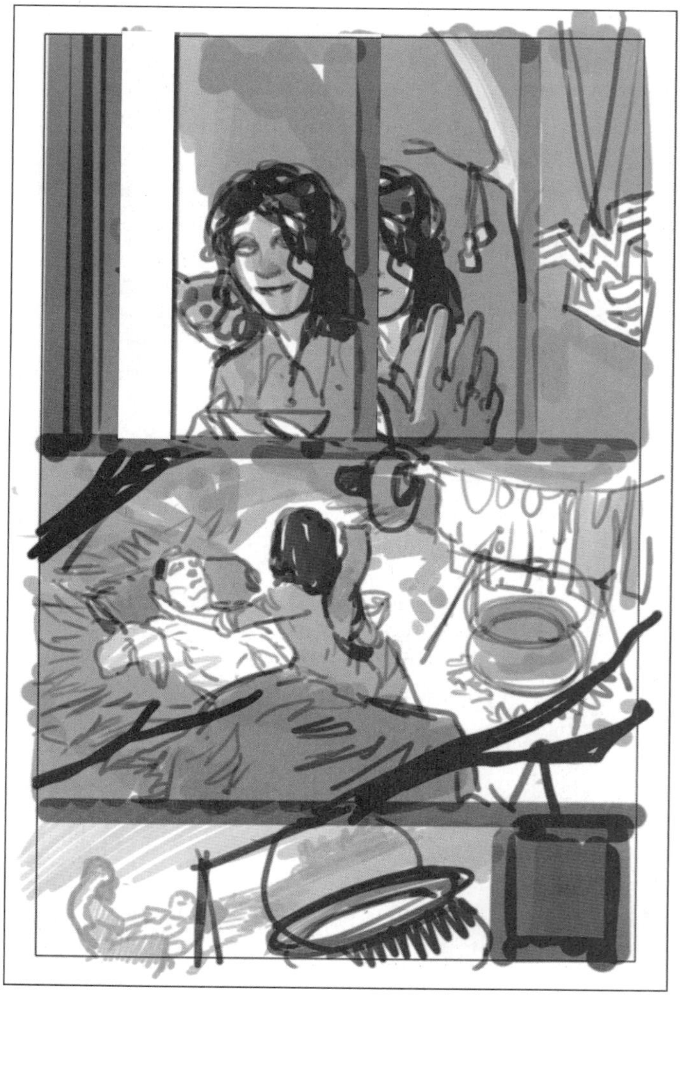

MM: [*laughs*] How did the *Return of Bruce Wayne* gig come about?

FRAZER: Marts emailed me. These things always have that inauspicious start, and despite my trying to sex it up, the answer is almost always as simple as that. The dude emailed and seemed to ask if I was interested. I don't know if he was playing or if he genuinely thought I might say no to a gig like that. I know that Grant had said that he wanted me on it, and that is documented in the many interviews he has given on the subject, so I can only assume he gave Mike his list of who he wanted and it was Mike's job to hunt us down like the scurvy dogs we are.

MM: In working on issue #2, did you have any foresight into the first installment in terms of design and story, or even what would come after your own? Did this in turn affect how you broached the assignment?

FRAZER: I had seen the pencils to issue #1 so I could get a handle on the story, and I knew what the basic outline was for the rest, but that didn't matter to me. I knew Grant had picked me because my style would be very different to those on either side. In fact, it seems he has this idea a lot, mixing the art styles up for big gigs like *Seven Soldiers*, *Batman*, *Multiversity*, etc., and I totally fit in with that. The only concerns I had were that if I invented something such as that big tentacle monster on page one, then it had to be something other artists could draw without difficulty later on in their chapters.

MM: Key moments really stand out in this issue in terms of your own progression as an artist. The fractured panel sequence that draws the eye to the Superman/Wonder Woman pendant, the color palette for the colonial Gotham, and the amazing forest scene come to mind. What does the issue represent for you in your own evolution in style and design?

FRAZER: It marked the end of a way of working where I was laying down more washy lines than I needed. I mean, it suited this story, but it was laborious and also made a lot of panels unclear, so for me it was the end of an indulgent and decadent period of drawing and caused me to revise my method in order to achieve greater clarity. I was pleased with the new brushes I had made for the forest scenes, and the contrast with the super-hero moments was quite nice, though it all printed darker than I expected, something I corrected for the *Batman* stuff later.

MM: I've read that you were supposed to follow Frank Quitely on *Batman and Robin*. Was that a mistake?

FRAZER: I was told that I would be doing the arc after Cameron Stewart, but it wasn't nailed down at the time. Things always change behind the scenes in comics, and often I'm the last to know. [*laughs*]

MM: It seems that between bumping covers or selecting artists for assignments, so much is hanging in the balance and only at the whim of the editorial team. Would you say that's indicative of both writing and art, or more on the illustrative side of the industry?

FRAZER: I hear it from all over the place, and the actions of these artists and writers can also affect it. We are all part of a massive, moving thing, and sometimes stuff happens to affect others and it isn't always communicated well. In the early days I was convinced editors hated me, that they thought I was a tedious British squit, but it seems they were just assuming I was doing okay and didn't need any input. I quite like the way they leave me alone to do my thing now, actually.

MM: You had to still be working on your *Return of Bruce Wayne* issue when you started your run on Morrison's sister title, *Batman and Robin*, correct? Were you aware of what Morrison was planning, and did this affect your approach to the pages and the varied designs of Batman Bruce versus Batman Dick?

FRAZER: I started *Batman and Robin* after *Return of Bruce Wayne*, so there was no overlap.

I didn't know what was going to happen in *Batman and Robin*, as Grant kept his cards very close to his chest on that. I only really knew when I got the scripts to the actual issues, but that just made it more compelling for me. It would have helped a little if I had known more in advance, as there were some design aspects that I dropped the ball on when they came around for the second time in the story. Because I knew I was going to be drawing the two different Batmen I made the choice to base Wayne on a more robust and Dredd-like face and base Grayson on a lithe angular face, though whether that actually worked is another matter. [*laughs*]

Previous Page: Frazer's sketch for *The Return of Bruce Wayne* #2, page 3, along with his tones for panel 5 of the page. **Below:** Frazer's tones for *Batman and Robin* #13, page 20.

Bruce Wayne, Robin, The Joker and all related characters ™ and © DC Comics.

MM: What design aspects do you feel you dropped the ball on and why? Looking back at Bruce and Dick, do you feel those approaches worked?

FRAZER: Now when I look back at the pages I can't pick out the bits that I felt let it down. It's possible I compensated later on and have just forgotten what it was, but there was a definite feeling halfway through that if I had known what was going to happen I would have drawn some parts differently. It may well have been the overall illustrative style, or perhaps details like the design of the atom bomb in the last part of issue #15. Perhaps I would have made it cleaner, but it's passed now and if it doesn't bug me when I look at the book, then it can't have been that important. As for Wayne and Grayson—I can't call them Bruce and Dick without giggling like a naughty schoolboy—I think the differences are there enough, though I would have preferred to have

made them even more different. These are the lessons I take with me to the next gig and so on, learning and refining each time.

MM: After talking with Grant about his process and reading the script for *Batman and Robin #13*, I know you received the script only in parts. How did that interrupt or delay your own design and storytelling? Were you forced to revise or alter anything?

FRAZER: There were no revisions as such, but it did mean that each time I finished pages my art engine cooled down, and this forced me to do all the warming up again for the next set of pages, which added delays to the whole shebang. I got into the groove by the end of the run, but that first issue was a bit disconcerting, not just because I only got chunks, but also because I knew the pressure was on to perform.

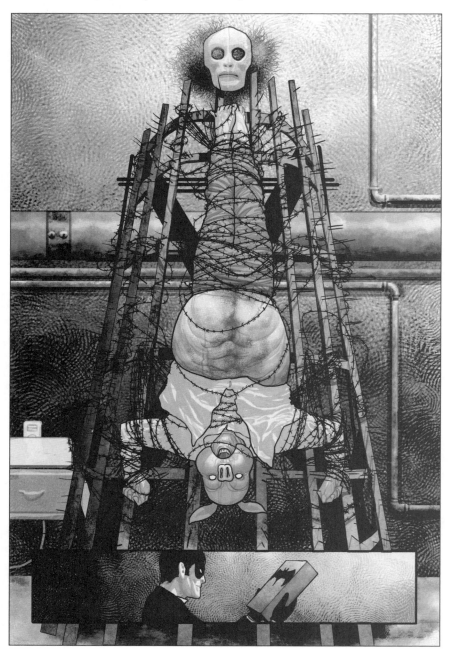

MM: Few can probably appreciate the collaborative efforts between you and Grant on this series, but having seen the script and comparing them with the pages is simply amazing just how close they are, almost natural. Is it the hive mind or something in the water supply there in the UK?

FRAZER: It's mushrooms. [*laughter*] Seriously, I didn't think I played it that close. I always feel like I'm tampering with writers' works when I draw them. I get it big time with *Gutsville*, and I felt it a lot with *Days Missing*, but the writers always seem happy with it, so I don't worry too much anymore. With Grant's scripts I feel it a great deal because he leaves so much space to experiment, though maybe what I see as differences in the script and art comparison are perceived differently by people like yourself. I play it close enough so that if the script says, "Gordon tied to a gurney on a stage," and I do a crazy fisheye thing that isn't asked for, you will still just note that I did at the very least put Gordon on a gurney on a stage. In that respect I play it as close as I can, because otherwise I'm telling a different story.

MM: We've also discussed the variations between what you see in your designs on screen versus the limitations of the printing process to duplicate your art. How have you had to alter your own approach to accommodate those limitations, and are there any aspects of your more current work that stand out as examples of these conflicts? I ask because page seven, panel two in the script calls for a shadowed figure I don't want to reveal and I'm curious if you inserted it in the actual page or not.

FRAZER: Funny you should say that, as I only just noticed it. [*laughter*] Grant formats his scripts in some weird way that means none of my software can read it without jumbling the words all over the place, regardless of the formats I use, so in some cases sentences made no sense and I had to do some detective work to figure it out. That one little bit of text must have completely eluded me. When I work on a script, I scribble basic layouts as I read, getting the first impressions. That's the best way to find out what is important in each panel, and I work with that, referencing the script to refine ideas and stuff, but clearly on that panel I had an idea based on the basic description and I just went with it. It didn't seem to affect the storytelling, and reading the script now I think it actually would have cluttered the story a little had I put the figure in.

Regarding print and screen conflicts, *Return of Bruce Wayne* was the worst case, where entire pages became dark, muddy messes in print, and so I simply adjusted the controls on both my screens to reflect the printed version and that's the workspace I use now to draw. The *Xombi* pages are quite close to what I see on the screen now, and this won't be an issue anymore until I start making art for the iPad or web, because that will mean recalibrating it all.

MM: Is that print and screen conflict something more indicative of working digitally as opposed to using traditional methods, or was it something specific to DC's printing methodologies, i.e., something you've not encountered on other projects?

FRAZER: Oh, no, they're all like that. Luckily they all seem to be the same these days, but back in the early 2000s each publisher had a slightly different take on it, and it was a nightmare calibrating. 2000 *AD* always overcooked the cyan on their pages, so I adjusted for that, then the DC stuff was too red, etc. Teething problems, eh?

MM: Seeing Grant's script pages is perhaps the best way to witness the style you so prefer as an artist, particularly his descriptions of the Joker, Batman, and Robin, or Batman and Gordon on the Bat Rail. Can you take me through how you decide and assign color to those moments since Grant's words allow for such open expression?

FRAZER: It's often dictated by the environment. The Bat Rail scene was underground

and would probably need to have subdued lighting to conserve energy as well as keep it all secret, so I figured "red" was the way to go. It's also a factor of separating scenes by color. I couldn't have red in the following scene, as it would seem like they were in the same place, so that became blue. Any scene with the Joker, however, is going to need his signature color scheme in it, as he is so identified by his green hair, white skin, and red lips—I added yellow teeth, too—but that always worked regardless of the color schemes I used, as the colors relate by value not hue. Other times it's all about the mood, and then finding an environmental facet that can justify the choices, like the blues in the graveyard are moonlight,

Previous Page: Tones for *Batman and Robin* #14, page 6, featuring one of writer Grant Morrison's more disturbing creations—and that's saying something— Professor Pyg.
Above: A "Batman and Robin action pose" for the variant cover of *Batman and Robin* #13.

Batman, Robin, Professor Pyg and all related characters ™ and © DC Comics.

Below and Next Page: Frazer's digital sketch and finished inks with gray tones for the variant cover of *Batman and Robin* #15. The darker lines you see in the sketch are done on a separate layer. When it comes time to ink, Frazer simply removes the light, rough layer so the finer detail of the darker lines are clearly visible.

oranges of the theater are the tobacco-stained surfaces reflecting light or the fire of the burning wall, the grisly puke-greens of the interrogation chamber are rust and human fluids rotting on the walls, etc. In the interrogation scene, the script did call for more stark contrast, like *Sin City*. I, however, felt that all that black would be a lost opportunity, and opted to fill it with textures to make the situation less stark and more sickly. Everything the Joker did was sick, and I wanted to convey that visually utilizing the "hidden actor," which is the background. Instead of showing just brutality, I wanted to hint at how fundamentally wrong Damian's actions were, even though he didn't know it.

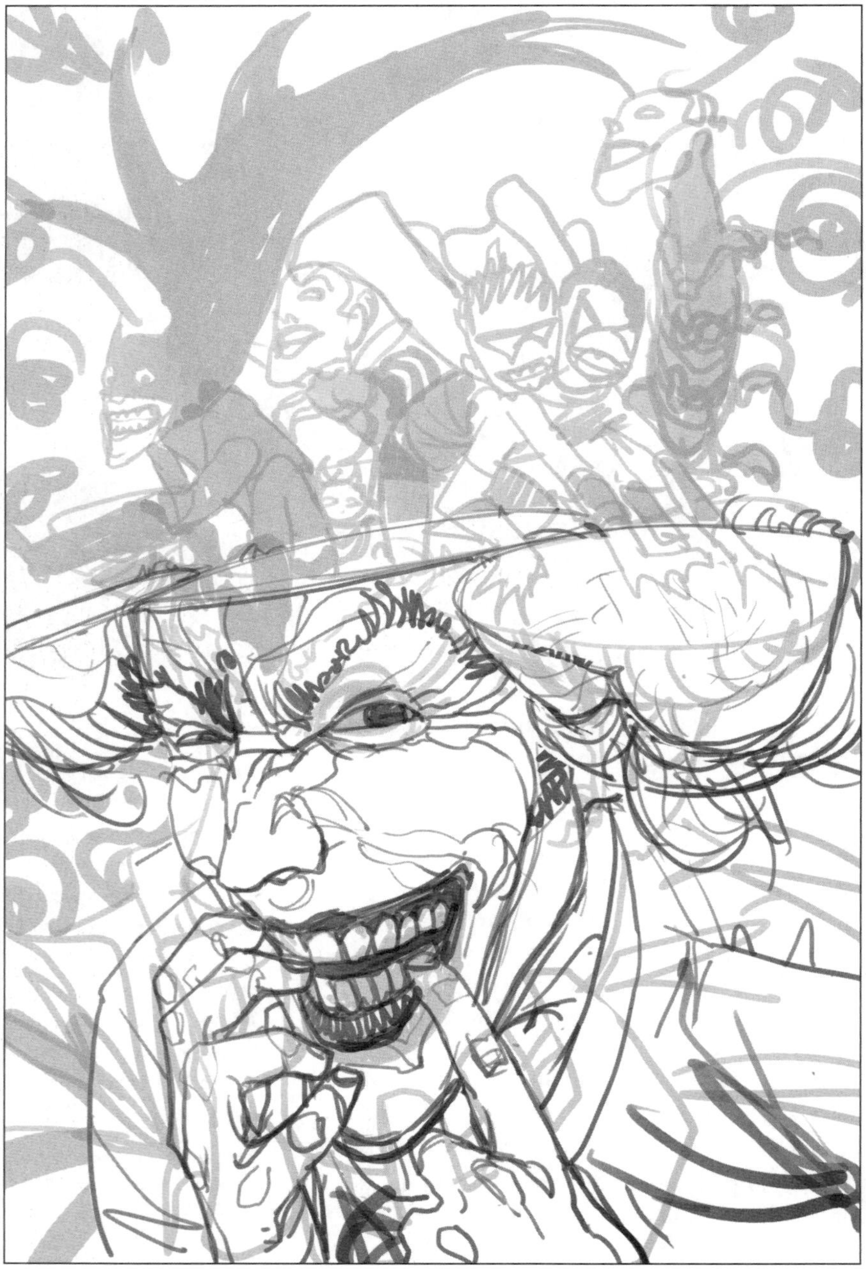

MM: One item that stood out was how different the dialogue was between the early script and the published comic.

FRAZER: Grant changes a lot of dialogue during subbing, more so than others I have worked with, but I know most writers would like the opportunity to modify the words once the pictures are made. I think it's the best way to do it, and produces more cohesive comics, but it's not always possible if the art is late or if the editor is swamped with other stuff. I never feel like I need to go back and change stuff when that happens, because the writers always modify it to improve the comic, never to disrupt it. Grant's revisions were a revelation. I would read the printed book and be amazed at how the story was so fresh and different, how the characters became so much more alive with new information growing out of dialogue which was so different to what I assumed would be there. Some dialogue is very basic and almost patronizing in the script, but the magic is when the writer changes it to allow the art to carry more of the storytelling and uses the dialogue to convey information in a less obvious manner.

MM: Is it at all strange to design a variant cover for the issue you're also illustrating? Did you have any correspondence with Frank Quitely? Were the covers done before you knew what the interiors would be? What guidance did you have in those cover designs?

FRAZER: I have spoken to Mr. Quitely once, and that was at a con for about five seconds. All of his covers were done before mine, and were in some cases the only clues I had as to what was going on in that issue. I also had to make covers in advance of getting scripts due to solicitation deadlines, which meant that my *Batman and Robin* covers bear no relation to the narrative within the book. The first two covers I had simple guides from Marts. He asked for a "Batman and Robin action pose" for issue #13 and "Batman and Robin fighting a group of shadowy figures" for issue #14, and I had to run with that. For issue #15 I suggested a mental Joker image, and he just said, "Go for it."

MM: Issue #15 is perhaps the most iconic cover of the three because of the true insanity. How did you go from the Joker playing with Batman and Robin hand-puppets to the explosive nature of figures and characters in his head?

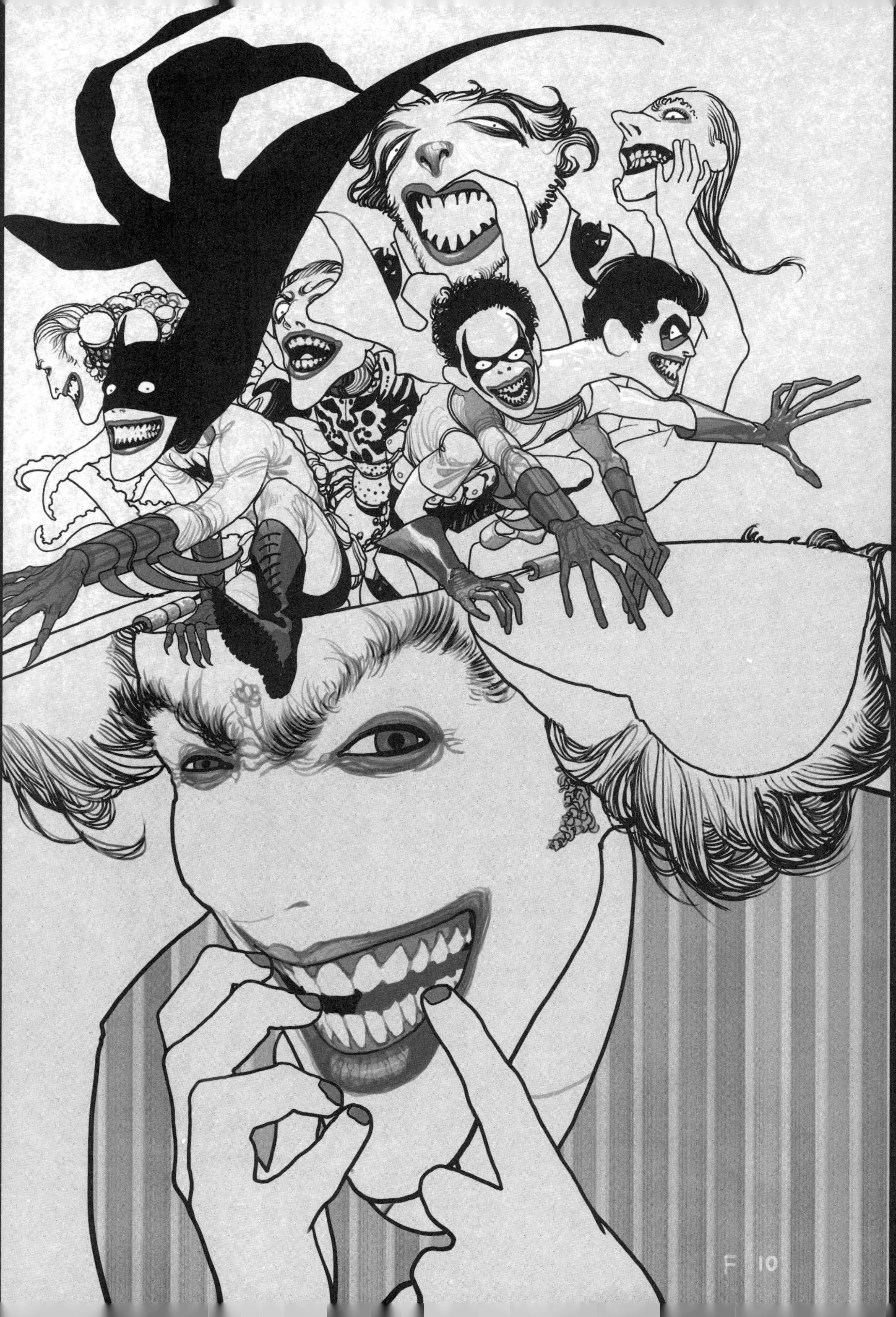

FRAZER: The portrait shot was more along the lines of what I wanted to do, but I figured I should offer them some variations with a more narrative nature, so the glove puppets were done after the portrait shot. That image is pretty much how I see the Joker, and it's something I knew I could do easily and have a lot of fun with, though I'm still surprised Mike picked it, because I thought it would be a little too generic.

MM: *Batman and Robin #16* stands out in a series that has so many great issues. I know you've worked with other artists on a single project before, but how did this arrangement work between you, Cameron Stewart, and Chris Burnham, as the original solicits only listed one artist involved?

FRAZER: Truth? I had heard that Cameron was drawing that issue and I was a bit angry, as it was just one more issue and I wanted that whole collected edition for myself, but I figured there must be good reasons. Then, I discovered, when talking to Cameron at SDCC, that he didn't even know about it. Thinking there was some mix-up here I spoke to Marts about it and discovered a bit of a communication break-down happening, so I mentioned that if Cameron couldn't do it due to his Ubisoft gig, then I would be happy to step in. A mixture of utter selfishness and utter selflessness. Later on I heard from Marts that Cameron was indeed drawing it now, but only the first part, and Grant had written the script to work with different artists drawing different

scenes, and did I want to do a bit of it? More importantly, he was concerned I wouldn't have the time, but I assured him I could do ten pages in twelve days, no problemo. It was a bit messy—as it transpired there were seven pages of a scene set aside for another artist and all the chosen ones had bailed, so in a moment of organization I suggested Chris Burnham to Kristan, and the next thing I know he's doing the pages. Whether or not it was down to my suggestion I will never know, but it was good to see him get the break. Ultimately, the three of us jammed on our scenes and made the last issue a very vibrant one, but it does show some of the complexities involved with making Batman comics with such vast and voracious egos such as mine involved.

MM: Tell me about how the final page—the money shot, if you will—of Bruce announcing his new endeavor served as an end to your run with the series. What did that mean for you?

FRAZER: It meant I could sleep again. [*laughter*] It was a bit sad, as I was just getting into the characters and here I was sending them off into a new world which I wasn't a part of, but I guess that happens a lot with writers when they end their arcs, so I got over it.

MM: As you move into *Xombi* in early 2011, audiences see you shifting your style yet again. You'd mentioned before that *Xombi* was one of those moments of change, but what spurred you to make that shift in your process for the series?

FRAZER: It was clarity issues on *Batman and Robin*. The method made for some muddy artwork and I wanted to see if I could clean that up, so I reduced the amount of stuff that went into each panel and, boom, it was clearer. The simpler lines, the less cluttered shadows, it all makes it clearer to read without losing anything important, though halfway through my run now I see that I perhaps made it a little too clean and clinical, and I'm once again tweaking the knobs to bring it back a little bit. The issue is what is effective versus what is comfortable and efficient. The ideal balance can be struck where the flow of art is relaxed and organized as well as totally open for me to create very simple as well as very complicated imagery in the same panel if I need to. I'm closer now than ever before, but I reckon there may be more tweaking ahead.

MM: With *Xombi*, one of the most fascinating aspects is Kim's movement on pages six and seven of issue #1. Absent any panels, was this something John Rozum called for in the script or something you came up with yourself?

FRAZER: That was my thing. Like with issue #1 of *Gutsville*, I felt John's script wasn't really doing anything with that scene other than following standard comic notions of story-telling, when in reality it was an opportunity to break the rhythm of the previous pages and really define this relationship David and Chet have using a distinctive visual trick. I assumed they would reject it for being wacky, but it turned out John loved it and so I was given the greenlight. I would have been annoyed had I been told to change it, as I thought it worked perfectly well, but one can never be too sure. Since then, John and I have become far more collaborative when it comes to pacing and stuff, which is awesome, though I try to avoid peppering too many

variations into the strip, as it would then become inconsistent and confusing. Things like that must be used sparingly in a comic like *Xombi*, in order for them to stand out.

MM: Obviously, as a professional artist you cannot please everyone, and nor should you. Do you ever feel restricted though by "playing" in the super-hero or mainstream genres of American comics versus your experiences with 2000 *AD* or more independent projects?

FRAZER: Not anymore. Once I found my own step, it became just as free and fun as anything else, and I welcome each new gig as an opportunity to expand and explore my skills for a wider and more diverse audience.

Previous Page and Above: Rough sketch, finished inks, and gray tones for the cover of *Xombi* #1. Though the grays appear rather dark here, the finished colors range from bright pink to deep purple, with the grays adding depth of tone.

Xombi ™ and © Milestone Media Partners, Inc.

91

Below: Rough sketch and gray tones for page 2 of *Xombi* #3. This time the lighter grays in the rough are the more detailed lines and will be what Frazer inks.
Next Page: Here, Frazer uses one-point perspective in his pencils to get the proper feeling of depth in this cover for *Xombi* #3.

This is one reason why I took on *Xombi*, as I knew it would be a different audience in some respects to the Grant Morrison crowd I had played to on *Batman and Robin*.

MM: I think few would argue that change is often difficult to come by in American comics, or if it does occur, it is temporary at best and largely a commercial gimmick. Your style and approach seem to run counter to what is largely a very static industry here in the U.S. Is that a concern for you when working on company toys such as Batman or Iron Man?

FRAZER: I like to delude myself that they choose me specifically because they need a bit of weird to spice things up a bit. Whether or not I do the job how they would like is another matter.

MM: When you receive a script and begin generating visuals about the characters and design, do you immediately set out to put these down on the Cintiq or do you have to give it time to sink in?

FRAZER: I like to read the script once before doodling, but in many cases there's no time, so I give it a once over and then start scribbling. I like the immediacy of that, though I also like to be able to let some ideas and themes sink in gradually, like with *Xombi*.

MM: How often would you say that your preliminary designs and concepts match up with the final products of how characters turn out the pages? What, for you, best explains that transformation?

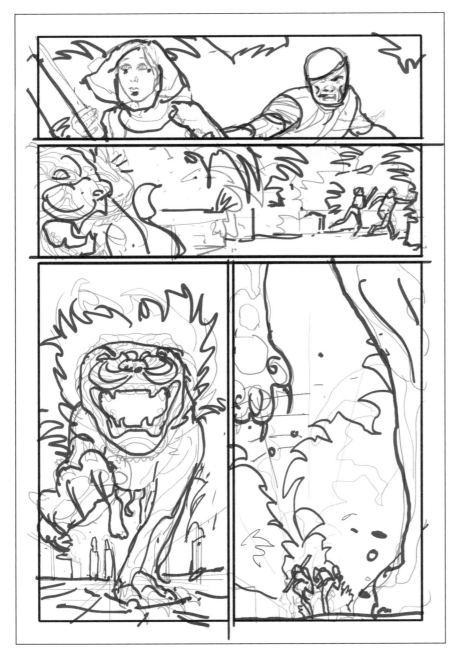

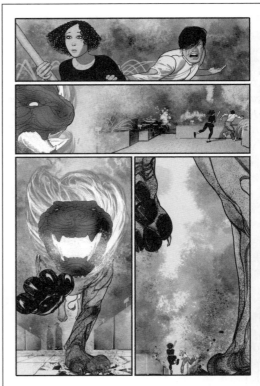

FRAZER: They always evolve over the course of the story. This would happen regardless of how much prep I did or how long I worked on the characters, because the art evolves by itself and needs room to breathe. Look at any major work by modern comic artists and you will see an evolution in terms of design as well as storytelling over the work as they get comfortable with some aspects and revise some which they didn't like. Unless I have prepared every aspect of the story to suit a specific visual gimmick I already had in my toolbox —such as with the stuff I'm writing—then there's going to be a lot of exploring on the page itself, and there is where the evolution happens.

MM: Does that inherently vary depending on the assignment, i.e., a one-shot versus a three-issue mini-series, versus a six-issue run?

FRAZER: One-shots never get the chance to evolve, so they are single statements. The longer the run, the more it grows and the better it will get.

MM: In developing and retooling your approach to digital technology, what do you feel you have lost in regards to traditional methods? Although we've discussed the benefits, what are some of the limitations and drawbacks you've encountered?

FRAZER: Power cuts, data corruption, expensive hardware upgrades, hard to draw in a café, etc., would be the limits. The loss of original art doesn't really bother me.

MM: What about the market for original art, though, at conventions?

FRAZER: The money I made from selling pages was minimal, due not only in part to the low value they had—because of the project's inherent value on the market and my name at the time—but also because none of the pages were complete, meaning that they were always quite sparse to allow for color, and that makes them far less attractive as items or investments to the art market. I also had a senti-mental attachment to a lot of art, which explains why none of my "Necronauts" pages are out there, as I wanted to keep them. So not having original art makes almost no difference to me, and the benefits of having the almost limitless options presented to me in the digital realm far, far outweigh any small income the restrictive practices of drawing ink on paper would offer up.

MM: I realize that the script determines the level and power of the art you design, but if a script was solid and sound, are there any corporate characters you would enjoy drawing or illustrating simply because of the character?

FRAZER: Nope. It's all about the story, the schedule, and the money. [*laughter*]

MM: Finally, with so much time spent in the industry thus far, how do you continue to challenge yourself to improve, and where do you look for inspiration in such challenges?

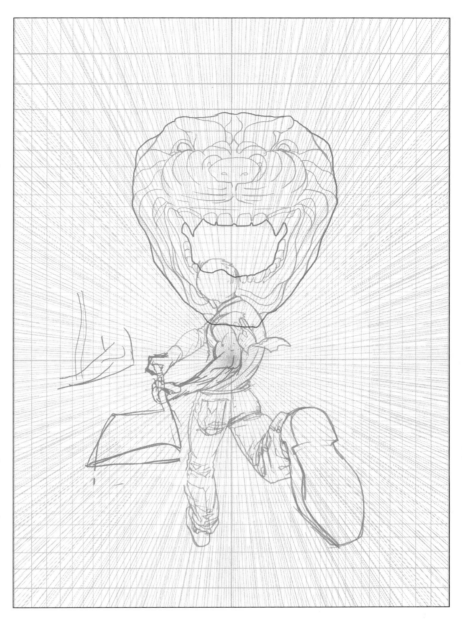

FRAZER: I look at others to inspire me. My peers are a constant source of competition, and this drives me to refine and develop what I do to impress them in the same way if I can. I also see the flaws in every panel and I am constantly working on this list of things I must improve on, like the variety of nose I draw—I need to study more noses and eyebrows. Also, I have personal projects that I want to make happen and they demand a great deal of preparation and input from me on an illustrative level, and the story compels me like a wicked mistress to beef my art muscle up and get it waxed and oiled, etc. I feel like after eleven years as a pro now that I have finally reached the stage where I am confident with my work in that I can start to make things look like they did in my head for the previous 39 years of my life, which is like saying I feel like now I can walk, I can start to trot, and then one day I may run or even sprint.

Frazer Irving

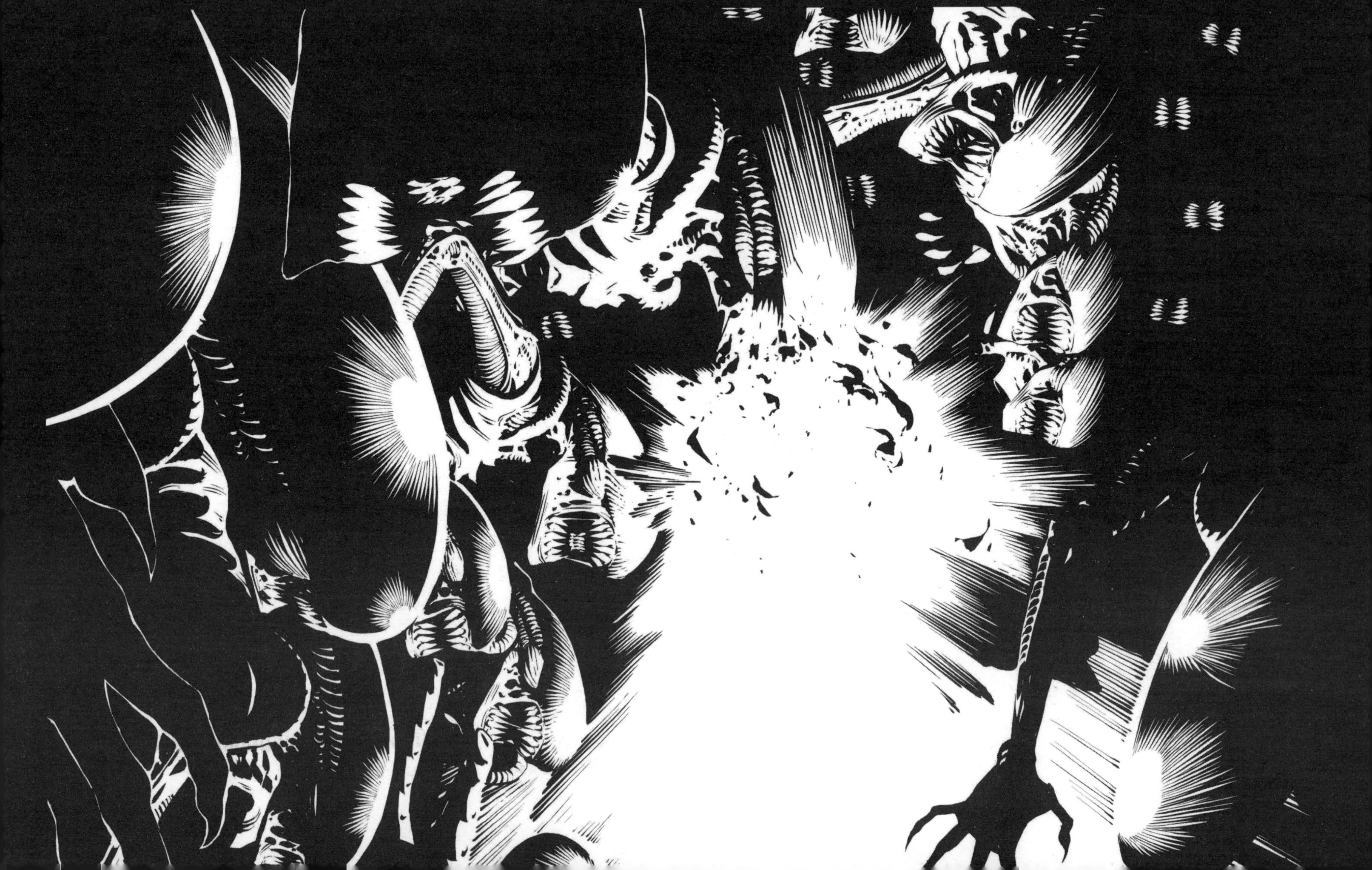

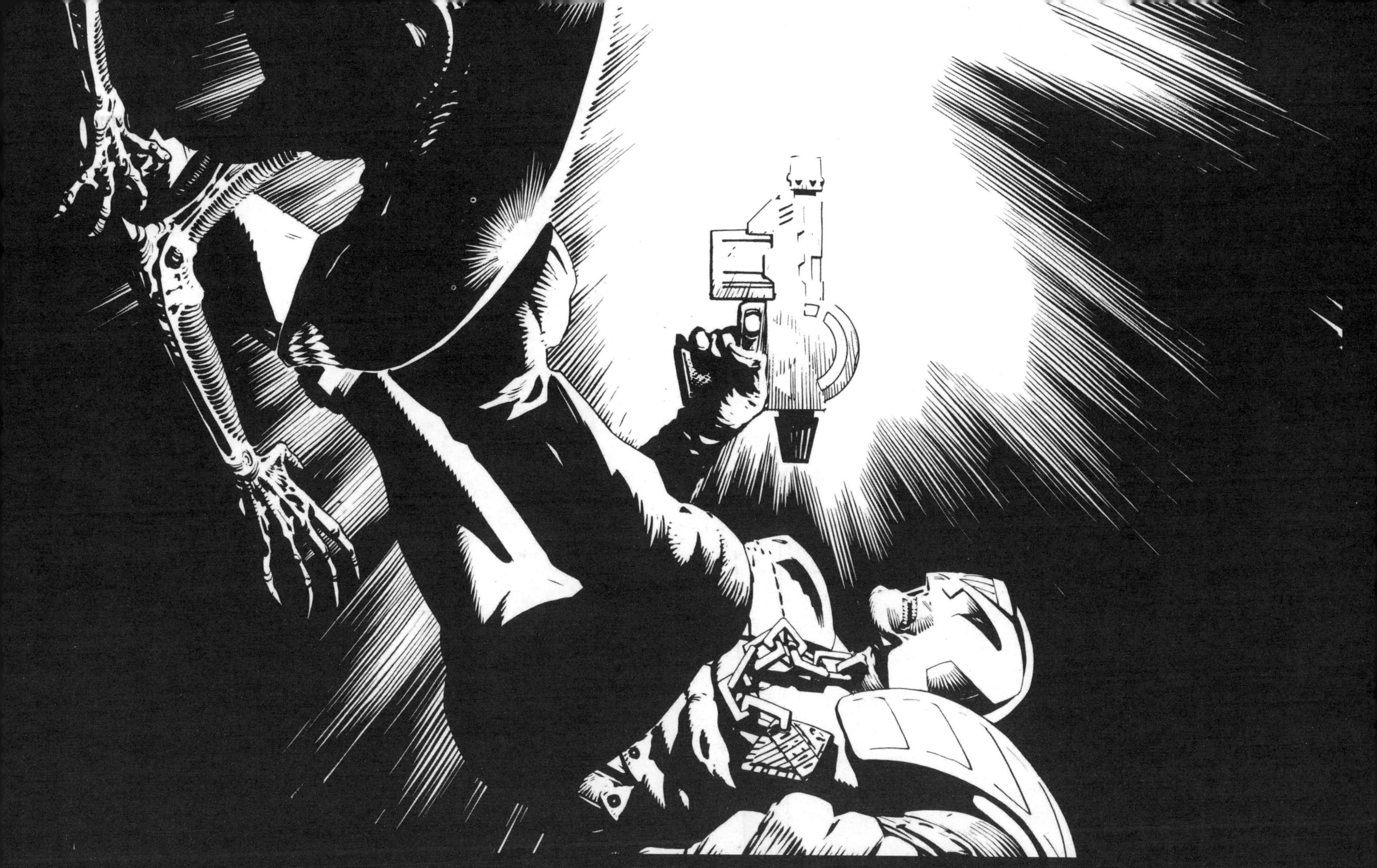

Art Gallery

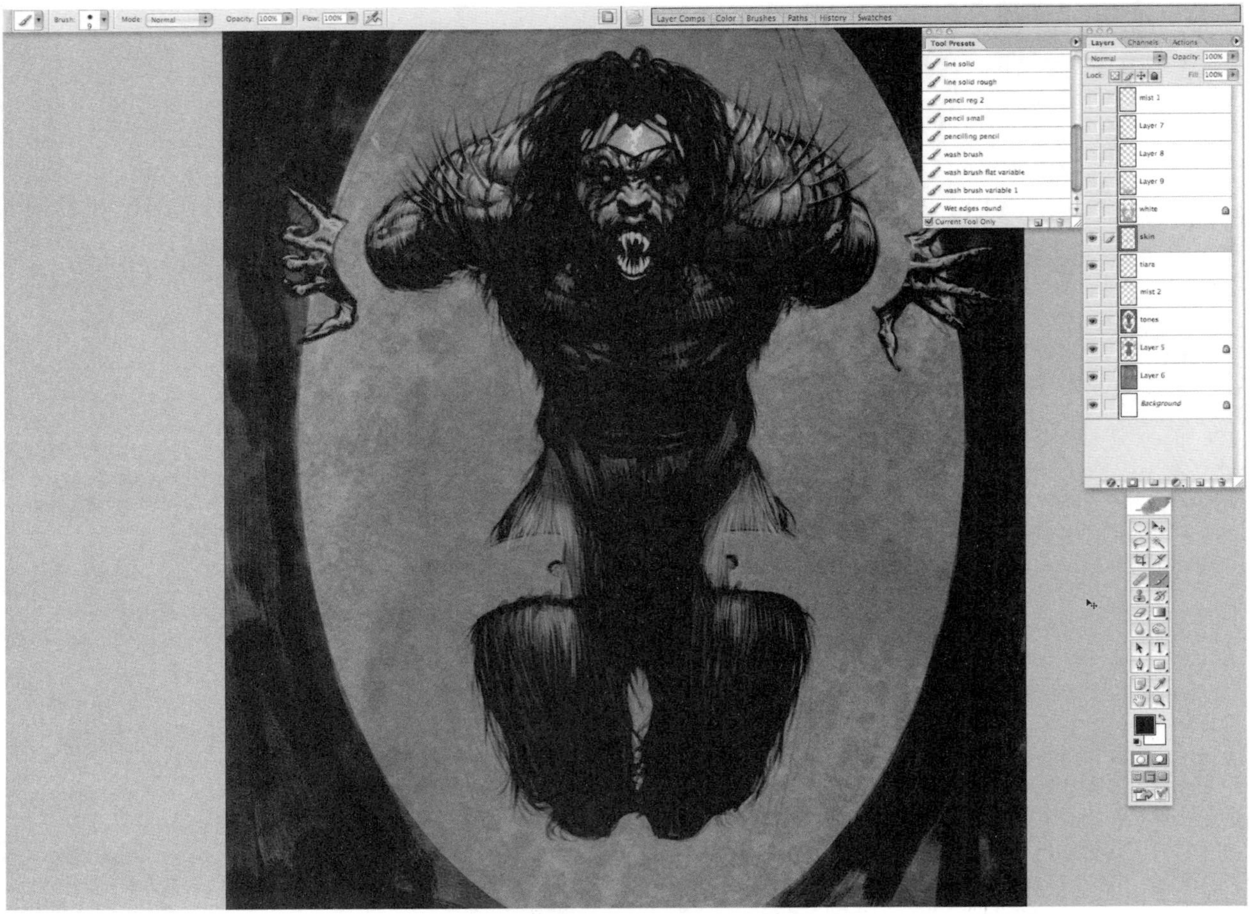
Brush:
Mode: Normal
Opacity: 100%
Flow: 100%
Layer Comps
Color
Brushes
Paths
History
Swatches
Tool Presets
line solid
line solid rough
pencil reg 2
pencil small
pencilling pencil
wash brush
wash brush flat variable
wash brush variable 1
Wet edges round
Current Tool Only
Layers
Channels
Actions
Normal
Opacity: 100%
Lock:
Fill: 100%
mist 1
Layer 7
Layer 8
Layer 9
white
skin
tiara
mist 2
tones
Layer 5
Layer 6
Background

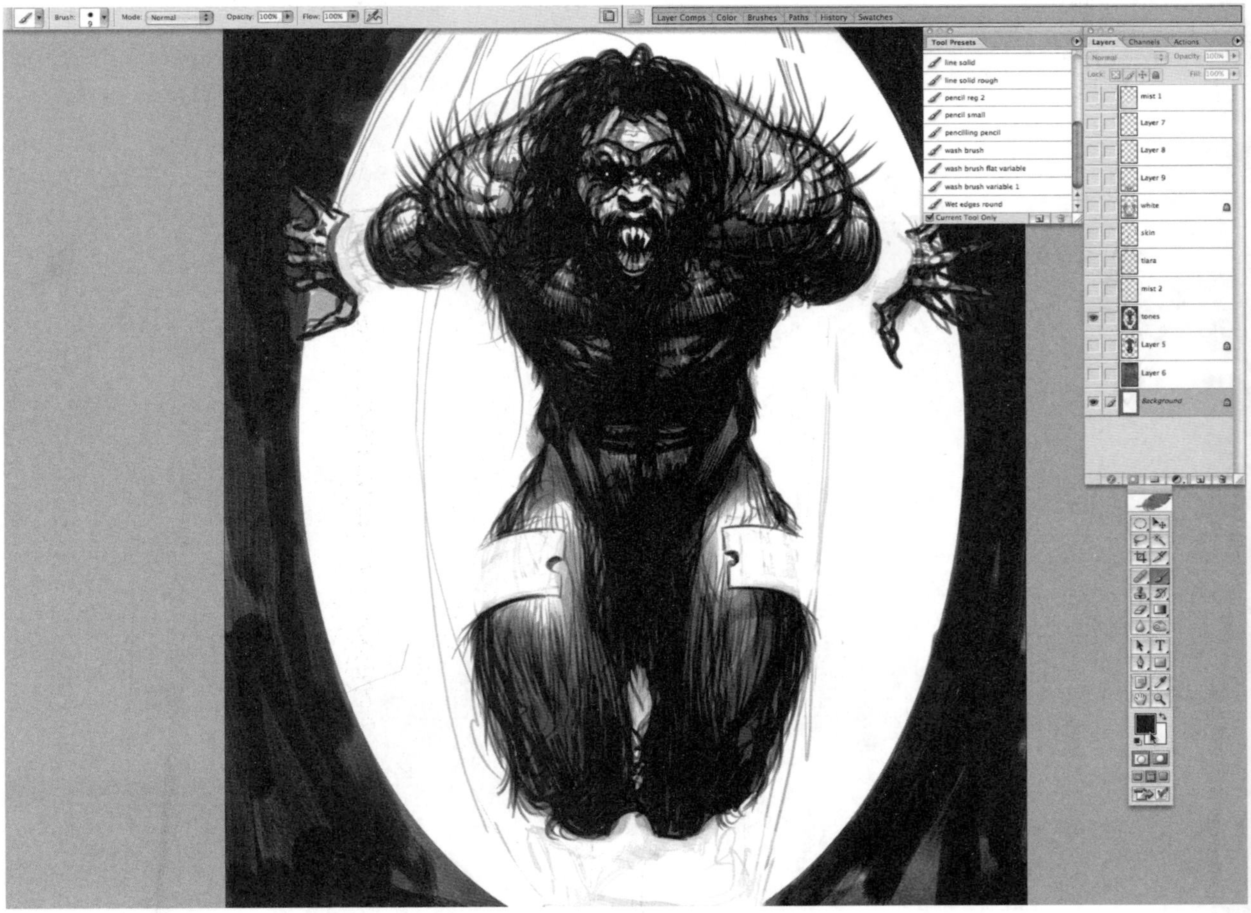
Brush:
Mode: Normal
Opacity: 100%
Flow: 100%
Layer Comps
Color
Brushes
Paths
History
Swatches
Tool Presets
line solid
line solid rough
pencil reg 2
pencil small
pencilling pencil
wash brush
wash brush flat variable
wash brush variable 1
Wet edges round
Current Tool Only
Layers
Channels
Actions
mist 1
Layer 7
Layer 8
Layer 9
white
skin
tiara
mist 2
tones
Layer 5
Layer 6
Background

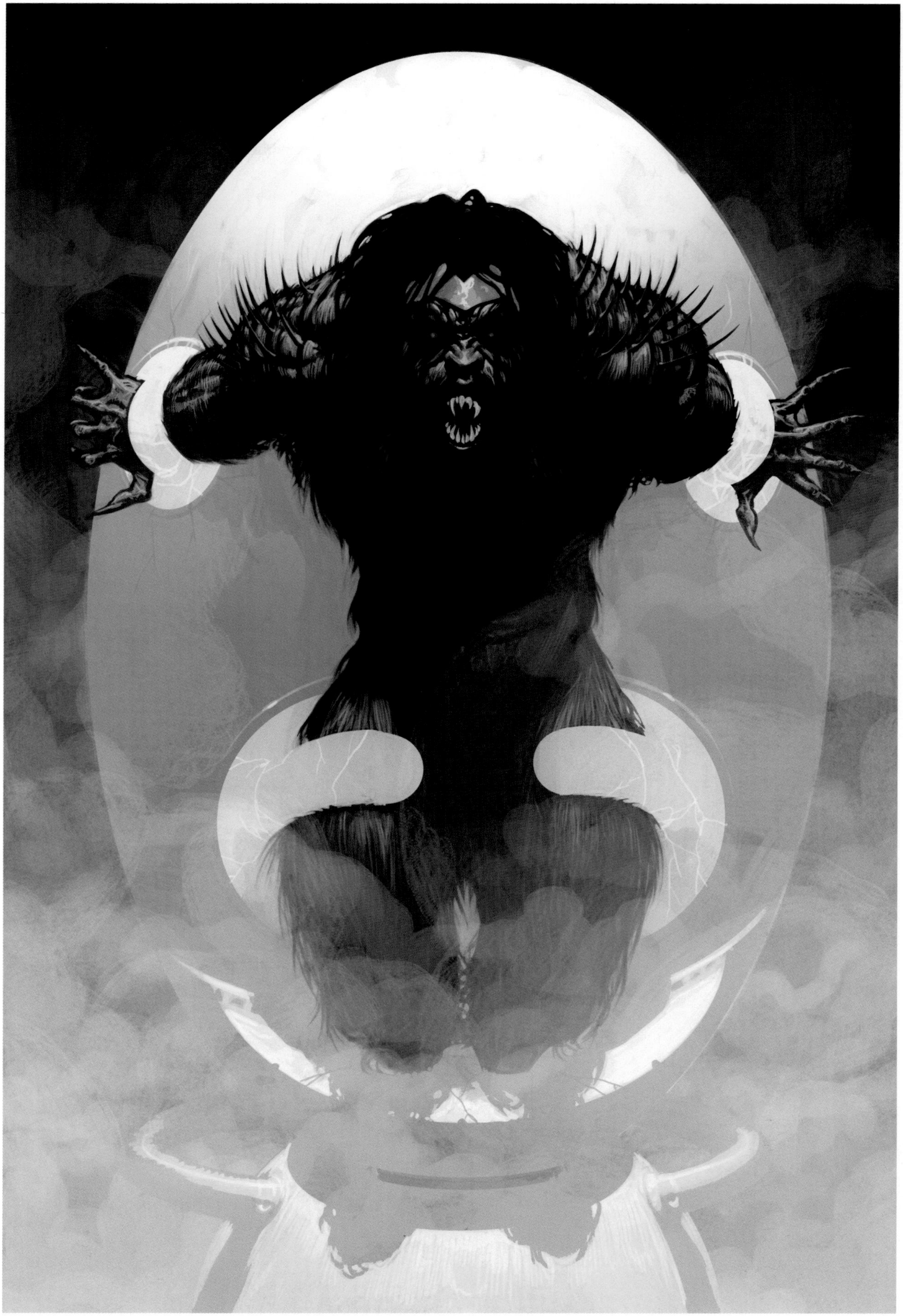

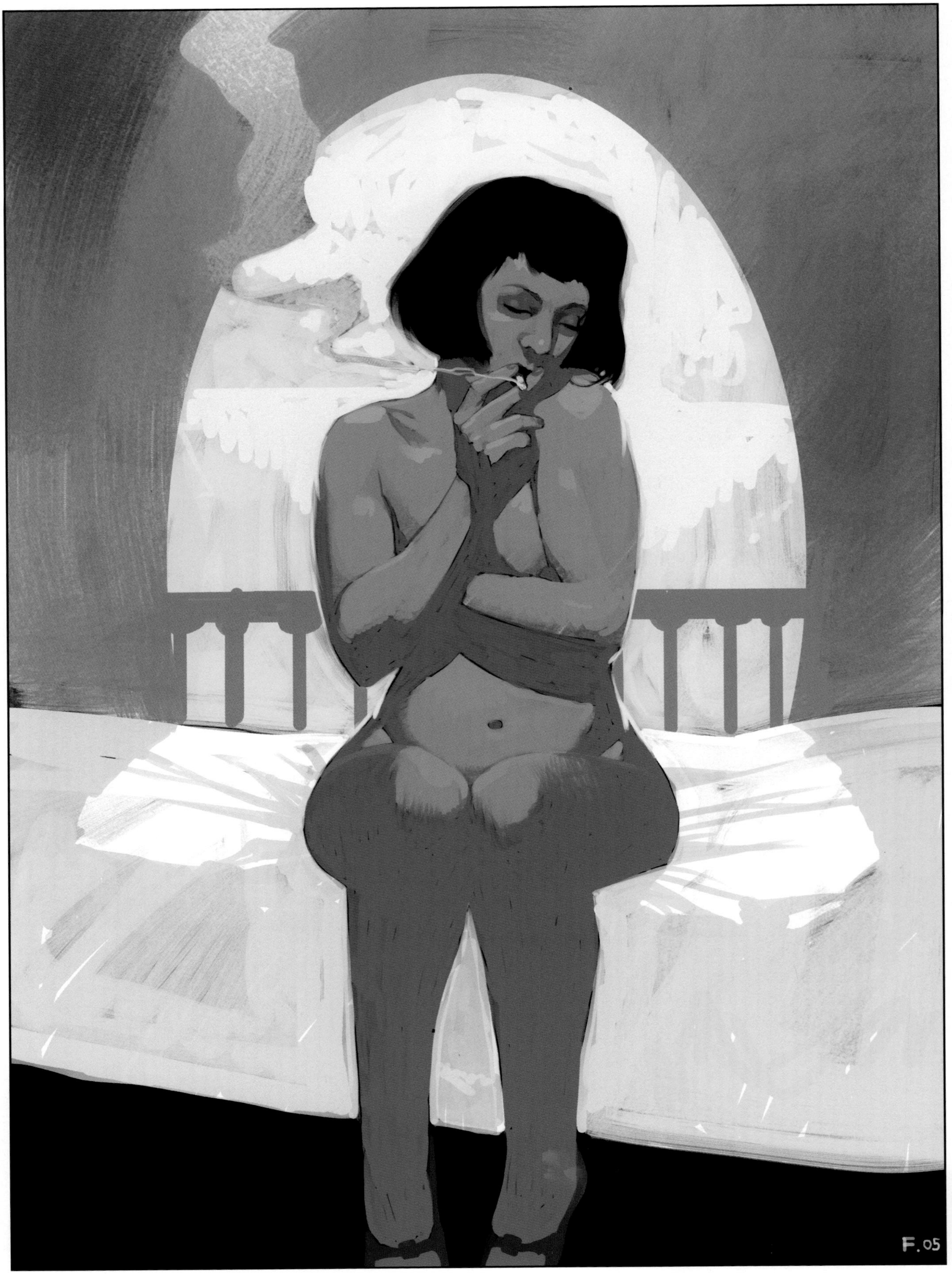
F.05

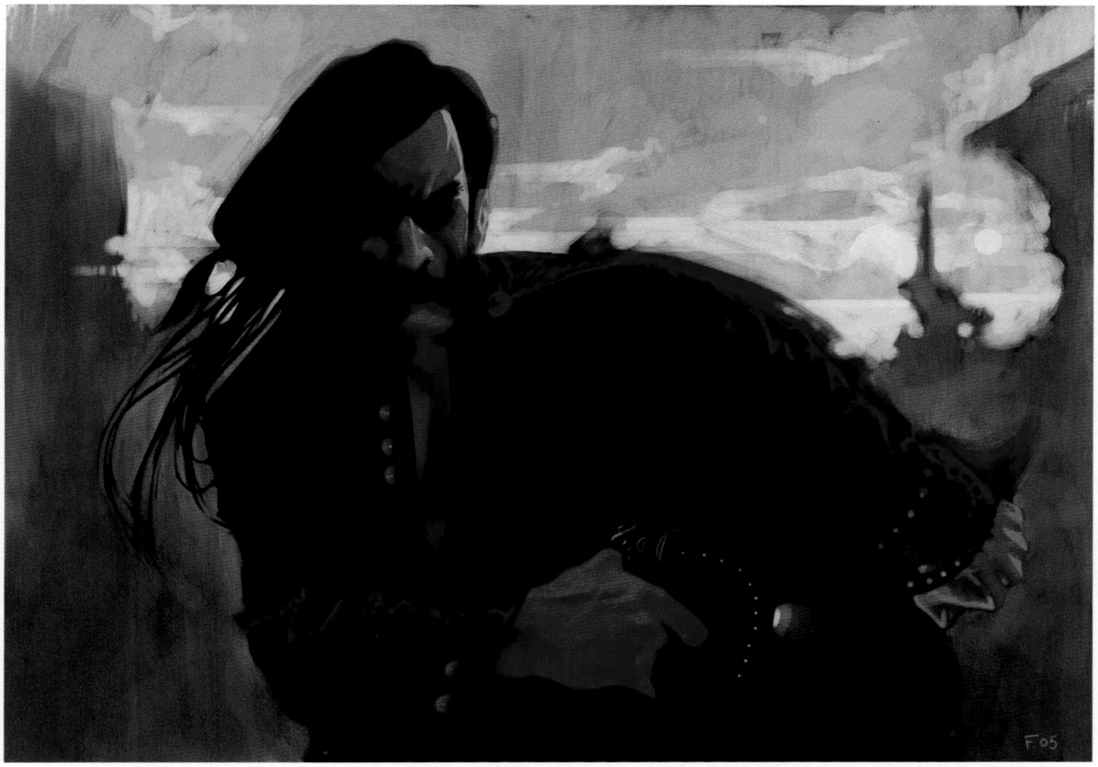
F05

Pages 94-95: Cover art for *Judge Dredd Versus Aliens: Incubus* #3.
Pages 96-97: Preliminary steps and final artwork for *Silent War* #1, page 22. The screen grabs show two layers of the process Frazer used to create the finished page. As you can see from the tool bars, Frazer uses several different custom brushes in his work and he works in a large number of layers in order to get the finished look he wants.

Previous Page: "The Smoker," 2005 digital illustration.
Above: "The Gunslinger," 2005 digital illustration.
Right: "Tongues," digital illustration.
Page 100: An Iron Man digital illustration, which Frazer did on his own and not as part of the *Iron Man: Inevitable* mini-series.
Page 101: Artwork for the cover of *Gutsville* #1.

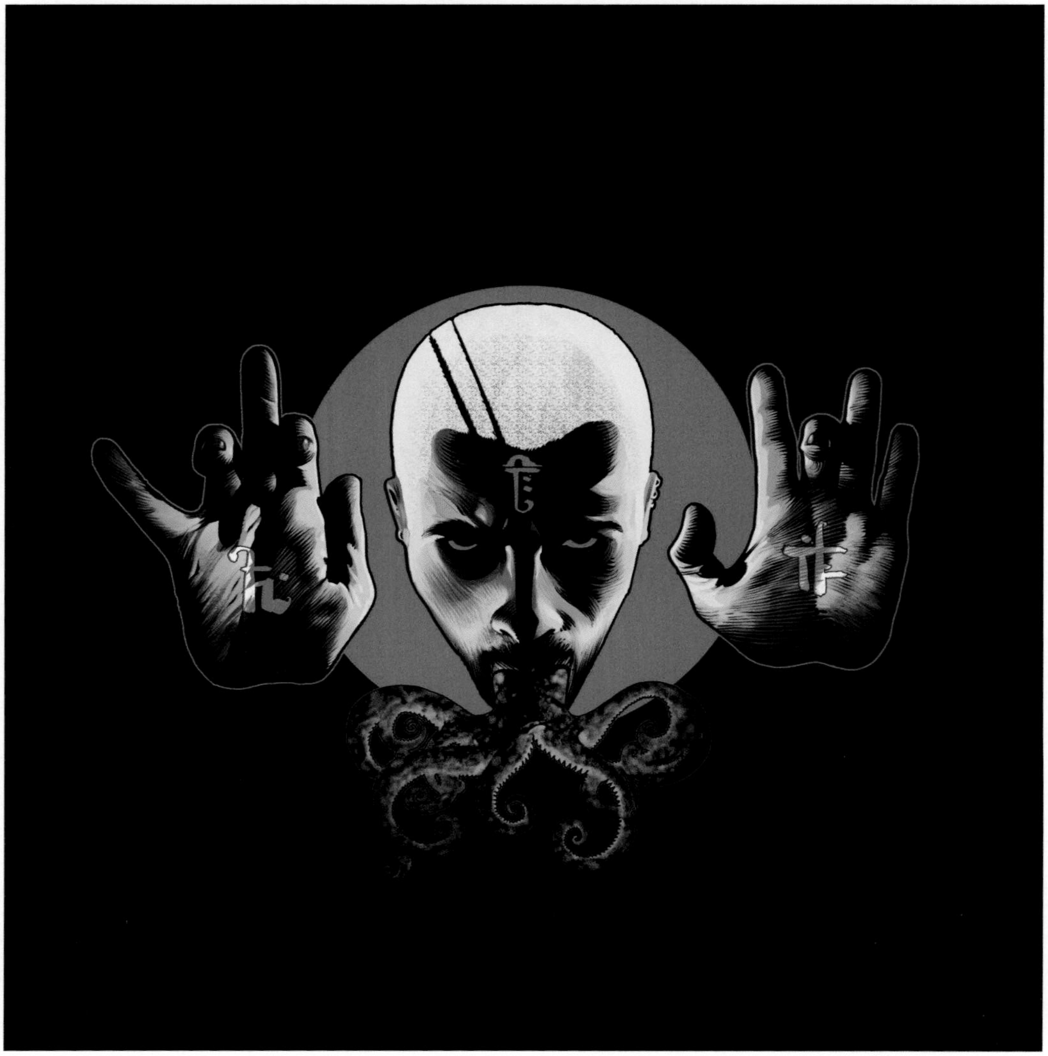

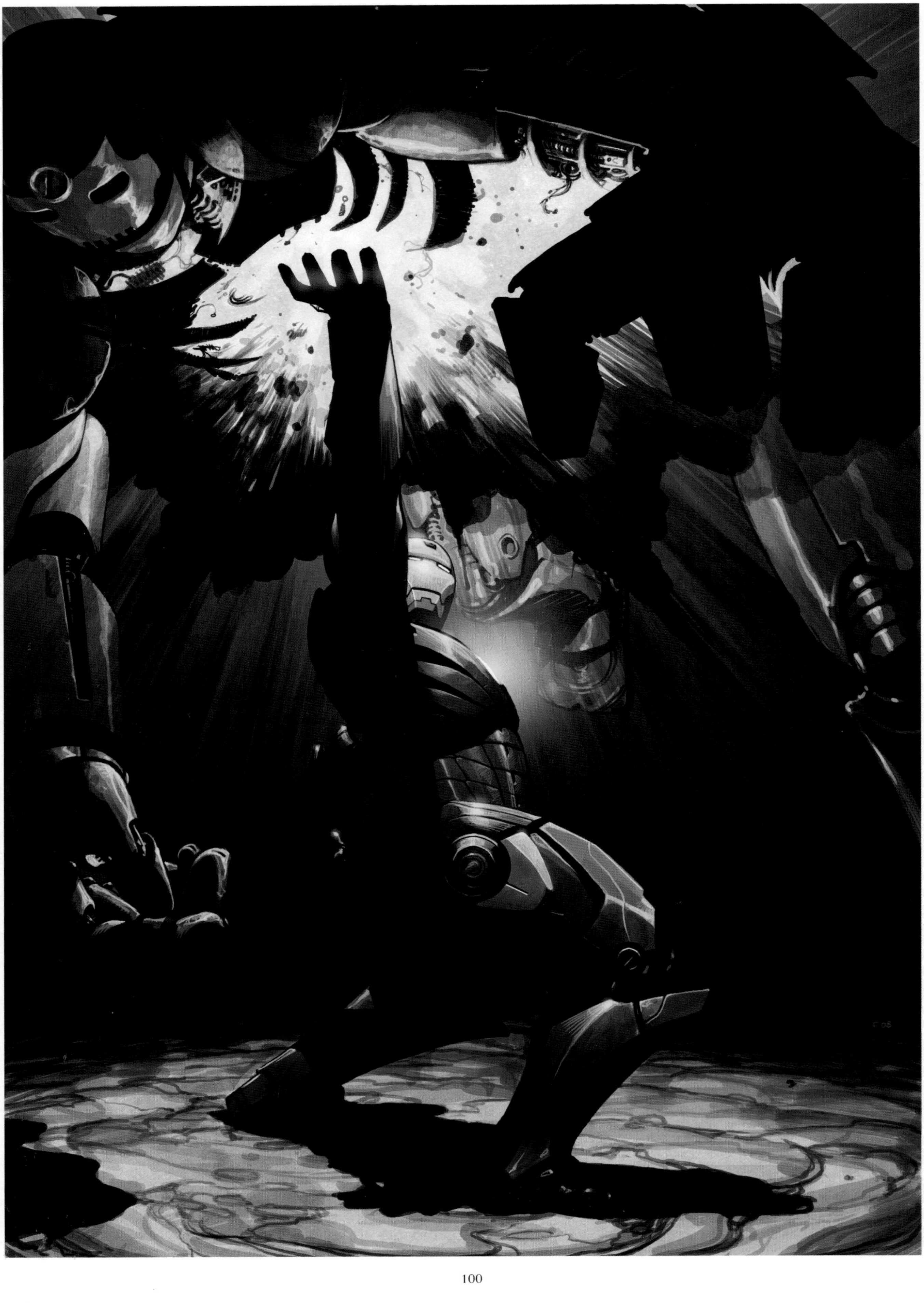

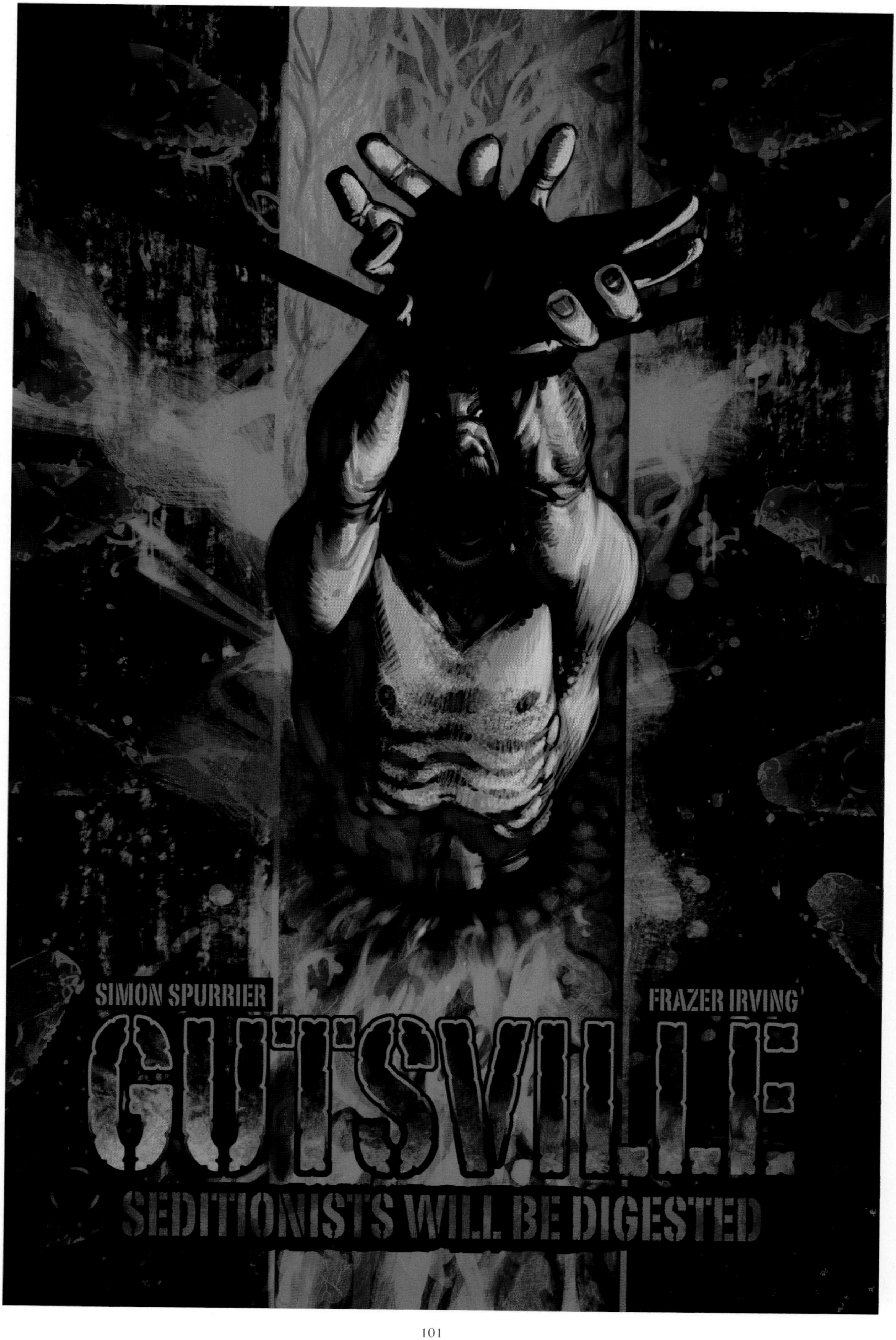
SIMON SPURRIER
FRAZER IRVING
GUTSVILLE
SEDITIONISTS WILL BE DIGESTED

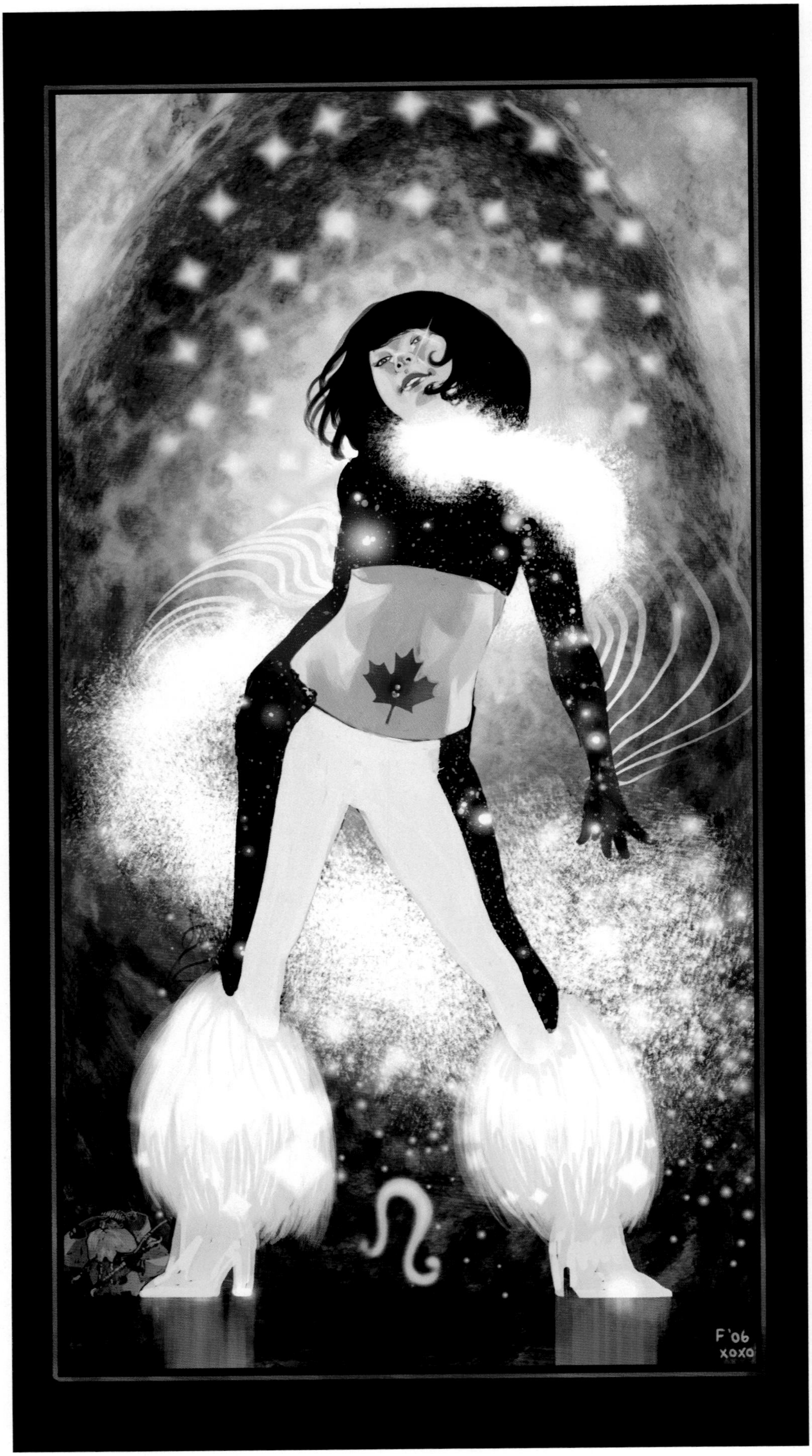
F'06
xoxo

"I see all the weaknesses in every image I draw, and I'm constantly chipping away at that massive pile of errors. Neal Adams said that your style is whatever you draw 'wrong,' and I go along with that totally. Richard Corben draws 'wrong' in many ways, but that is what makes his art distinctive. Kirby would draw vastly exaggerated perspectives; Corben draws distorted anatomy; I use very unrealistic colors. My color work is utterly "wrong," yet it's also the most emotive and immediate aspect of my art. These things are wrong in the sense that they defy the reality we observe, and thus they become the aspects that stand out and give the art character."

— Frazer Irving

Left: Oh, Canada! This digital illo was based on photo reference of Canadian artist, Fiona Staples.
Next Page: Page 8 of *Batman and Robin* #14. The sickly green backlighting of the drug-addled crowd contrasting with the fuschia primary lighting adds to the sense of horror and impending violence. It may not be "realistic," but it is very effective.
Page 104: A far-out page from "Storming Heaven."
Page 105: Pencils for "Storming Heaven."

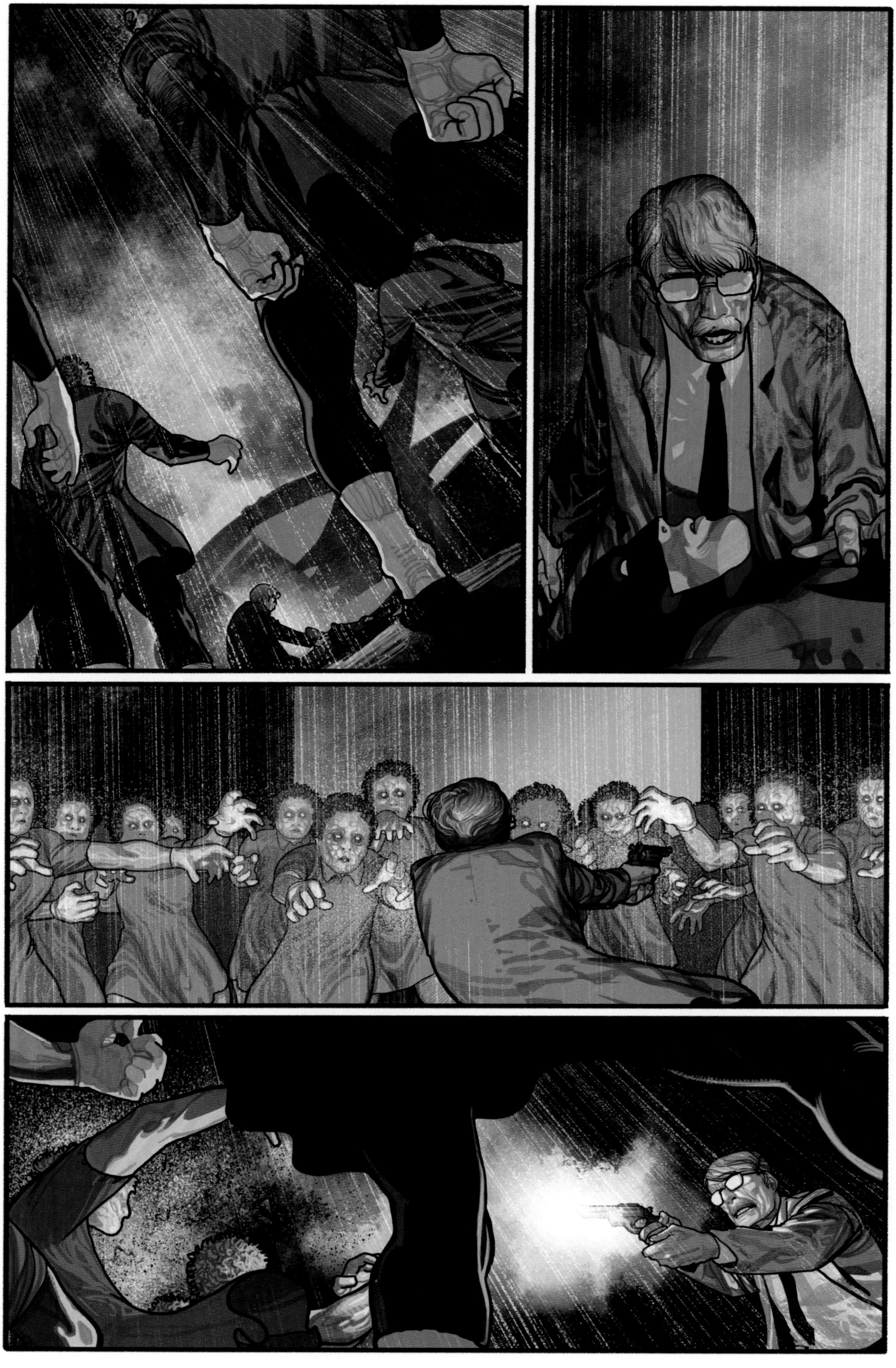

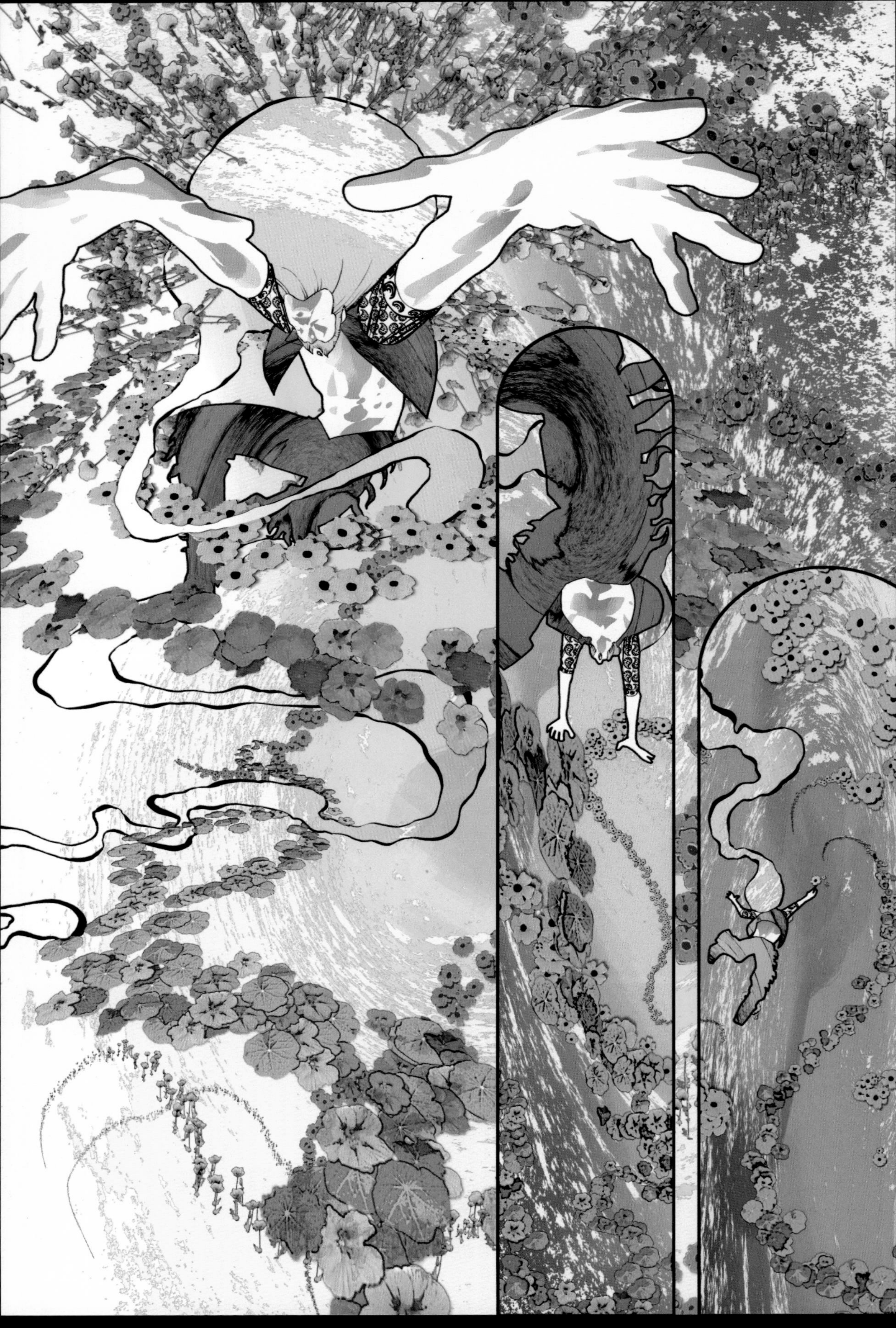

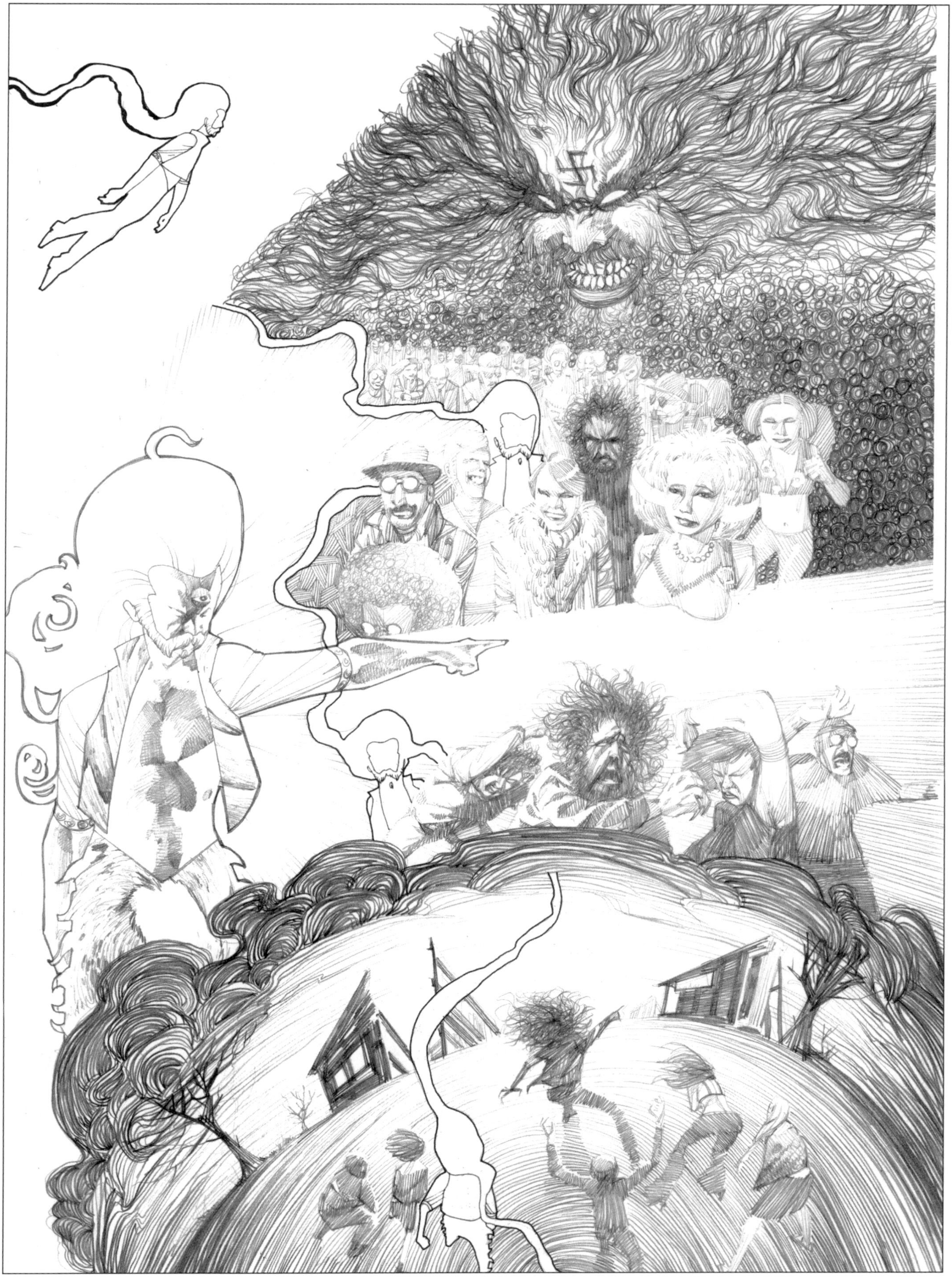

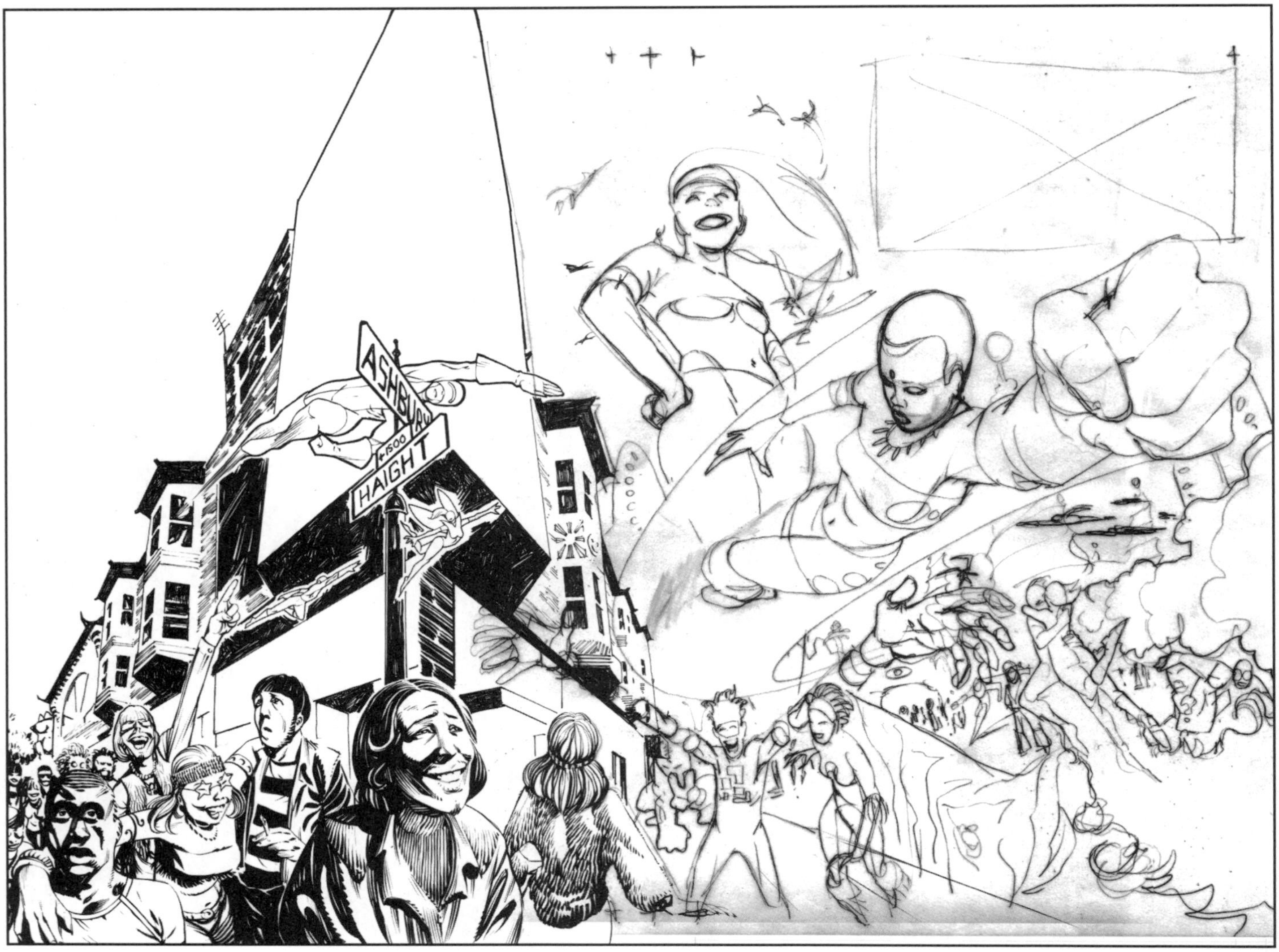
HAIGHT

This Page: Partially inked two-page spread for "Storming Heaven." Frazer inked the main figure on a separate sheet of paper.
Next Page: Pencils for "Storming Heaven."
Pages 108-109: Finished artwork for the black-&-white "Judge Death" strip in *2000 AD*.
Page 110-111: Digital pencils and traditional inks for the opening page of *Seven Soldiers: Klarion the Witch Boy* #2.

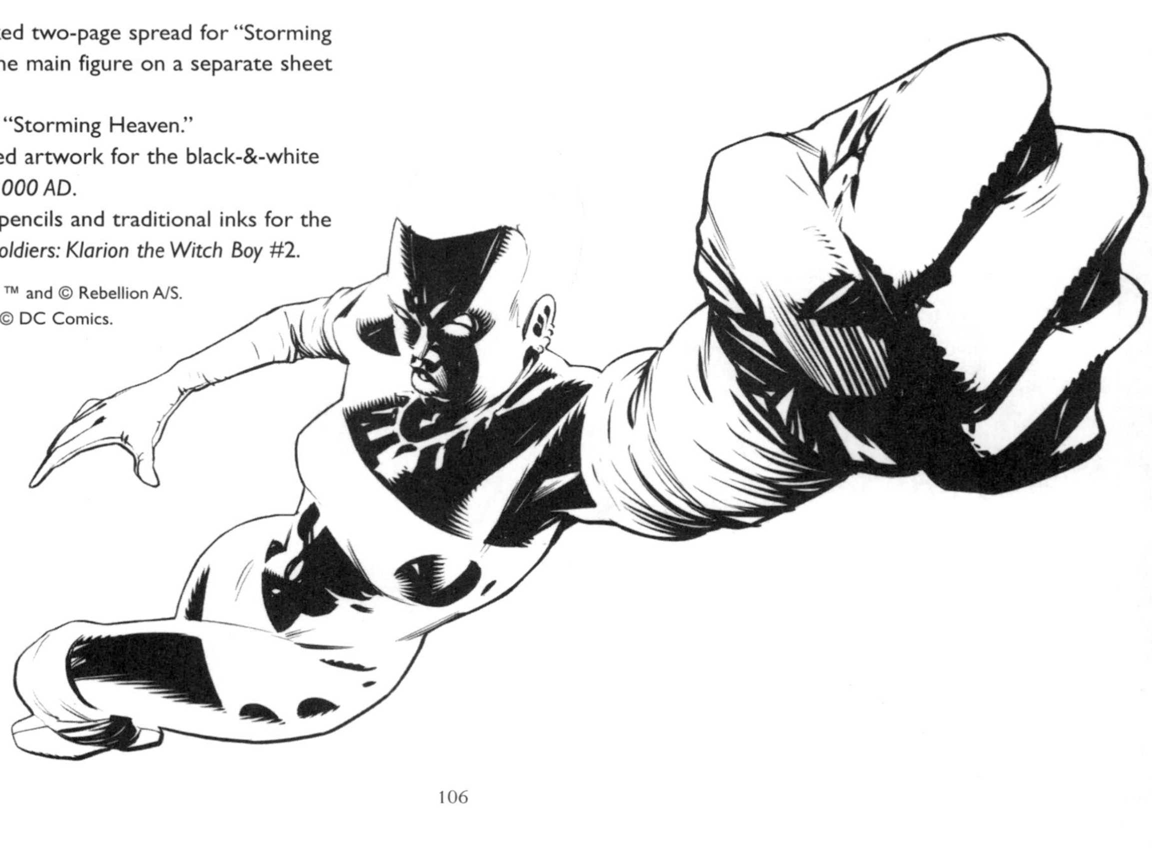

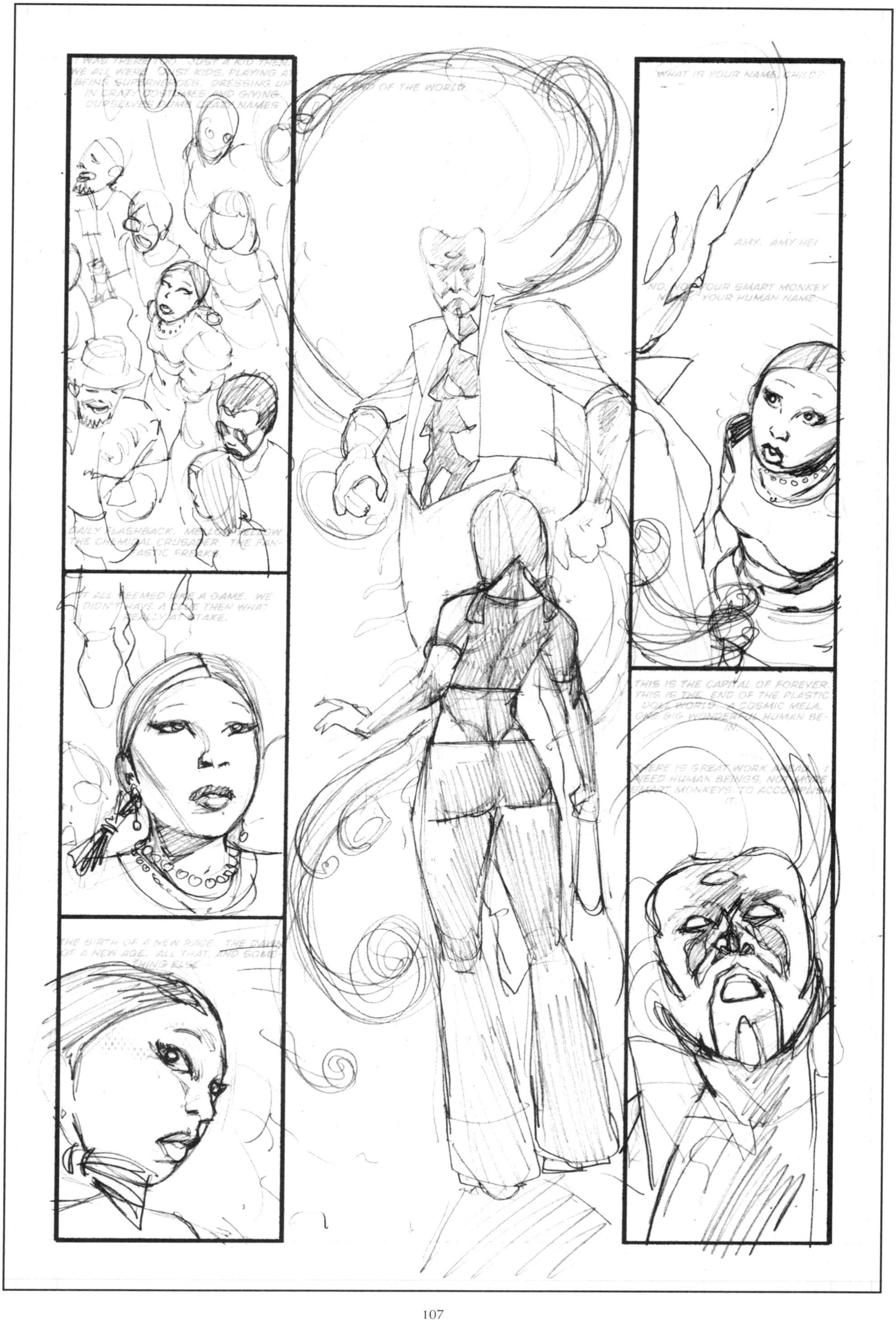
I WAS THERE TOO. JUST A KID THEN.
WE ALL WERE. JUST KIDS, PLAYING AT BEING SUPERHEROES. DRESSING UP IN CRAZY COSTUMES AND GIVING OURSELVES SOME CRAZY NAMES
DAILY FLASHBACK. MELLOW YELLOW. THE CHEMICAL CRUSADER. THE FANTASTIC FREAKS.
IT ALL SEEMED LIKE A GAME. WE DIDN'T HAVE A CLUE THEN WHAT REALLY AT STAKE.
THE BIRTH OF A NEW RACE. THE DAWN OF A NEW AGE. ALL THAT, AND SOMETHING ELSE
OF THE WORLD.
WHAT IS YOUR NAME, CHILD?
AMY. AMY HEI
NO, NOT YOUR SMART MONKEY NAME. YOUR HUMAN NAME.
THIS IS THE CAPITAL OF FOREVER. THIS IS THE END OF THE PLASTIC DOLL WORLD. A COSMIC MELA, ONE BIG WONDERFUL HUMAN BE-IN.
THERE IS GREAT WORK AHEAD. I NEED HUMAN BEINGS, NOT MORE SMART MONKEYS TO ACCOMPLISH IT.

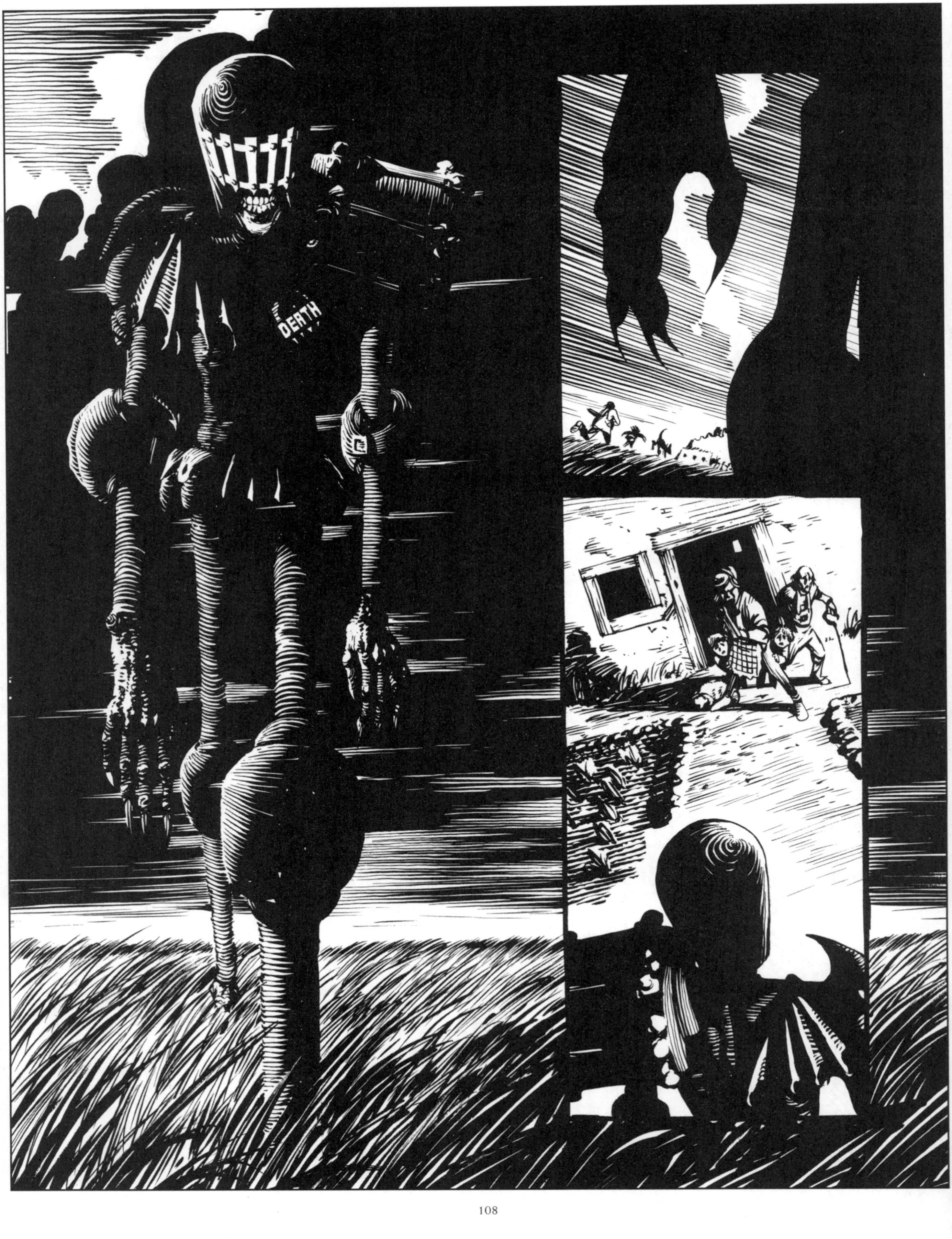
DEATH

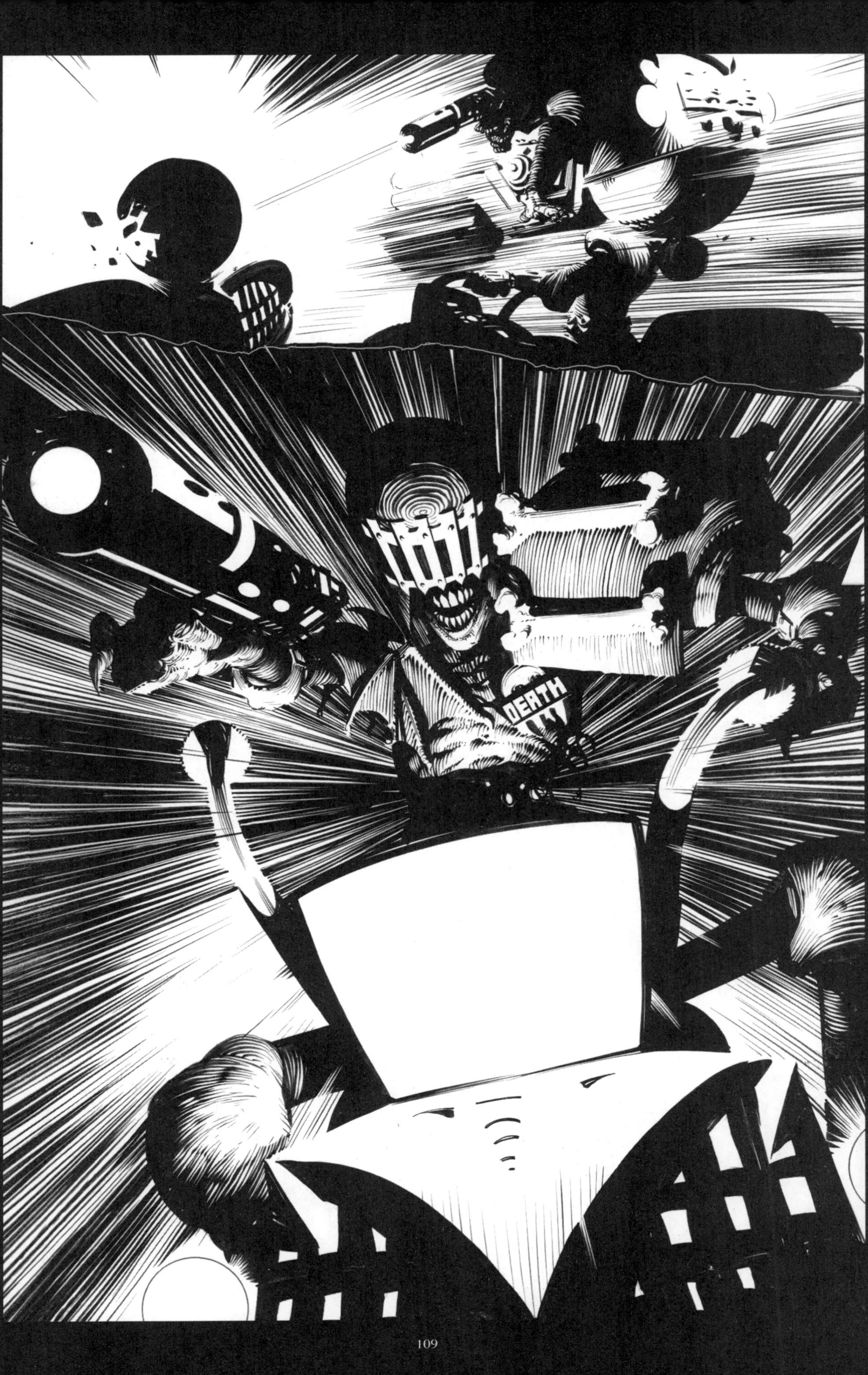
DEATH

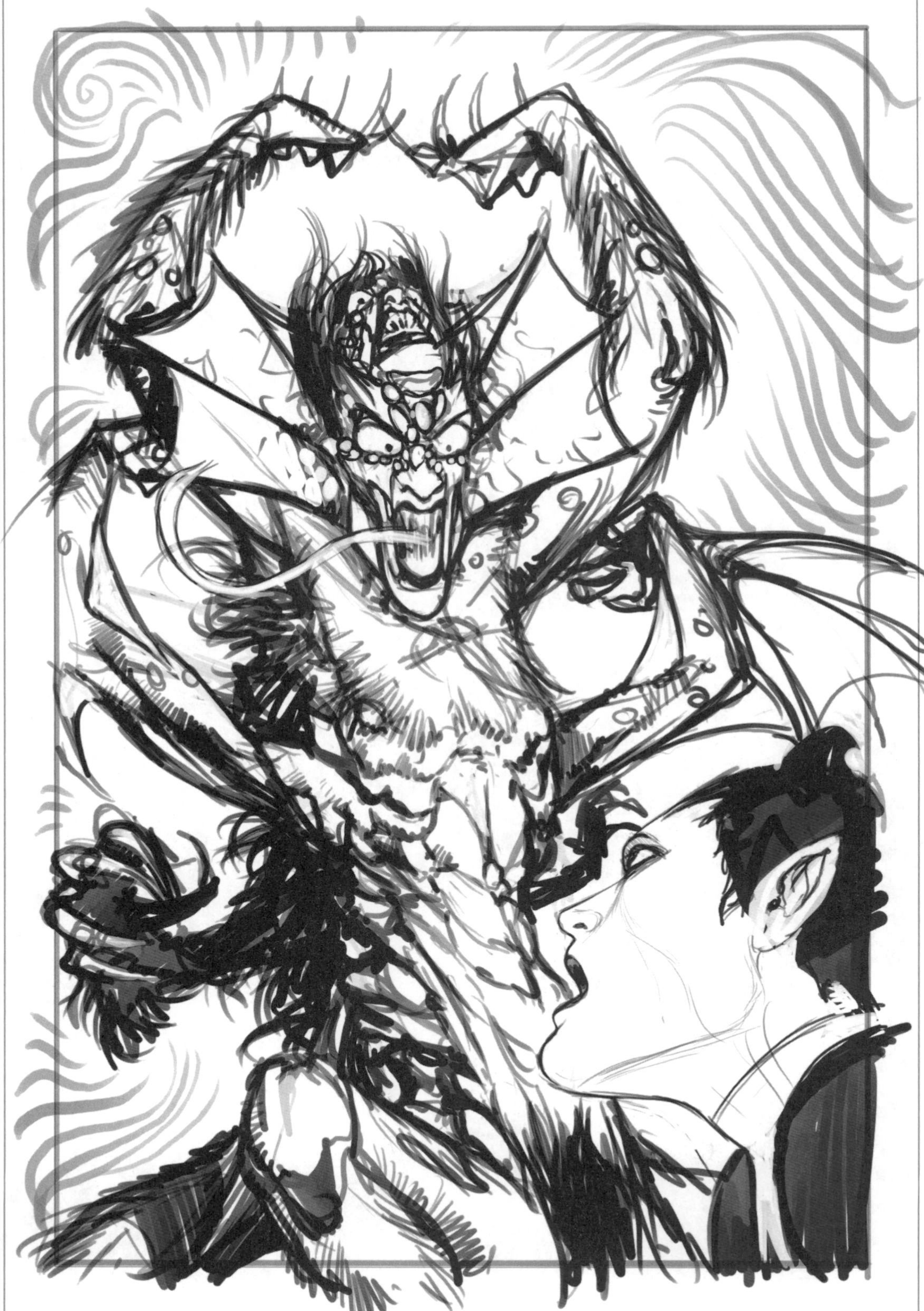

F. IRVING F. IRVING 1
SEVEN SOLDIERS: KLARION 2

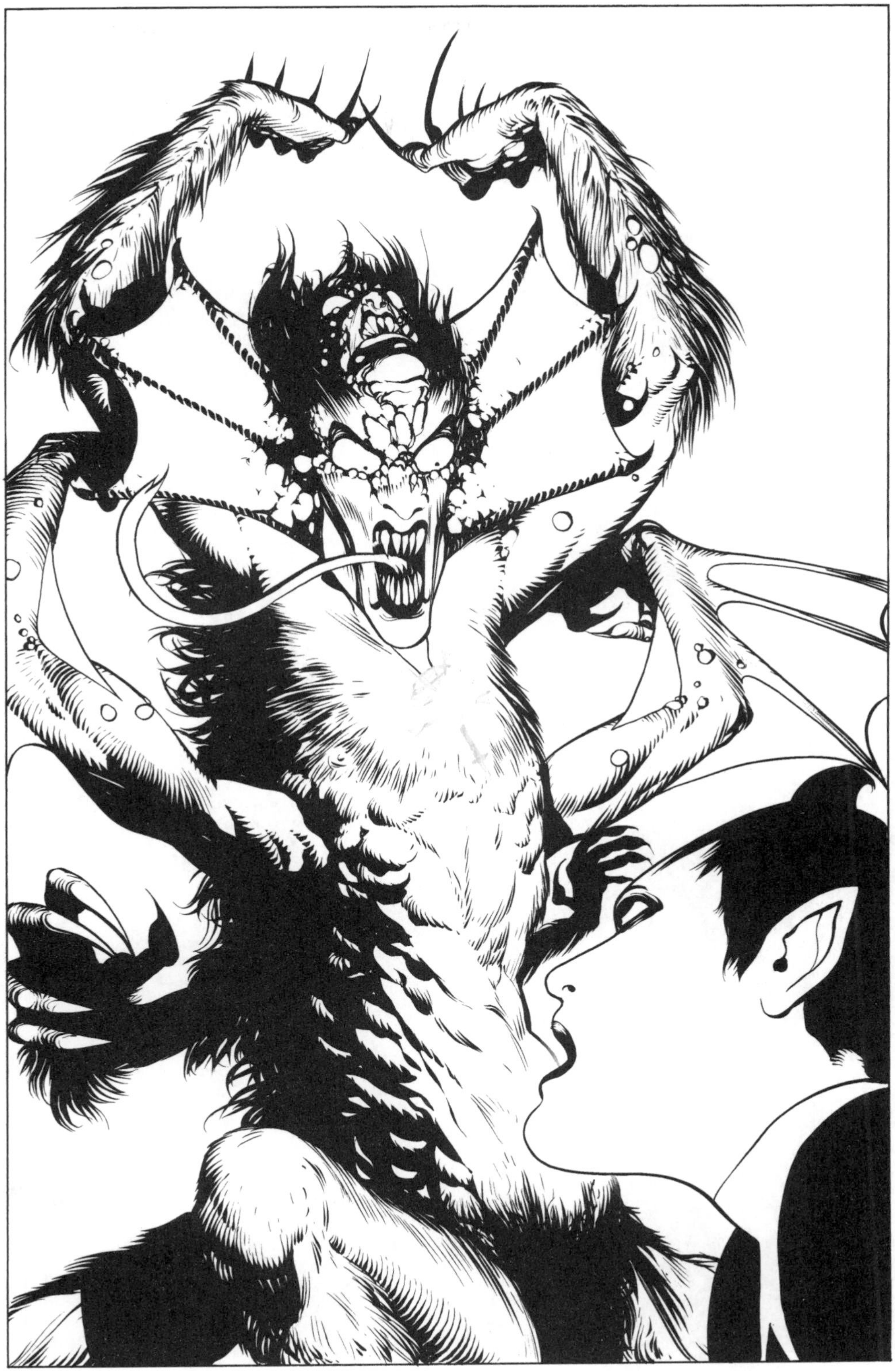

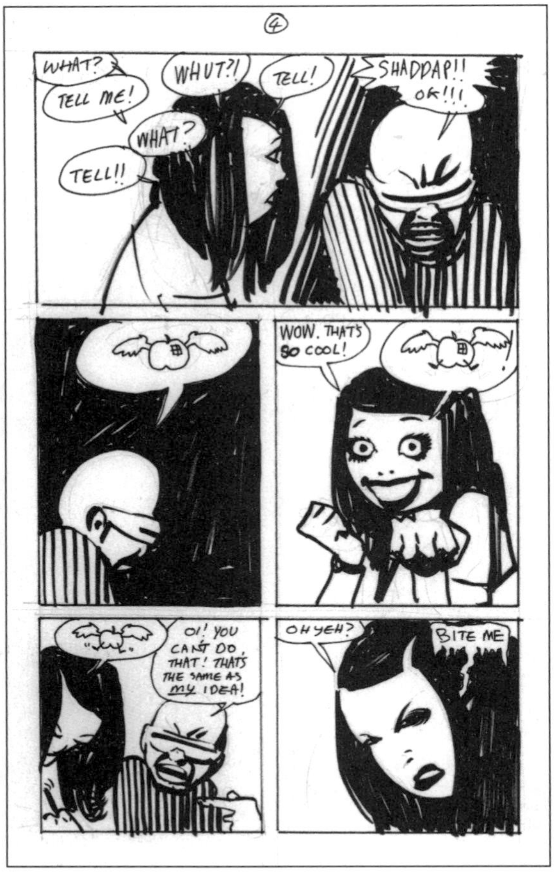
4
WHAT?
TELL ME!
WHUT?!
TELL!
WHAT?
TELL!!
SHADDAP!! OK!!!
WOW. THAT'S SO COOL!
OI! YOU CAN'T DO THAT! THAT'S THE SAME AS MY IDEA!
OH YEH?
BITE ME

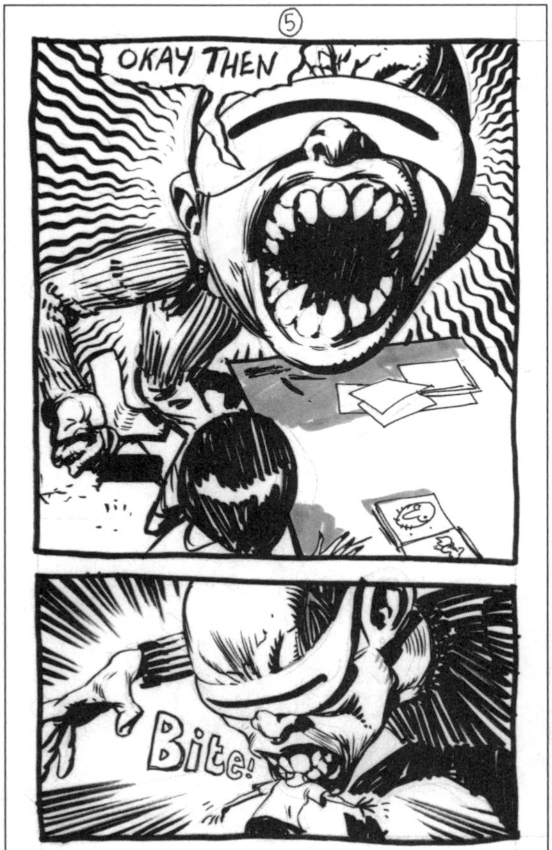
5
OKAY THEN
Bite!

Left and Below: Pages from "Bad Gramma," Frazer's 24-page story done over 15 hours during 2006's 24-Hour Comic Book Day at Comic-Kazi in Calgary, Alberta. Why Canada? Frazer responds, "I went to Canada because, once again, I was chasing my libido. The comic shop that hosted the event was close to where I was staying and the girl I was wooing worked there... It was chaos, because I had no idea what I was doing with this comic, and I was also using brushes and ink, which isn't good for high-speed art. I mean, I can do 24 pages of layouts in a day, but that's not the same, plus it's a lot of very hard work which leaves me depleted for ages afterwards... I was making it up from page to page, trying to do it *Lost* style, and I got lost. The pencil stuff was because the pages up 'til then sucked, and I was the only professional in the shop, so I sort of felt pressure to perform."

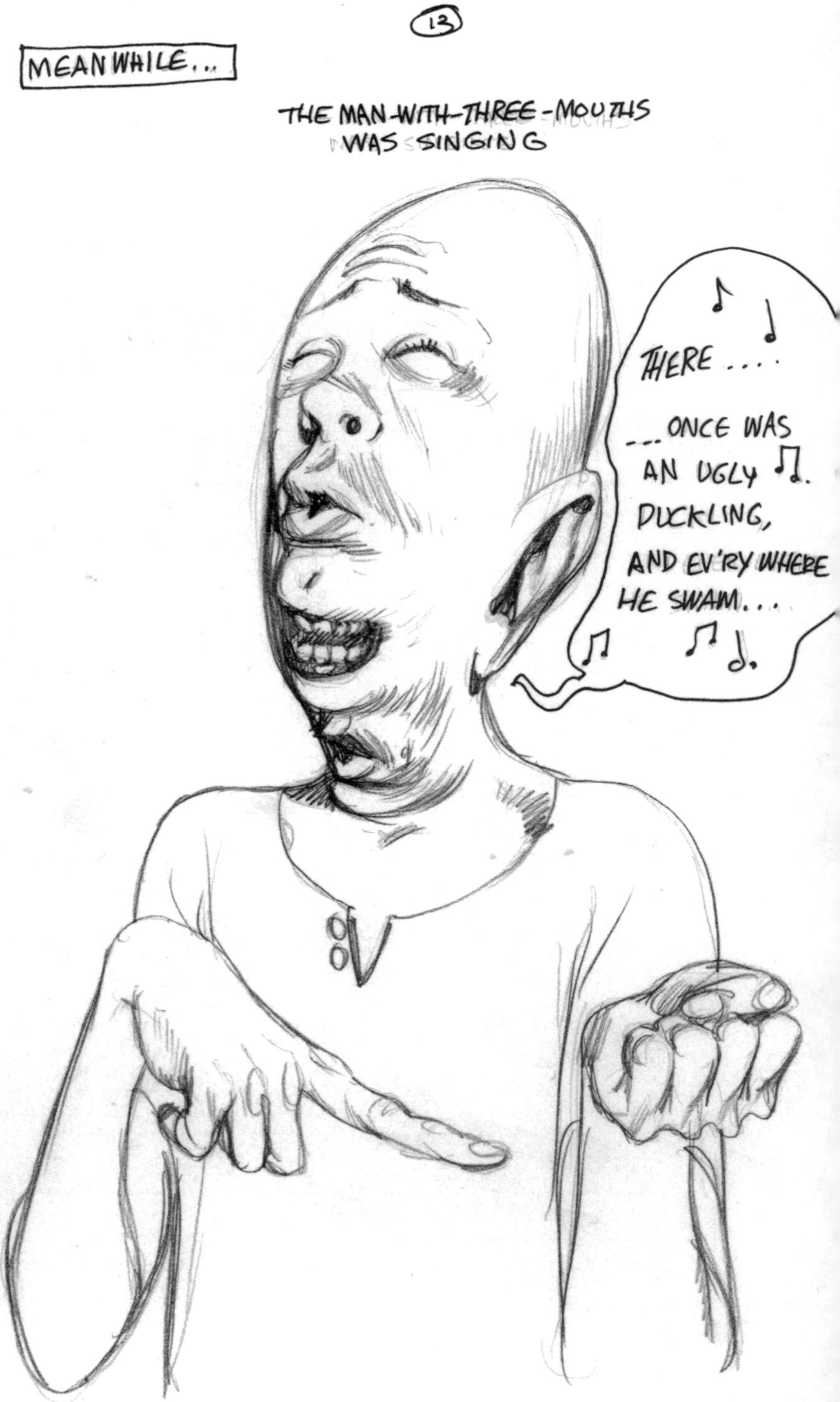
13
MEANWHILE...
THE MAN-WITH-THREE-MOUTHS WAS SINGING
THERE....
...ONCE WAS AN UGLY DUCKLING, AND EV'RY WHERE HE SWAM...

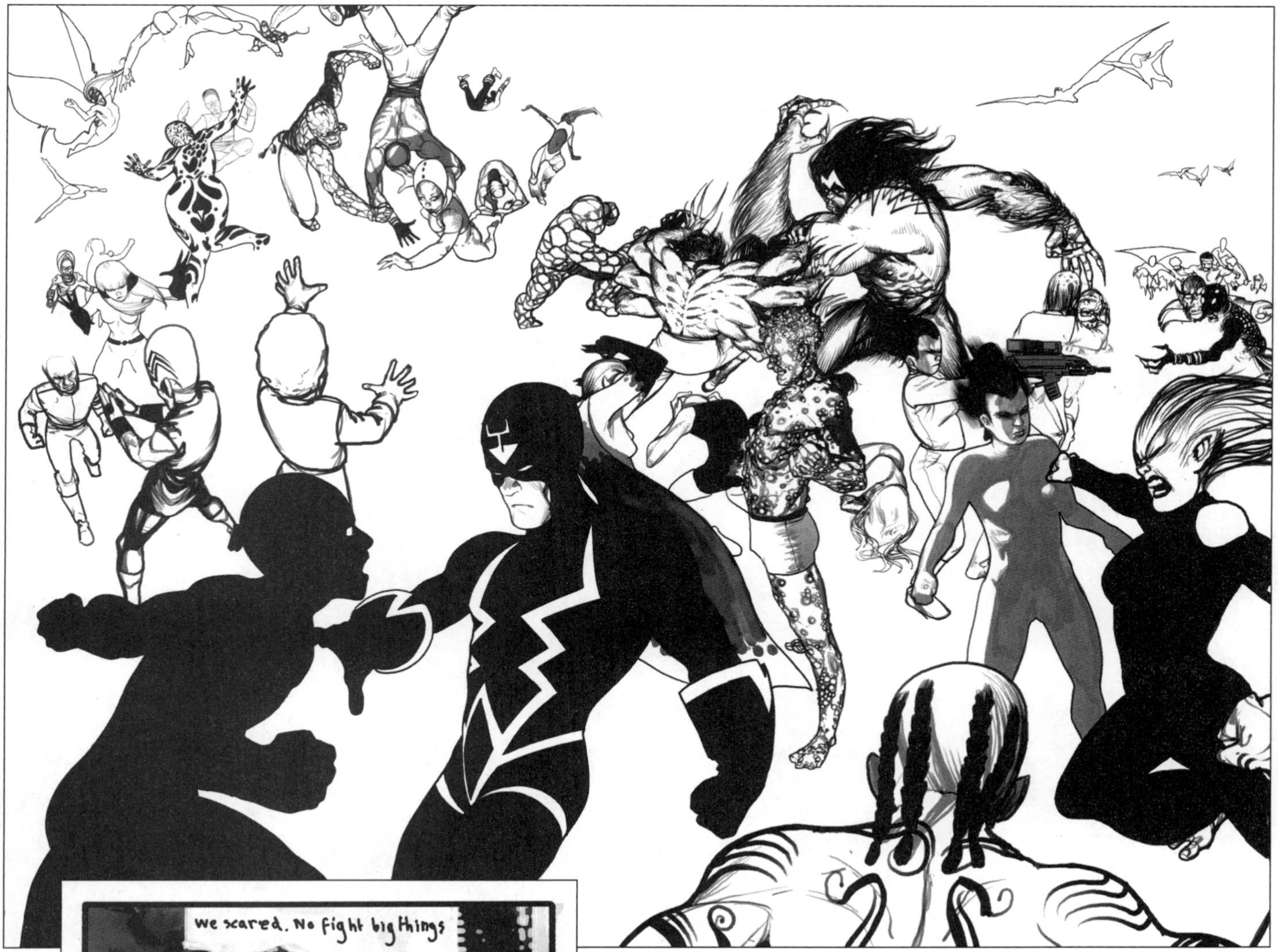

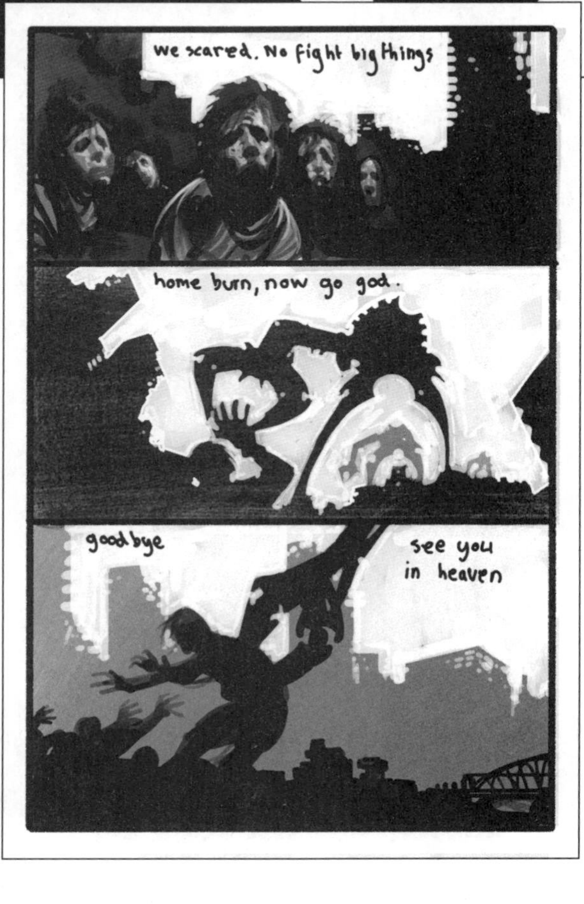

we scared. No fight big things
home burn, now go god.
goodbye
see you in heaven

Above: Inks for a double-page spread for *Silent War* #6.
Left: The opening page of "8 Green Bottles," Frazer's 2007 entry for 24-Hour Comic Book Day. This time around, Frazer was in Edmonton, Alberta, at Happy Harbor Comics: "I had a small, portable Wacom tablet and my laptop. I made sure to plan the story more in advance instead of winging it. I could draw faster, and I could also see the pages at a glance in the Finder, but the basic improvement this time was planning. I had become a *Lost* fan and was at that time very into story structures, and once you have that the rest of the imagery flows a lot better. I was pleased with the way the pictures and the text complemented each other, instead of restating the content, and I think that had a bit to do with the fact I could revise the text at any point, which is a digital boon.
Pages 114: *Gutsville* #3, page 18. Frazer is pitch-perfect with the poses and facial expressions.
Page 115: Page 19 of the yet to be published *Gutsville* #4. Here, Emelia's eyes tell the story.

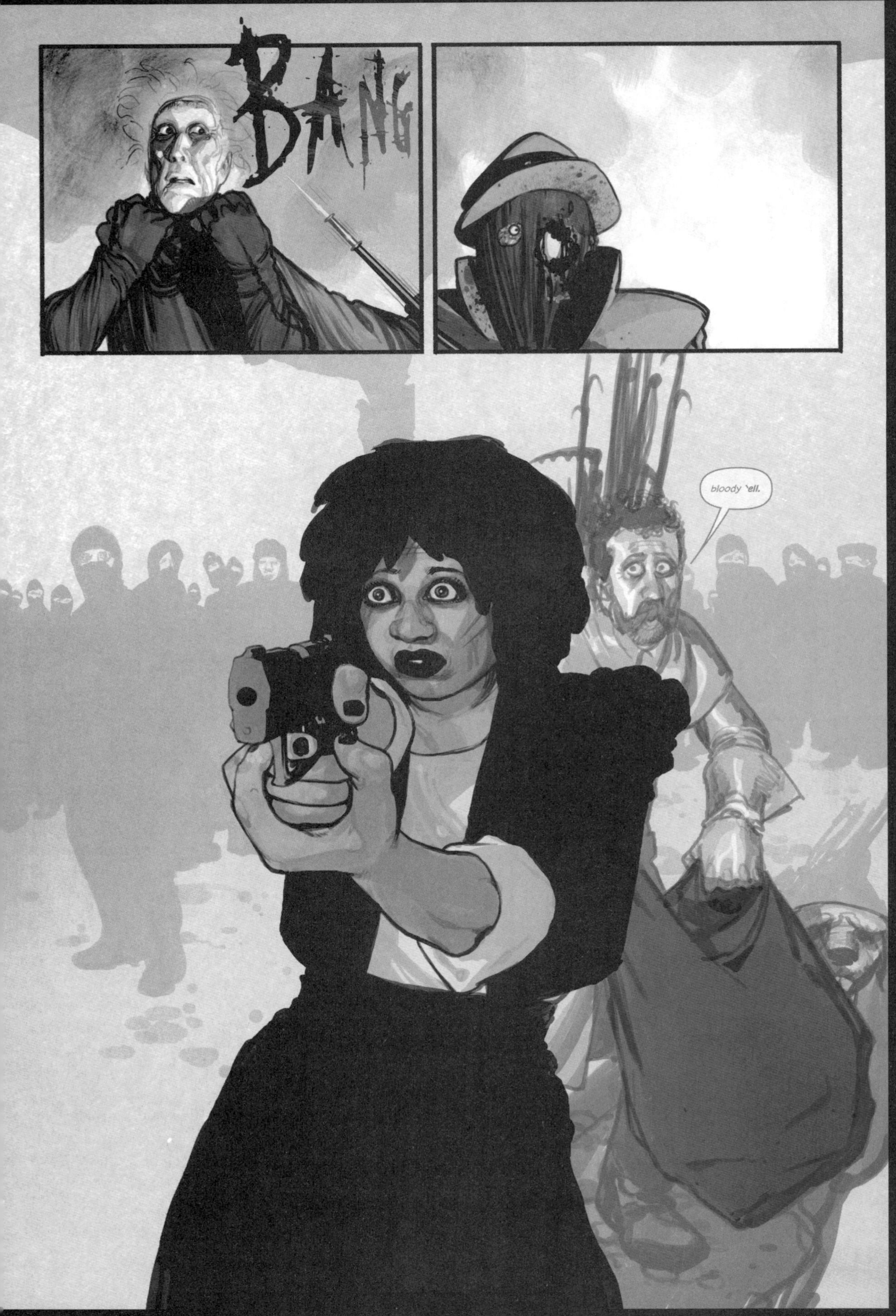
BANG
bloody 'ell.

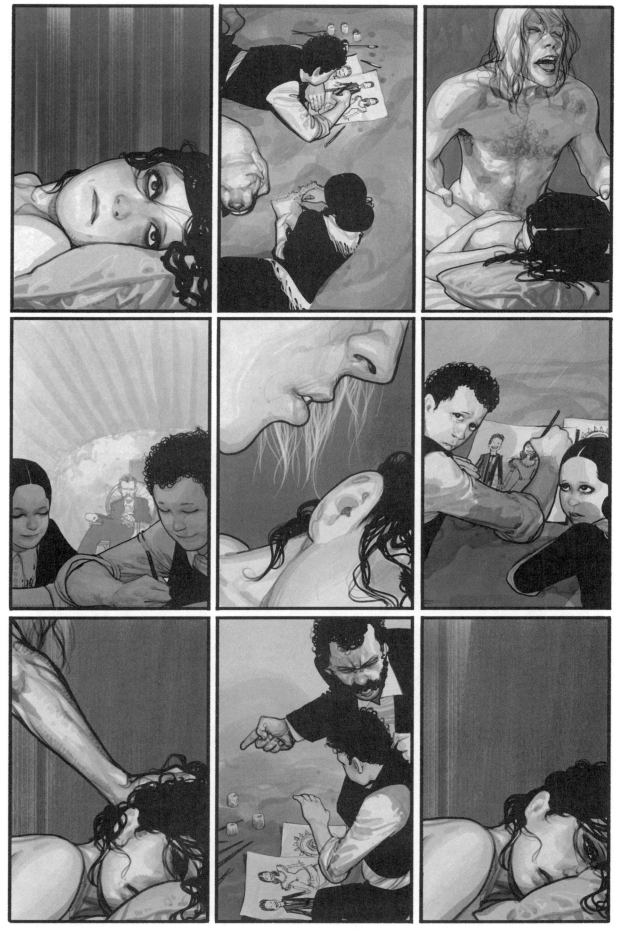

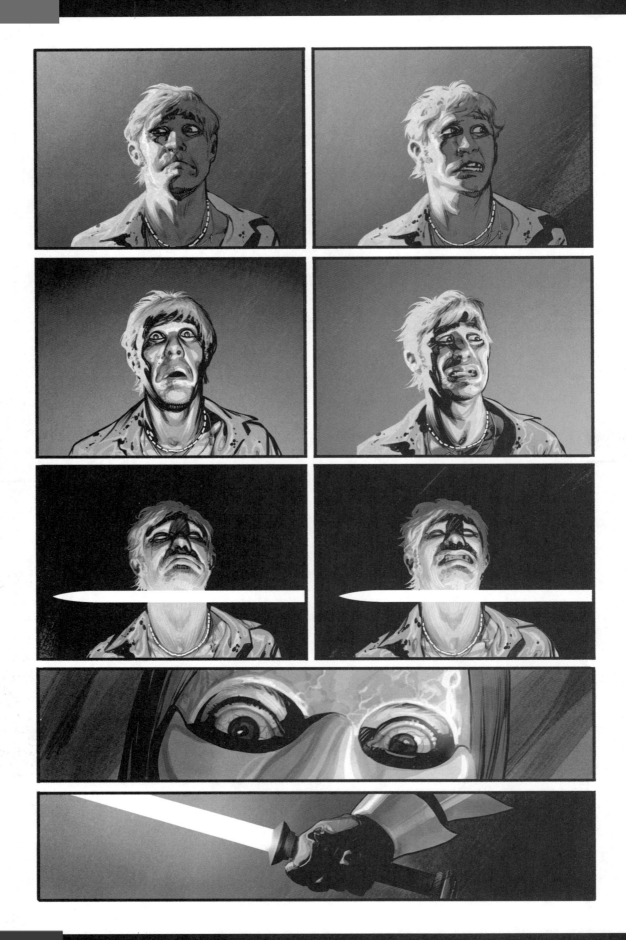

Previous Page: Frazer's gray tones for the opening page of *Azrael: Death's Dark Knight* #1.
Below: Gray tones for the money shot in *Batman: The Return of Bruce Wayne* #2.

Right: That's Frazer on the far right playing bass with his band, Atom Heart Brothers.

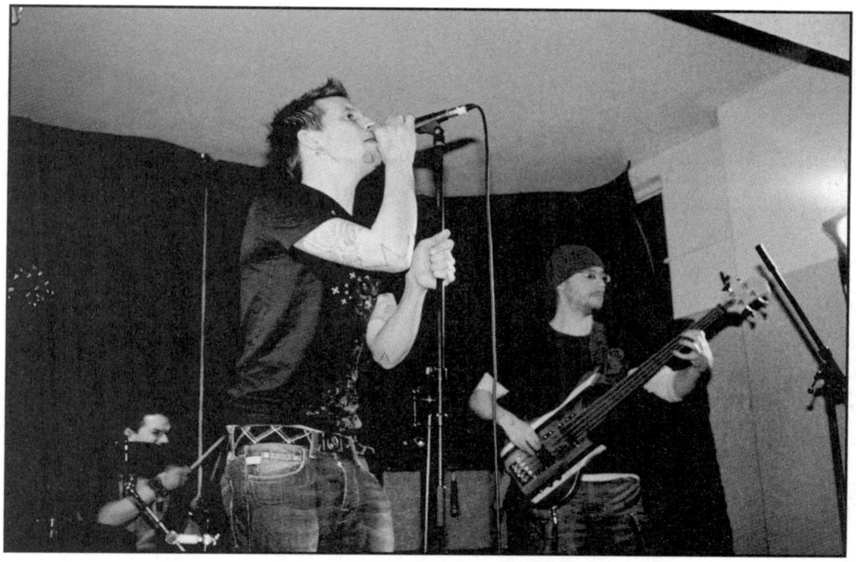

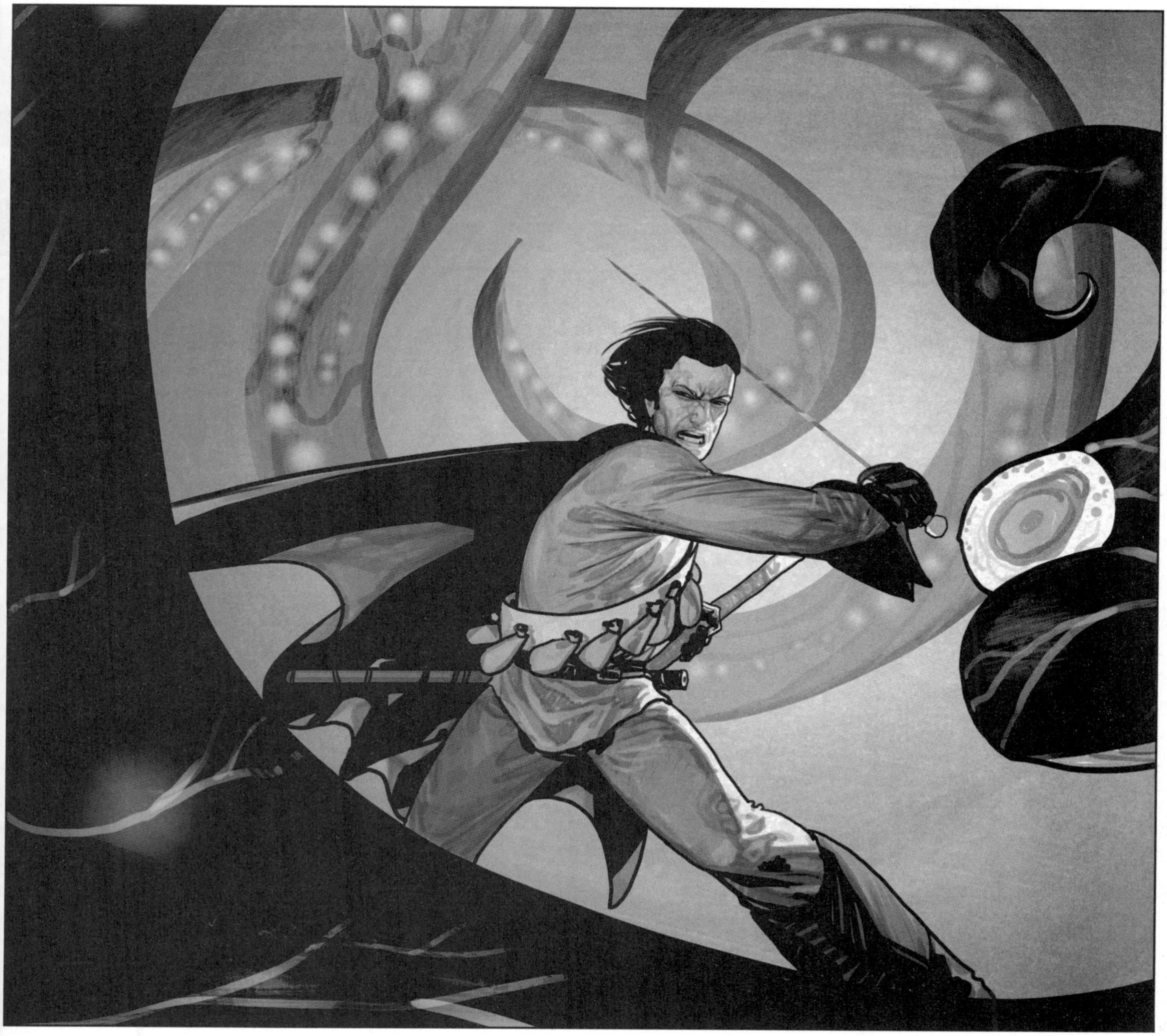

THE MODERN MASTERS SERIES

Edited by **ERIC NOLEN-WEATHINGTON**, these trade paperbacks and DVDs are devoted to the **BEST OF TODAY'S COMICS ARTISTS!** Each book contains **RARE AND UNSEEN ARTWORK** direct from the artist's files, plus a **COMPREHENSIVE INTERVIEW** (including influences and their views on graphic storytelling), **DELUXE SKETCHBOOK SECTIONS**, and more!

And don't miss the companion **DVDs,** showing the artists at work in their studios!

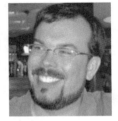

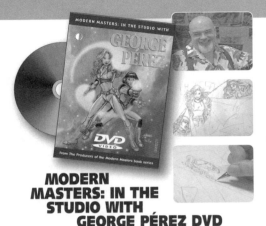

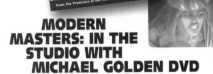

MODERN MASTERS: IN THE STUDIO WITH
GEORGE PÉREZ
DVD VIDEO
From The Producers of the Modern Masters book series

MODERN MASTERS: IN THE STUDIO WITH GEORGE PÉREZ DVD

Get a **PERSONAL TOUR** of George's studio, and watch **STEP-BY-STEP** as the fan-favorite artist illustrates a special issue of **TOP COW's WITCHBLADE!** Also, see George as he sketches for fans at conventions, and hear his peers and colleagues—including **MARV WOLFMAN** and **RON MARZ**—share their anecdotes and personal insights along the way!

(120-minute Standard Format DVD) **$29.95**
(Bundled with **MODERN MASTERS: GEORGE PÉREZ** book) **$37.95**
ISBN: **9781893905511** • UPC: **182658000011**
Diamond Order Code: **JUN053276**

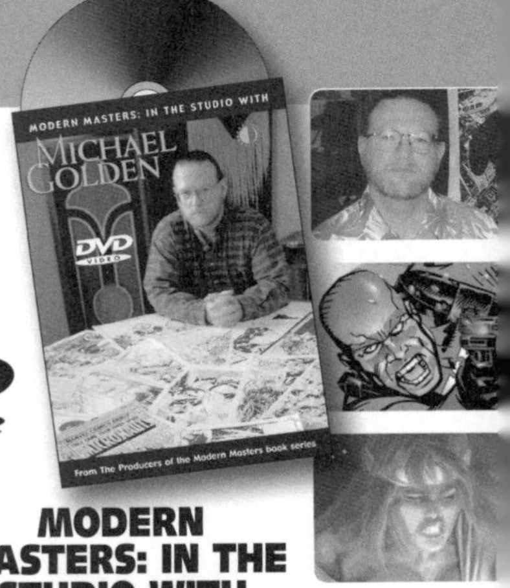

DVD VIDEO

MODERN MASTERS: IN THE STUDIO WITH
MICHAEL GOLDEN
DVD VIDEO
From The Producers of the Modern Masters book series

MODERN MASTERS: IN THE STUDIO WITH MICHAEL GOLDEN DVD

Go behind the scenes and into Michael Golden's studio for a **LOOK INTO THE CREATIVE MIND** of one of comics' greats. Witness a modern master in action as this 90-minute DVD provides an exclusiv look at the **ARTIST AT WORK,** as he **DISCUSSES THE PROCESSES** h undertakes to create a new comics series.

(90-minute Standard Format DVD) **$29.95**
(Bundled with **MODERN MASTERS: MICHAEL GOLDEN** book) **$37**
ISBN: **9781893905771** • UPC: **182658000028**
Diamond Order Code: **FEB088012**

Bundle the matching BOOK & DVD for just $37.95!

MODERN MASTERS VOLUME ONE
ALAN DAVIS

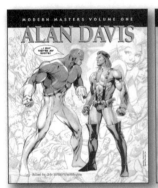

Modern Masters: ALAN DAVIS

by Eric Nolen-Weathington
(128-page trade paperback) **$14.95**
ISBN: **9781893905191**
Diamond Order Code: **JAN073903**

MODERN MASTERS VOLUME TWO:
GEORGE PÉREZ
Edited by Eric Nolen-Weathington

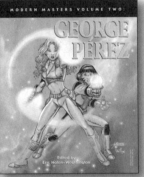

Modern Masters: GEORGE PÉREZ

by Eric Nolen-Weathington
(128-page trade paperback) **$14.95**
ISBN: **9781893905252**
Diamond Order Code: **JAN073904**

MODERN MASTERS VOLUME THREE:
BRUCE TIMM

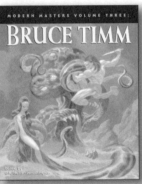

Modern Masters: BRUCE TIMM

by Eric Nolen-Weathington
(120-page TPB with **COLOR**) **$14.95**
ISBN: **9781893905306**
Diamond Order Code: **APR042954**

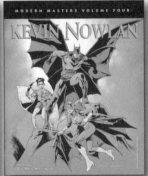

MODERN MASTERS VOLUME FOUR:
KEVIN NOWLAN

Modern Masters: KEVIN NOWLAN

by Eric Nolen-Weathington
(120-page TPB with **COLOR**) **$14.95**
ISBN: **9781893905382**
Diamond Order Code: **SEP042971**

MODERN MASTERS VOLUME FIVE:
J.L. GARCÍA LÓPEZ

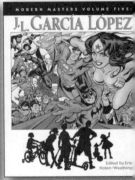

Modern Masters: GARCÍA-LÓPEZ

by Eric Nolen-Weathington
(120-page TPB with **COLOR**) **$14.9**
ISBN: **9781893905443**
Diamond Order Code: **APR053191**

MODERN MASTERS VOLUME SIX:
ARTHUR ADAMS

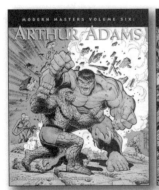

Modern Masters: ARTHUR ADAMS

by George Khoury &
Eric Nolen-Weathington
(128-page trade paperback) **SOLD OUT**
(Digital Edition) **$4.95**

MODERN MASTERS VOLUME SEVEN:
JOHN BYRNE

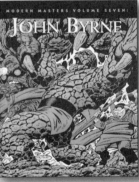

Modern Masters: JOHN BYRNE

by Jon B. Cooke & Eric Nolen-Weathington
(128-page trade paperback) **$14.95**
ISBN: **9781893905566**
Diamond Order Code: **FEB063354**

MODERN MASTERS VOLUME EIGHT:
WALTER SIMONSON

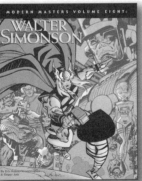

Modern Masters: WALTER SIMONSON

by Roger Ash &
Eric Nolen-Weathington
(128-page trade paperback) **SOLD OUT**
(Digital Edition) **$4.95**

MODERN MASTERS VOLUME NINE:
MIKE WIERINGO

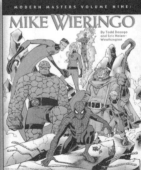

Modern Masters: MIKE WIERINGO

by Todd DeZago &
Eric Nolen-Weathington
(120-page TPB with **COLOR**) **$14.95**
ISBN: **9781893905658**
Diamond Order Code: **AUG063626**

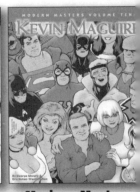

KEVIN MAGUIRE

Modern Masters: KEVIN MAGUIRE

by George Khoury &
Eric Nolen-Weathington
(128-page trade paperback) **$14.9**
ISBN: **9781893905665**
Diamond Order Code: **OCT06372**

Due to circumstances beyond our control, we've been unable to complete our planned volume on Darwyn Cooke as originally scheduled. Please visit www.twomorrows.com for updates as they become available.

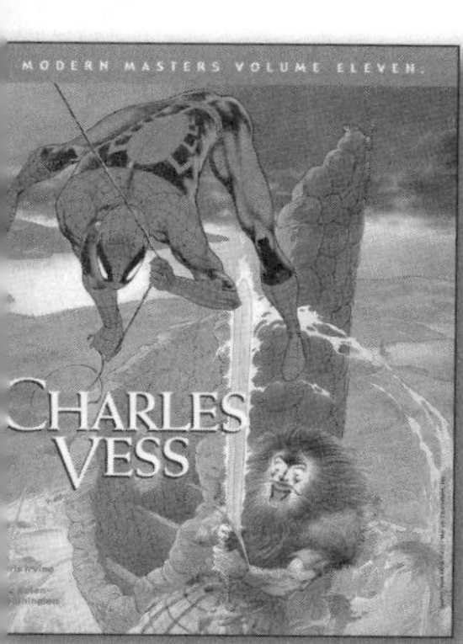
MODERN MASTERS VOLUME ELEVEN:
CHARLES VESS

Modern Masters:
CHARLES VESS
by Christopher Irving &
Eric Nolen-Weathington
(120-page TPB with **COLOR**) **$14.95**
ISBN: **9781893905696**
Diamond Order Code: **DEC063948**

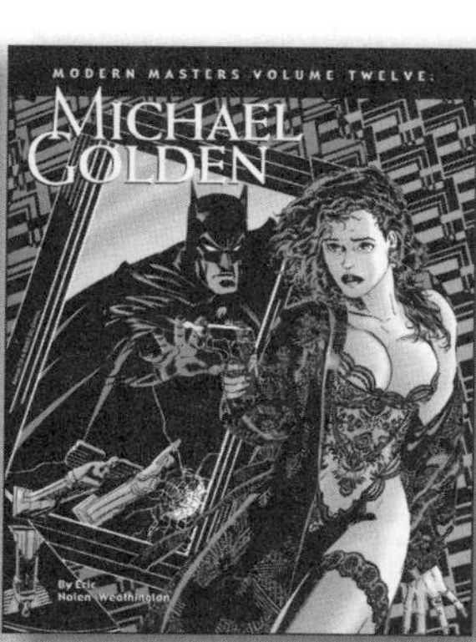
MODERN MASTERS VOLUME TWELVE:
MICHAEL GOLDEN

Modern Masters:
MICHAEL GOLDEN
by Eric Nolen-Weathington
(120-page TPB with **COLOR**) **$14.95**
ISBN: **9781893905740**
Diamond Order Code: **APR074023**

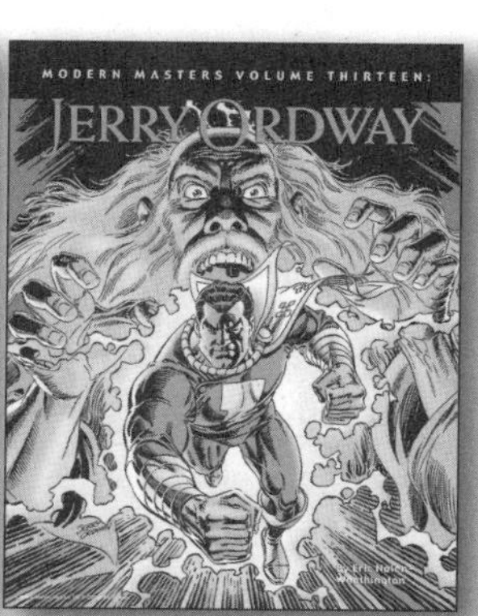
MODERN MASTERS VOLUME THIRTEEN:
JERRY ORDWAY

Modern Masters:
JERRY ORDWAY
by Eric Nolen-Weathington
(120-page TPB with **COLOR**) **$14.95**
ISBN: **9781893905795**
Diamond Order Code: **JUN073926**

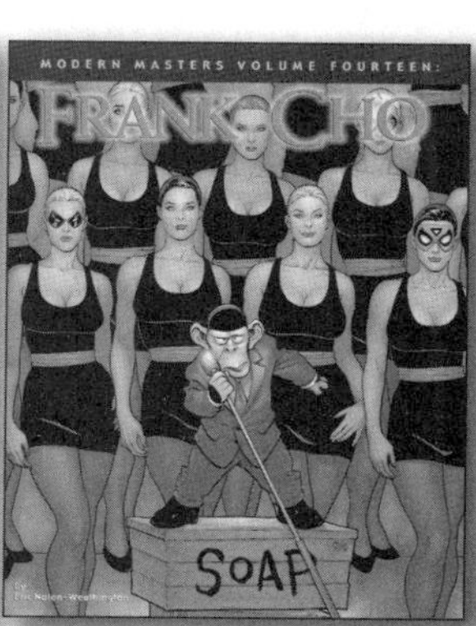
MODERN MASTERS VOLUME FOURTEEN:
FRANK CHO
SOAP

Modern Masters:
FRANK CHO
by Eric Nolen-Weathington
(120-page TPB with **COLOR**) **$15.95**
ISBN: **9781893905849**
Diamond Order Code: **JUL091086**

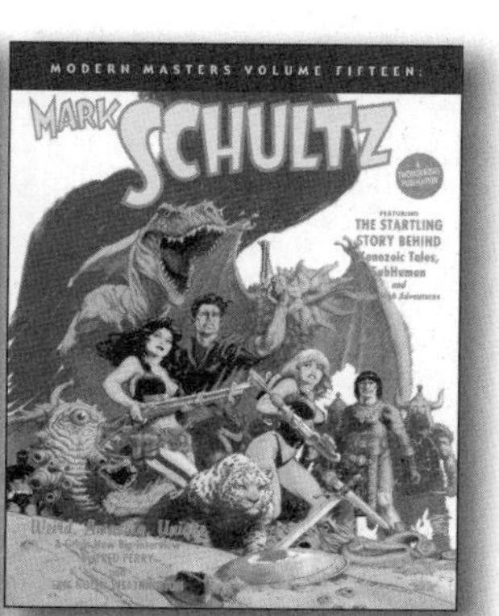
MODERN MASTERS VOLUME FIFTEEN:
MARK SCHULTZ

Modern Masters:
MARK SCHULTZ
by Fred Perry & Eric Nolen-Weathington
(120-page TPB with **COLOR**) **$14.95**
ISBN: **9781893905856**
Diamond Order Code: **OCT073846**

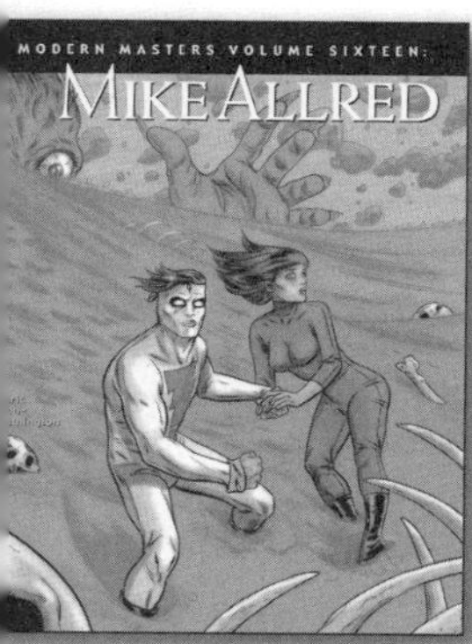
MODERN MASTERS VOLUME SIXTEEN:
MIKE ALLRED

Modern Masters:
MIKE ALLRED
by Eric Nolen-Weathington
(120-page TPB with **COLOR**) **$14.95**
ISBN: **9781893905863**
Diamond Order Code: **JAN083937**

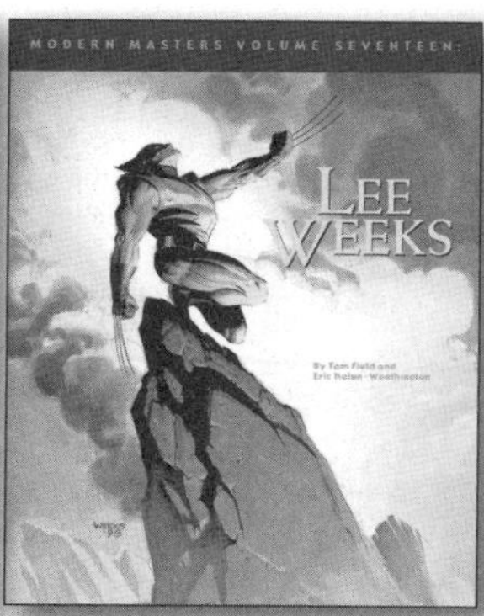
MODERN MASTERS VOLUME SEVENTEEN:
LEE WEEKS

Modern Masters:
LEE WEEKS
by Tom Field & Eric Nolen-Weathington
(128-page trade paperback) **$14.95**
ISBN: **9781893905948**
Diamond Order Code: **MAR084009**

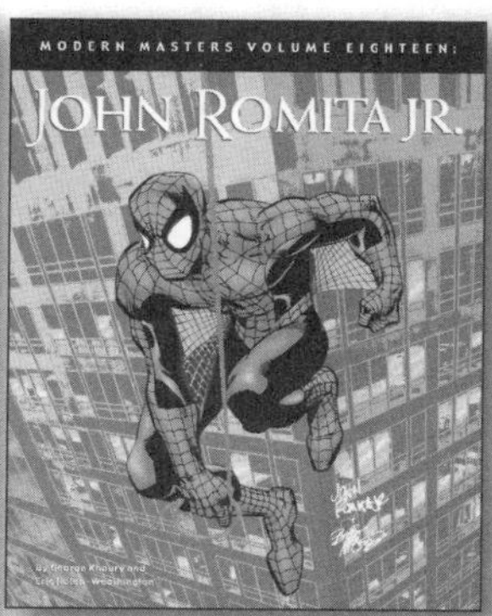
MODERN MASTERS VOLUME EIGHTEEN:
JOHN ROMITA JR.

Modern Masters:
JOHN ROMITA JR.
by George Khoury & Eric Nolen-Weathington
(128-page trade paperback) **$14.95**
ISBN: **9781893905955**
Diamond Order Code: **MAY084166**

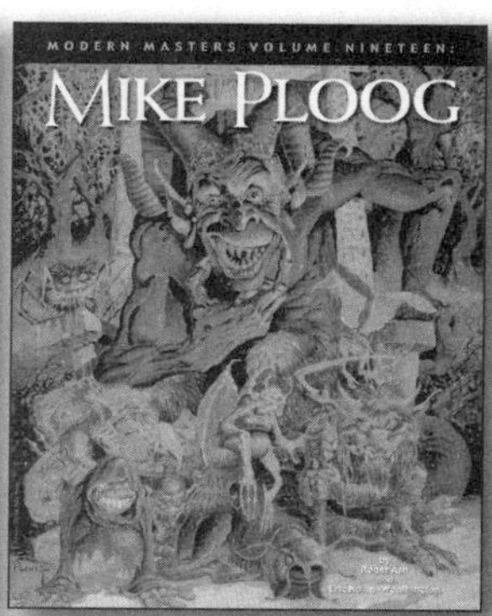
MODERN MASTERS VOLUME NINETEEN:
MIKE PLOOG

Modern Masters:
MIKE PLOOG
by Roger Ash & Eric Nolen-Weathington
(120-page TPB with **COLOR**) **$14.95**
ISBN: **9781605490076**
Diamond Order Code: **SEP084304**

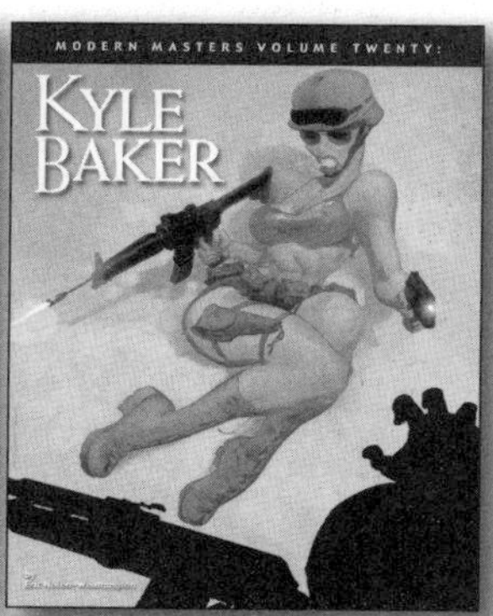
MODERN MASTERS VOLUME TWENTY:
KYLE BAKER

Modern Masters:
KYLE BAKER
by Eric Nolen-Weathington
(120-page TPB with **COLOR**) **$14.95**
ISBN: **9781605490083**
Diamond Order Code: **SEP084305**

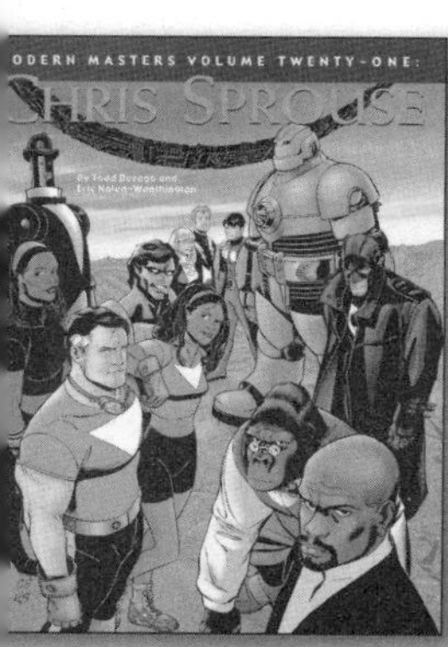
MODERN MASTERS VOLUME TWENTY-ONE:

Modern Masters:
CHRIS SPROUSE
by Todd DeZago &
Eric Nolen-Weathington
(120-page TPB with **COLOR**) **$14.95**
ISBN: **97801605490137**
Diamond Order Code: **NOV084298**

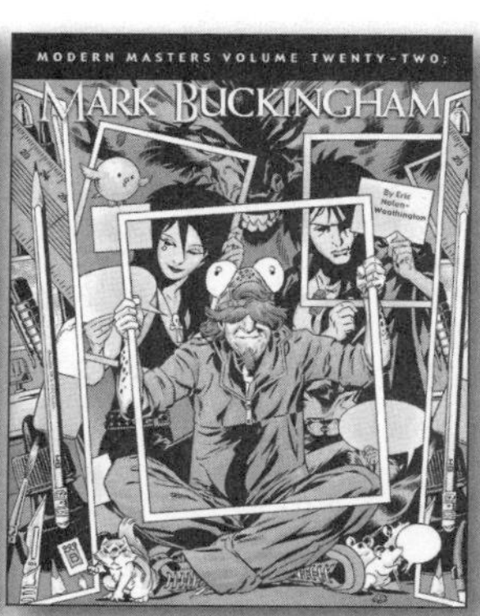
MODERN MASTERS VOLUME TWENTY-TWO:
MARK BUCKINGHAM

Modern Masters:
MARK BUCKINGHAM
by Eric Nolen-Weathington
(120-page TPB with **COLOR**) **$15.95**
ISBN: **9781605490144**
Diamond Order Code: **NOV090929**

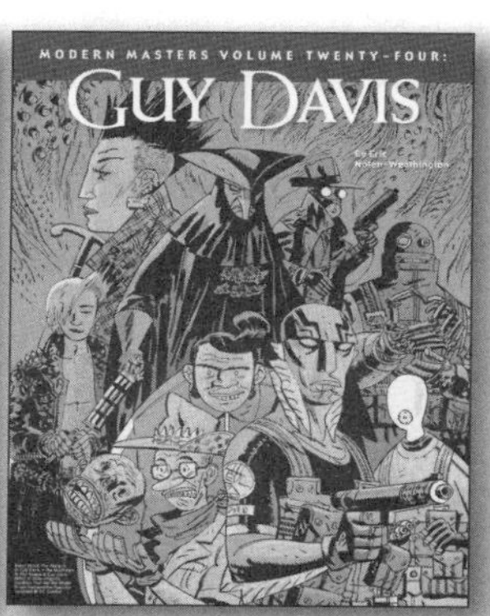
MODERN MASTERS VOLUME TWENTY-FOUR:
GUY DAVIS

Modern Masters:
GUY DAVIS
by Eric Nolen-Weathington
(120-page TPB with **COLOR**) **$15.95**
ISBN: **9781605490236**
Diamond Order Code: **AUG091083**

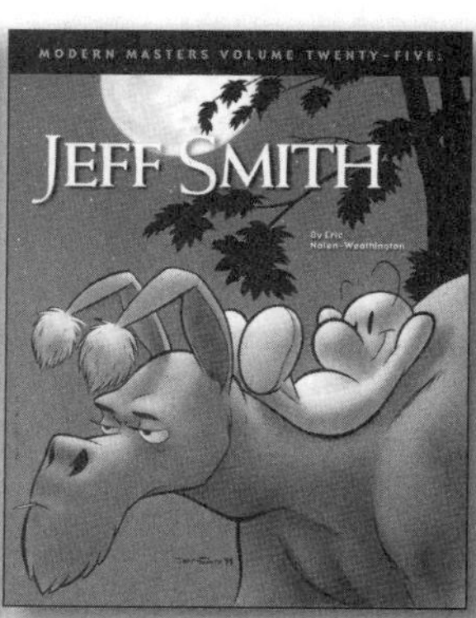
MODERN MASTERS VOLUME TWENTY-FIVE:
JEFF SMITH

Modern Masters:
JEFF SMITH
by Eric Nolen-Weathington
(120-page TPB with **COLOR**) **$15.95**
ISBN: **9781605490243**
Diamond Order Code: **DEC101098**

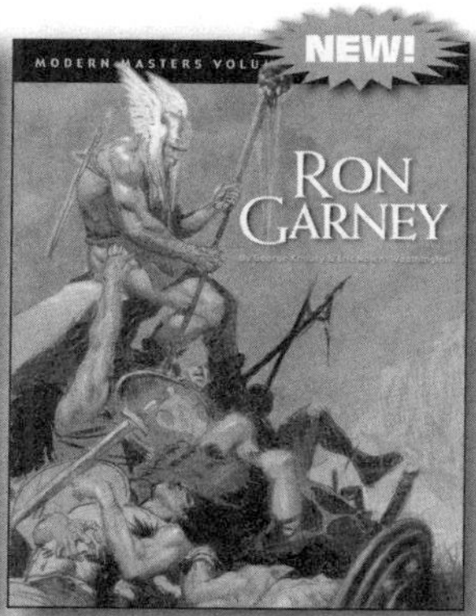
NEW!
RON GARNEY

Modern Masters:
RON GARNEY
by George Khoury &
Eric Nolen-Weathington
(120-page TPB with **COLOR**) **$15.95**
ISBN: **9781605490403**

More MODERN MASTERS are coming soon!
Check our website for release dates and updates!

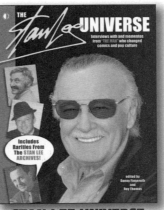